DEDICATION

This report is dedicated to the crew of the
Space Shuttle *Challenger*, Flight 51-L:

FRANCIS R. SCOBEE
Mission Commander

MICHAEL J. SMITH
Pilot

JUDITH A. RESNIK
Mission Specialist

ELLISON S. ONIZUKA
Mission Specialist

RONALD E. MCNAIR
Mission Specialist

GREGORY B. JARVIS
Payload Specialist

S. CHRISTA MCAULIFFE
Payload Specialist

"They had a hunger to explore the Universe and discover its truths. . . . They, the members of the Challenger *crew, were pioneers. . . . The future doesn't belong to the faint-hearted. It belongs to the brave. The* Challenger *crew was pulling us into the future, and we'll continue to follow them."*
—PRESIDENT RONALD REAGAN

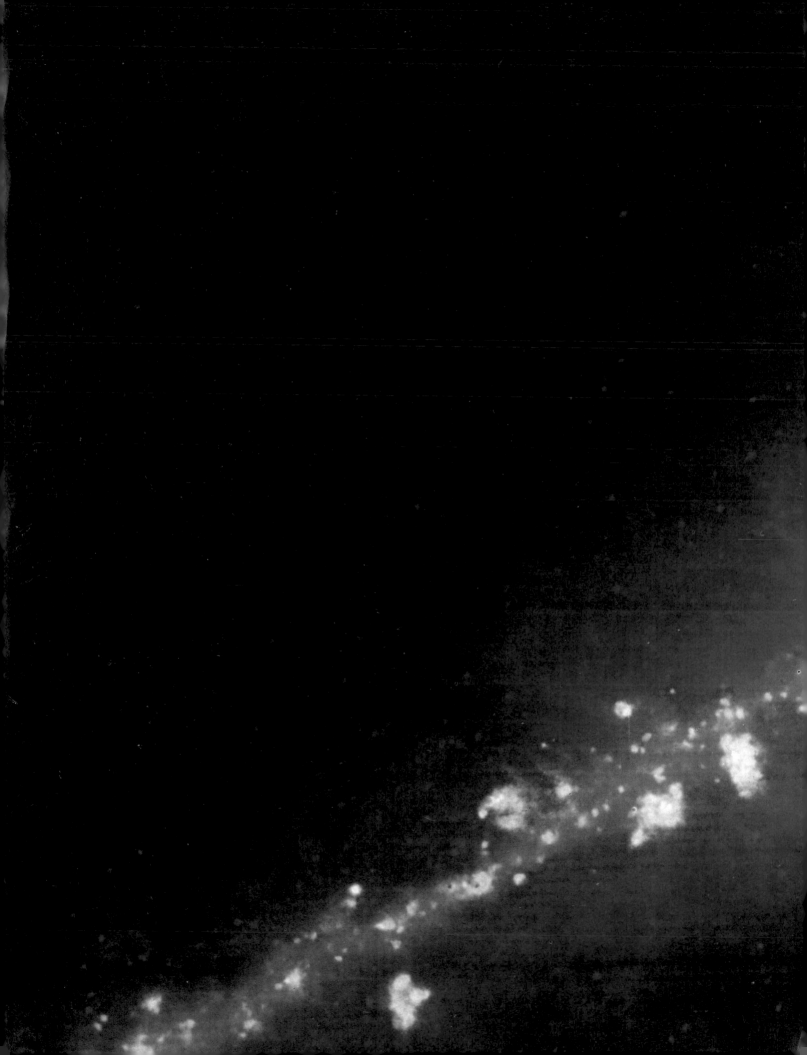

PIONEERING
THE
SPACE FRONTIER

The Report of the National Commission on Space

BANTAM BOOKS
TORONTO · NEW YORK · LONDON · SYDNEY · AUCKLAND

PIONEERING THE SPACE FRONTIER
A Bantam Book / May 1986

*The original artwork created for this report was not prepared at
Government expense.*

Cover: A settlement on Mars in the 21st Century. Courtesy Robert McCall.

Book design by Barbara N. Cohen
Cover art and inside illustrations copyright © 1986 by Bantam Books, Inc.
For information address: Bantam Books, Inc.

Library of Congress Cataloging-in-Publication Data

United States. National Commission on Space.
   Pioneering the space frontier.

   Bibliography: p. 203
   1. Outer space—Exploration—United States.
   2. Astronautics—United States.   I. Title.
   TL789.8.U5U565   1986   629.4'0973   86-7958
   ISBN 0-553-34314-9

Published simultaneously in the United States and Canada

PRINTED IN THE UNITED STATES OF AMERICA

WAK   0   9   8   7   6   5   4   3   2   1

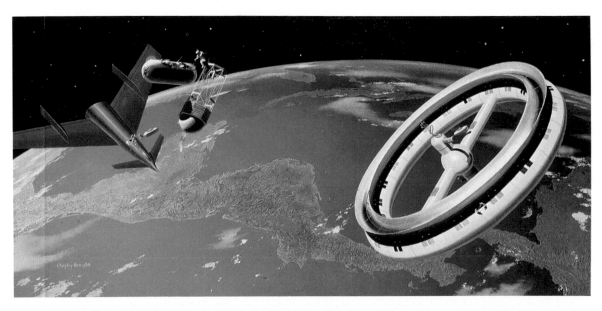

While predicting the future can be hazardous, sometimes it can be done. In 1951, Wernher von Braun and Chesley Bonestell predicted a future in space, above, with a reusable launch vehicle, a space telescope, and a rotating space station. Below is an illustration by Robert McCall which shows this vision coming true. The space shuttle is a reality, the Hubble Space Telescope will be launched in the near future, and the Space Station will be in operation by the mid-1990s.

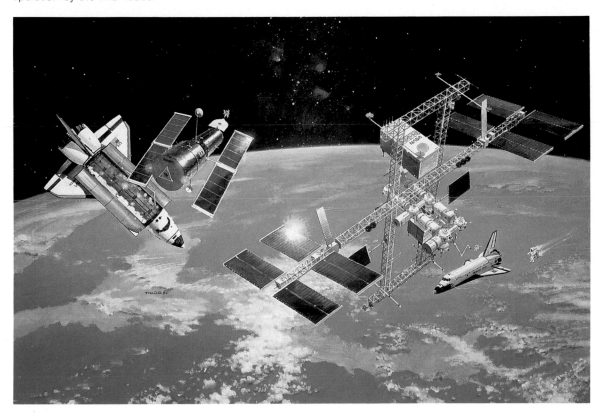

LOOKING FIFTY YEARS INTO THE FUTURE

The year is 1935. Pan American Airways is inaugurating trans-Pacific service, with additional flying boats on order to open trans-Atlantic service in 1939. The last Pony Express rider turns over his mail pouch to a young biplane pilot while newsreel cameras grind. Almost nobody expects to fly the Atlantic—that's for daredevils like Lindbergh—but half a million people per year cross in ocean liners. Washington's chief concern is the Federal Deficit: $30 billion in revenues versus $50 billion in outlays (1985 dollars).

The year is 1985. Could we explain to a visitor from 1935 that more than 25 million people now fly the Atlantic every year? That 16 years ago astronauts flew at 24,790 miles per hour to the Moon? That communication satellites are flashing color television signals around the world? That a spacecraft has transmitted pictures and data from Uranus across 1.8 billion miles, and is now flying on to Neptune? That supercomputers are being used to design next-generation spacecraft that will drastically reduce the cost of space travel? Washington's grappling with the Federal Budget deficit might sound familiar, but 50 years of cumulative technological advance would be beyond comprehension.

What will 2035 be like? The National Commission on Space has been charged by the Congress and the President to look into the future to propose civilian space goals for 21st-century America. It is as challenging for us today to envision the advanced world of 2035 as it was to foresee today's world back in 1935. Even the most visionary science fiction writer then failed to foresee the scale of the resources that would be needed to initiate the Space Age, and that no one imagined these would become available within 25 years. Looking to the future, we are confident that the next century will see pioneering men and women from many nations working and living throughout the inner Solar System. Space travel will be as safe and inexpensive for our grandchildren as jet travel is for us. Our vision and our recommendations are outlined in this report. **Through vigorous leadership on the space frontier, America can make this happen.**

CONTENTS

DECLARATION FOR SPACE

A PIONEERING MISSION FOR 21st-CENTURY AMERICA

To lead the exploration and development of the space frontier, advancing science, technology, and enterprise, and building institutions and systems that make accessible vast new resources and support human settlements beyond Earth orbit, from the highlands of the Moon to the plains of Mars.

A lunar settlement in the 21st century. (COURTESY ROBERT MCCALL)

RATIONALE FOR EXPLORING AND SETTLING THE SOLAR SYSTEM

Our Vision: The Solar System as the Home of Humanity

The Solar System is our extended home. Five centuries after Columbus opened access to "The New World" we can initiate the settlement of worlds beyond our planet of birth. The promise of virgin lands and the opportunity to live in freedom brought our ancestors to the shores of North America. Now space technology has freed humankind to move outward from Earth as a species destined to expand to other worlds.

Our Purpose: Free Societies on New Worlds

The settlement of North America and other continents was a prelude to humanity's greater challenge: the space frontier. As we develop new lands of opportunity for ourselves and our descendants, we must carry with us the guarantees expressed in our Bill of Rights: to think, communicate, and live in freedom. We must stimulate individual initiative and free enterprise in space.

Our Ambition: Opening New Resources to Benefit Humanity

Historically, wealth has been created when the power of the human intellect combined abundant energy with rich material resources. Now America can create new wealth on the space frontier to benefit the entire human community by combining the energy of the Sun with materials left in space during the formation of the Solar System.

Our Method: Efficiency and Systematic Progression

In undertaking this great venture we must plan logically and build wisely. Each new step must be justified on its own merits and make possible additional steps. American investments on the space frontier should be sustained at a small but steady fraction of our national budget.

Our Hope: Increased World Cooperation

In his essay *Common Sense,* published in January of 1776, Tom Paine said of American independence, " 'Tis not the affair of a City, County, a Province, or a Kingdom; but of a Continent. . . . 'Tis not the concern of a day, a year, or an age; posterity are virtually involved in the contest, and will be more or less affected even to the end of time, by the proceedings now." Exploring the Universe is neither one nation's issue, nor relevant only to our time. Accordingly, America must work with other nations in a manner consistent with our Constitution, national security, and international agreements.

Our Aspiration: American Leadership on the Space Frontier

With America's pioneer heritage, technological preeminence, and economic strength, it is fitting that we should lead the people of this planet into space. Our leadership role should challenge the vision, talents, and energies of young and old alike, and inspire other nations to contribute their best talents to expand humanity's future.

Our Need: Balance and Common Sense

Settling North America required the sustained efforts of laborers and farmers, merchants and ministers, artisans and adventurers, scientists and seafarers. In the same way, our space program must combine with vigor and continuity the elements of scientific research, technological advance, the discovery and development of new resources in space, and the provision of essential institutions and systems to extend America's reach in science, industry, and the settlement of space.

Our Approach: The Critical Lead Role of Government

As formerly on the western frontier, now similarly on the space frontier, Government should support exploration and science, advance critical technologies, and provide the transportation systems and administration required to open broad access to new lands. The investment will again generate in value many times its cost to the benefit of all.

Our Resolve: To Go Forth "In Peace for All Mankind"

When the first Apollo astronauts stepped onto the Moon, they emplaced a plaque upon which were inscribed the words, "We came in peace for all mankind." As we move outward into the Solar System, we must remain true to our values as Americans: To go forward peacefully and to respect the integrity of planetary bodies and alien life forms, with equality of opportunity for all.

A NEW LONG-RANGE CIVILIAN SPACE PROGRAM

Program Thrusts

The National Commission on Space proposes a future-oriented civilian space agenda with three mutually-supportive thrusts:

- **Advancing our understanding of our planet, our Solar System, and the Universe;**
- **Exploring, prospecting, and settling the Solar System; and**
- **Stimulating space enterprises for the direct benefit of the people on Earth.**

We judge these three thrusts to be of comparable importance. They are described in Part I of our report: *Civilian Space Goals for 21st-Century America.*

To accomplish them economically, the Nation must make a long-range commitment to two additional thrusts:

- **Advancing technology across a broad spectrum to assure timely availability of critical capabilities; and**
- **Creating and operating systems and institutions to provide low-cost access to the space frontier.**

These two thrusts are described in Part II of our report: *Low-Cost Access to the Solar System,* including *Building the Technology Base,* constructing a *Highway to Space,* and establishing a *Bridge between Worlds.*

A Logical Approach

To meet the challenge of the space frontier, the Commission proposes a sustained step-by-step program to open the inner Solar System for exploration, basic and applied research, resource development, and human operations. This program will require a creative partnership of Government, industry, and academia of the type that has proved highly productive in previous

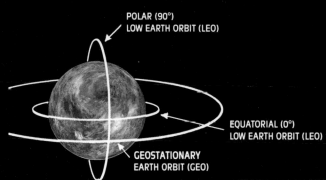

POLAR (90°)
LOW EARTH ORBIT (LEO)

LIBRATION POINT
(L1)

EQUATORIAL (0°)
LOW EARTH ORBIT (LEO)

MOON

GEOSTATIONARY
EARTH ORBIT (GEO)

EARTH–MOON SYSTEM

SUN   MERCURY VENUS   EARTH   MARS   ASTEROID
BELT

PLANET	DISTANCE FROM SUN (MILLION MILES)
MERCURY	36
VENUS	67
EARTH	93
MARS	142
ASTEROID BELT	205-308

INNER SOLAR SYSTEM

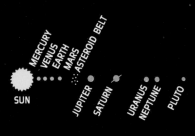

SUN   JUPITER SATURN URANUS NEPTUNE PLUTO

OORT
CLOUD
(COMETS)

PLANET	DISTANCE FROM SUN (MILLION MILES)
JUPITER	484
SATURN	887
URANUS	1784
NEPTUNE	2796
PLUTO	3668
OORT CLOUD	ABOUT 4,000,000

THE SOLAR SYSTEM

national enterprises. U.S. leadership will be based upon a reliable, affordable transportation system and a network of outposts in space. This infrastructure will allow us to extend scientific exploration and to begin the economic development of the vast region stretching from Earth orbit outward to the surface of our Moon, to Mars and its moons, and to accessible asteroids. We can achieve our recommended program most economically and with minimum risk through a systematic program structured in accordance with the inner Solar System's natural characteristics: energy, distance, signal delay time, and availability of resources. These characteristics lead to a natural progression for future space activities within the inner Solar System.

- **Low Earth orbits** are those just beyond Earth's atmosphere and are therefore the easiest to reach from Earth. They provide both our nearest orbital view of Earth and our nearest clear window for observation of the Universe. Freedom from strong gravitational effects allows experiments impossible on Earth and facilitates construction of large structures of low mass. In this region, our mother planet provides a sheltering skirt of magnetic field that protects us from the radiation produced by solar flares.
- **Geostationary orbit,** 22,300 miles above Earth's equator, is the orbit in which space-craft match Earth's 24-hour rotation and hold fixed longitudes. This valuable real estate is a tenth of the distance to the Moon and is the locale of today's entire civil communications satellite industry.
- **Lunar distance** is 240,000 miles. The Moon is our nearest nonterrestrial source of abundant materials. The energy required to bring materials from the Moon to high Earth orbit is less than a twentieth of that needed to lift an equal mass from Earth to such an orbit. Round-trip communication time for a television image traveling at the speed of light to arrive from lunar distance and for a responding command signal from Earth can be as low as three seconds. This short time may allow practical tele-operation of remote machines on the Moon by people on Earth.
- **Mars and the asteroids** are the nearest resource-rich bodies beyond our Moon. Because they are on the order of 1,000 times as far away, voyages to them require many months. Even at the speed of light, round-trip communication with them involves times of 10 to 40 minutes, so robotic machines on these Solar System bodies must be "smarter" than those on the Moon. However, certain distant objects with valuable resources can be reached with low energy expenditure, including the Martian moons Phobos and Deimos and some asteroids.
- **Work sites and energy.** We gain access to useful materials when we land on a moon or planet, but pay a price in propellants to descend to those surfaces. There we also lose full-time solar energy, which is valuable for industrial processing, and lose microgravity, which is advantageous for building large space structures. Early industrial production in space may, therefore, be best achieved by transporting raw materials from the Moon to high orbit for processing and fabrication into finished products in robotic factories powered by continuous solar energy. As on Earth, the economics of mining, processing, transportation, fabrication, and point of utilization will determine the best locations for transportation hubs and industrial centers within the inner Solar System.

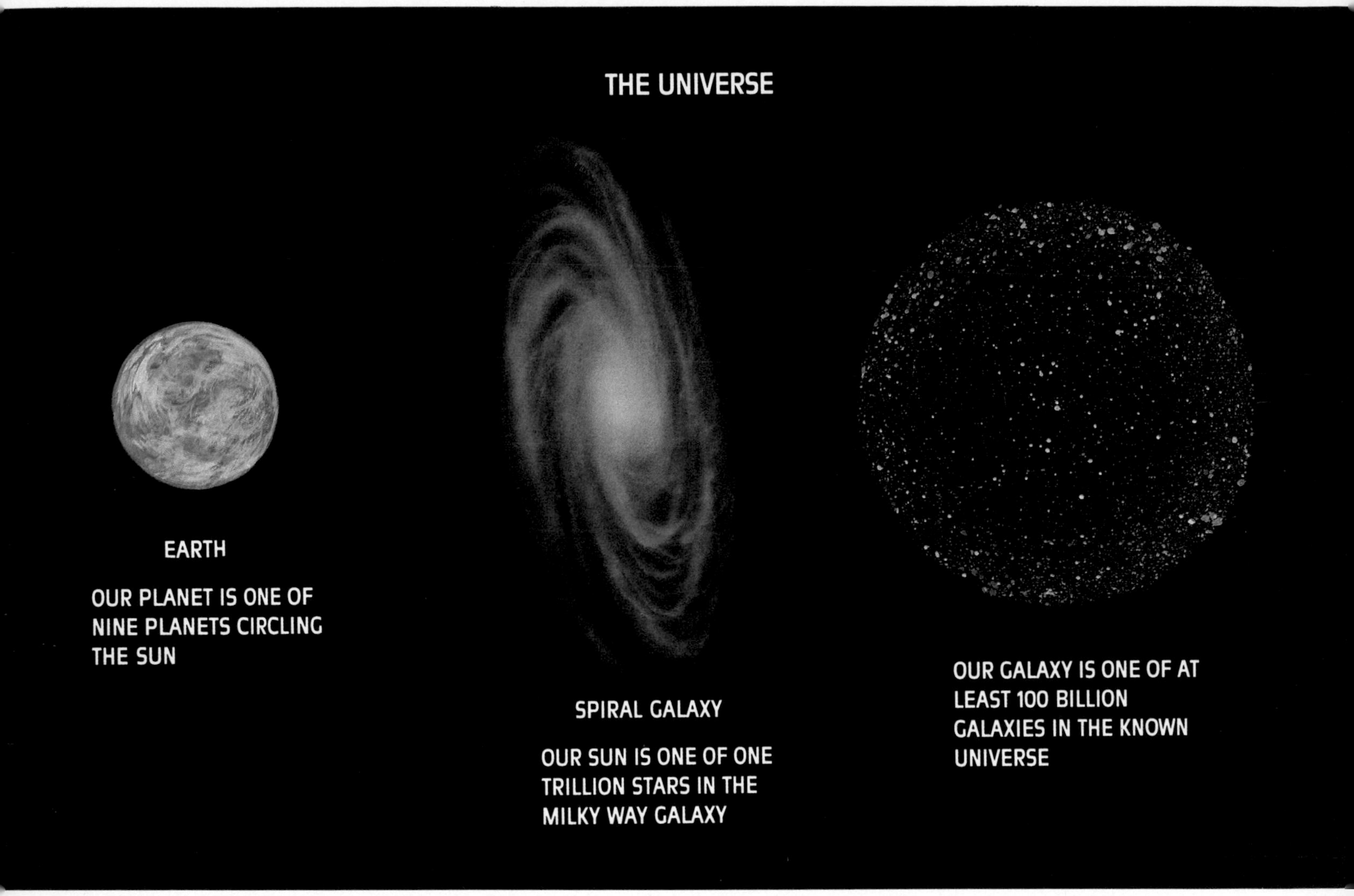

THE UNIVERSE

EARTH

OUR PLANET IS ONE OF
NINE PLANETS CIRCLING
THE SUN

SPIRAL GALAXY

OUR SUN IS ONE OF ONE
TRILLION STARS IN THE
MILKY WAY GALAXY

OUR GALAXY IS ONE OF AT
LEAST 100 BILLION
GALAXIES IN THE KNOWN
UNIVERSE

Principal Recommendations

Consistent with our proposed five basic thrusts and the logical approach outlined above, the major parts of our report that follow include a number of specific recommendations.

Advancing Science

We recommend an aggressive space science program with three major objectives: (1) understanding the structure and evolution of the Universe, our Galaxy, our Solar System, and planet Earth, including the emergence and spread of life; (2) applying this understanding to forecast future phenomena of critical significance to humanity; and (3) using the environment of spaceflight and the tools of space technology to study the basic properties of matter and life. We have reviewed the current plans of U.S. science advisory groups for orderly progress toward these goals in the several disciplines of science. We endorse these plans, and note that an exciting opportunity exists to integrate the research results from previously separate disciplines. In order to foster this integrated approach to research on fundamental questions in science, the Commission recommends:

A sustained program to understand the evolution of the Universe, through astronomical facilities of increasing power, precision, and sophistication at locations in more distant Earth orbits and at eventual locations on the Moon.

A study of the evolution of the Solar System by using samples returned from selected planets, moons, asteroids, and comets. With returned samples, we can use all of our sophisticated laboratory technologies to perform the analyses. The results will also contribute significantly to the future discovery and utilization of space resources.

A global study of planet Earth using both ground- and space-based instruments. The goal of the study is in-depth understanding of the processes that shape our planet's interior, oceans, atmosphere, and polar ice caps, with particular emphasis on phenomena which affect, or are affected by, life, and the means to forecast, quantitatively, such phenomena.

A study of the Sun and the vast region it influences, using remote sensing from Earth as well as interplanetary probes. We must seek to understand the generation of energy deep in the Sun, its transformation into radiations that affect Earth and planets as well as life, and its interaction with solar and planetary magnetic fields. The processes involved occur throughout all space, so our understanding will be broadly applicable.

A continuing program to search for evidence that life exists—or has existed—beyond Earth, by studying other bodies of the Solar System, by searching for planets circling other stars, and by searching for signals broadcast by intelligent life elsewhere in the Galaxy.

Provision of state-of-the-art facilities for laboratory experiments on the ground and on the Space Station to increase the returns from the Nation's investment in space science, with particular attention to computer modeling, data access, advanced graphics, and artificial intelligence software.

New research into the effects of different gravity levels on humans and other biological systems, as well as on processes in physics and chemistry. The planned space program and the extension proposed here provide both the opportunity and necessity to resolve fundamental questions and to solve pacing problems that depend on gravity. Particularly needed are long-duration studies of the reactions of humans and plants to the microgravity of free space, the one-sixth gravity of the Moon, and the one-third gravity of Mars.

Exploring, Prospecting, and Settling the Solar System

In addition to basic scientific research, we propose specific applied-science investigations to discover, study, and learn to use for human benefit the resources on the space frontier. These materials have special value because they do not have to be lifted from Earth and carried over a long supply line. As a natural consequence of these investigations, the future will see growing numbers of people working at Earth orbital, lunar, and, eventually, Martian bases, initiating the settlement of vast reaches of the inner Solar System.

Living in space will be practical even though for long-term good health, people and the food crops that support them require atmosphere, water, sunlight, protection from radiation, and probably some gravity. Technological advances will permit all of these requirements to be met in free space; food, oxygen, and water can be recycled within an artificial biosphere, shielding from cosmic and solar flare radiation can be provided by lunar soil transported from the Moon with little energy, and artificial gravity can be provided by rotation. In the event of illness or accident, we can return people to Earth from lunar distance within a few days. Thus, the Earth-Moon region is favored for initial industrial production and for testing prototype spaceships and life-support equipment for later voyages to Mars and its moons.

To support these activities the Commission recommends:

Continuing robotic prospector missions, using the techniques of remote sensing and of on-site measurements to discover and characterize usable materials on our Moon, Mars and its moons, and accessible asteroids. A very high priority should be given to discovering any resources that may be frozen near the lunar poles, to determining the potential water and hydrocarbon resources on the surfaces of Phobos, Deimos, and near-surface layers of Mars, and to charting and analyzing all of the asteroids that pass close to Earth.

Missions to obtain samples from selected sites on our Moon, Mars and its moons, and the most accessible asteroids. When prospector missions have identified the presence of valuable chemical elements, sample return missions will be needed to bring back enough material to characterize the minerals and initiate industrial process development based on the physical and chemical properties of the samples.

Robotic and human exploration and surveying of substantial areas and special features of the Moon and Mars. This effort will begin on the Moon with automated roving vehicles tele-operated from Earth, and on Mars with vehicles having substantial artificial intelligence. Robots will be followed by the first astronaut crews operating from lunar and Martian outposts and bases.

Human outposts and bases in the inner Solar System. On the space frontier, habitations with closed-ecology life-support systems and reliable power plants will be needed to support work crews and, eventually, their families for long-duration work. Maintenance of good health for people working on science, exploration, and enterprise in distant communities, some of them at less than Earth-normal gravity, requires more knowledge and the development of dependable new systems. The development of long-duration habitation in space, based upon local resources, is essential to the support of activities in all three of our primary areas: science, exploration, and enterprise.

Space Enterprise

Our proposals span the range from involving private enterprise more heavily in post-shuttle space transportation to the support of major new industries. We propose that NASA should have a role in encouraging new space enterprises through technological development and demonstration analogous to its traditional successful support of the private sector in aeronautical research. It is imperative that the private sector be much more heavily involved in defining the nature and specifications of future launch vehicles. This will help ensure the adoption of commercial practices that will reduce operating costs and make it possible to transfer operation of these vehicles to the private sector. Future vehicles for cargo and passenger transport should be designed to be readily operable by the private sector after development is complete and routine operation is reached. To accomplish this the Commission recommends: **That wherever possible the private sector be given the task of providing specified services or products in space, and be free to determine the most cost-effective ways to satisfy those requirements, consistent with evolving Federal regulations.** We also recommend: **That NASA initiate research and development now on systems and processes for application beyond low Earth orbit.**

These systems should include tele-operated machines to repair and refuel satellites in high orbit, and the machines of robotic lunar pilot plants. Lunar resource utilization will depend on automated and tele-operated machines which are reliable and easy to use. This equipment must be developed through the pilot-plant stage for robotic plants capable of transforming lunar and other non-terrestrial raw materials into propellants, shielding materials, structural elements, and industrial raw materials.

Building the Technology Base

The United States must substantially increase its investment in its space technology base. We recommend: **A threefold growth in NASA's base technology budget** to increase this item from two percent to six percent of NASA's total budget. This growth will permit the necessary acceleration of work in many critical technical fields from space propulsion and robotic construction to high-performance materials, artificial intelligence, and the processing of non-terrestrial materials. We also recommend: **Special emphasis on intelligent autonomous systems.** Cargo trips beyond lunar distance will be made by unpiloted vehicles; the earliest roving vehicles on the Martian surface will be unpiloted; and processing plants for propellants from the materials on asteroids, Phobos, or Mars will run unattended. To support these complex, automated, remote operations, a new generation of robust, fault-tolerant, pattern-recognizing automata is needed. They must employ new computers, sensors, and diagnostic and maintenance equipment that can avoid accidents and repair failures. These systems must be capable of taking the same common-sense corrective actions that a human operator would take. These developments by NASA should also have broad application to 21st-century U.S. industry.

We recommend demonstration projects in seven critical technologies:

- **Flight research on aerospace plane propulsion and aerodynamics;**
- **Advanced rocket vehicles;**
- **Aerobraking for orbital transfer;**

- **Long-duration closed-ecosystems (including water, air, and food);**
- **Electric launch and propulsion systems;**
- **Nuclear-electric space power; and**
- **Space tethers and artificial gravity.**

These base technology and demonstration programs are discussed in detail in Part II of our report: *Building the Technology Base.*

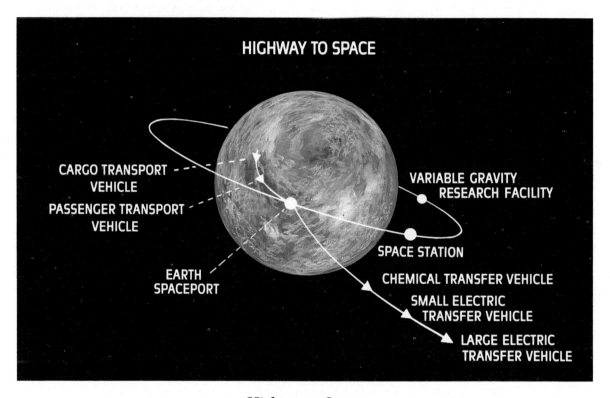

Highway to Space

The two most significant contributions the U.S. Government can make to opening the space frontier are to ensure continuity of launch services and to reduce drastically transportation costs within the inner Solar System. The shuttle fleet will become obsolescent by the turn of the century. Reliable, economical launch vehicles will be needed to provide flexible, routine access to orbit for cargo and passengers at reduced costs. A complementary system is needed for low-cost transport from low Earth orbit to geostationary orbit and lunar distance. To reduce space operation costs as soon as possible, the Commission recommends that: **Three major space transport needs be met in the next 15 years; the three major transport systems requirements are:**

- **Cargo transport to low Earth orbit;**

- **Passenger transport to and from low Earth orbit; and**
- **Round-trip transfer beyond low Earth orbit.**

For cargo transport, we propose that a new vehicle be put into operation by the year 2000 with a goal of achieving operation costs of $200 per pound delivered into orbit.

For passenger transport, we see two competing developments for the follow-on to the shuttle: an advanced reusable rocket vehicle, or an airbreathing aerospace plane. These piloted vehicles could carry both passengers and compact cargo. Accordingly, we propose an intensive technology-base program for the next five years to provide critical engineering data on both systems so the Nation can make a sound selection by 1992. Key technologies include computational fluid dynamics, dual-fuel rocket propulsion, supersonic combustion ramjet engines, high-performance materials, structures, aerodynamics, thermal shielding, and launch automation.

The airbreathing hypersonic propulsion has broad potential for a number of 21st-century applications, including intercontinental passenger transport, low-cost orbital transport, and a wide range of defense missions. **The Commission therefore supports a major national commitment to achieve early flight research with an experimental aerospace plane.** We also believe that in the next century the passenger transport system should be developed and operated privately for routine non-military operation between Earth and low Earth orbit.

For destinations beyond Earth orbit, a new transfer vehicle will be required. In the coming era of fully reusable Earth-to-orbit vehicles, the needs of Government and industry for the reliable emplacement of expensive satellites beyond low Earth orbit will require new space-based "workhorse" vehicles designed for flexibility through modular systems. Basic components should be capable of being ganged, or provided with extra tankage, for higher energy missions. They should be capable of transporting both cargo and people, be reusable, employ aerobraking, and be adapted to on-orbit servicing, maintenance, test, and repair. A transfer vehicle will be required to lift large payloads to geostationary orbit, to move payloads and crews to lunar orbit, to land payloads on the lunar surface, and to travel beyond the Earth-Moon system. Its Space Station base may be a critical pacing item. This vehicle should be designed for return to a low Earth orbit spaceport using aerobraking. The Commission recommends that: **The U.S. Space Station program be kept on schedule for an operational capability by 1994, without a crippling and expensive "stretch-out," and a space-based robotic transfer vehicle be developed to initiate a Bridge between Worlds.**

Bridge Between Worlds

Many of the systems needed for reaching outward to the planet Mars will be proven in the course of work in the Earth-Moon region. Others listed here are special to operations conducted at distances so remote from Earth that tele-operation and close mission support are not possible. To build the 21st-century Bridge Between Worlds that will open the Solar System, the Commission recommends:

BRIDGE BETWEEN WORLDS

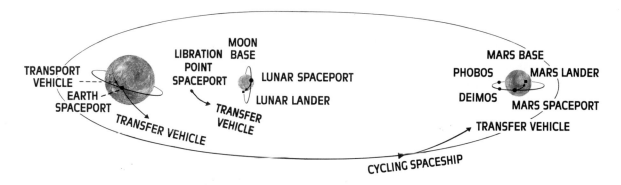

Developing reliable high-performance electric propulsion systems, including mass-drivers and ion propulsion able to operate throughout the entire Solar System. Candidate technologies should be pursued vigorously to ensure that they will be ready when needed. Mass-driver reaction engines would be able to use as propellants raw materials from Earth's Moon, Phobos, Deimos, or asteroids. They, and other electric thrusters, would be able to run on solar or nuclear electric power.

Developing fully self-sustaining biospheres independent of Earth. For routine operation beyond the Moon, it is essential that life support be maintained using on-site materials, without reliance on long supply lines.

Establishing initial outposts and bases on the Moon and Mars that combine objectives, including life-support, science, exploration, prospecting, resource development, material processing, automated rocket fuel production, and robotic fabrication. Long-term exponential growth into eventual permanent settlements should be the overarching goal.

An Economical, Phased Approach

In considering the financial resources required to carry out our recommended agenda and future civilian space budget levels needed to meet our goals, the Commission considered the potential growth of the U.S. economy from a number of perspectives, as discussed in Part IV of our report: *21st-Century America.* Based on what we believe to be realistic growth assumptions, we are confident that the long-range agenda we recommend can be carried out within reasonable civilian space budgets. Figure 1 outlines our phased approach to achieve low-cost access to the Solar System. The Highway to Space starts with economical new cargo and passenger transport vehicles, adding a transfer vehicle for destinations beyond low Earth orbit. These three systems would become operational in conjunction with an orbital spaceport within 15 years. In the following 5 years, the Bridge Between Worlds would support initial robotic lunar surface operations, followed by a permanent outpost to support astronaut operations. In 10 more years the space bridge would be extended out to Mars for detailed robotic exploration followed by a Mars outpost for human activity. To achieve this the Commission recommends that: **The phased space transportation network outlined in Figure 1 be developed and placed in operation.** It starts with simple components, but evolves over time into a system of spaceports, bases, and connecting transportation systems that will open the space frontier for large-scale exploration, science, and the initiation of economic development. Resources will be utilized where they are found, to minimize the need for resources transported from Earth. This inner Solar System network will ensure continuing American leadership in space in the next century.

Implementing the Program

The hallmarks of this program are the technological advances needed for major cost-reduction and capability extension. Figure 2 depicts the growth of the U.S. Gross National

LOW-COST ACCESS TO THE INNER SOLAR SYSTEM

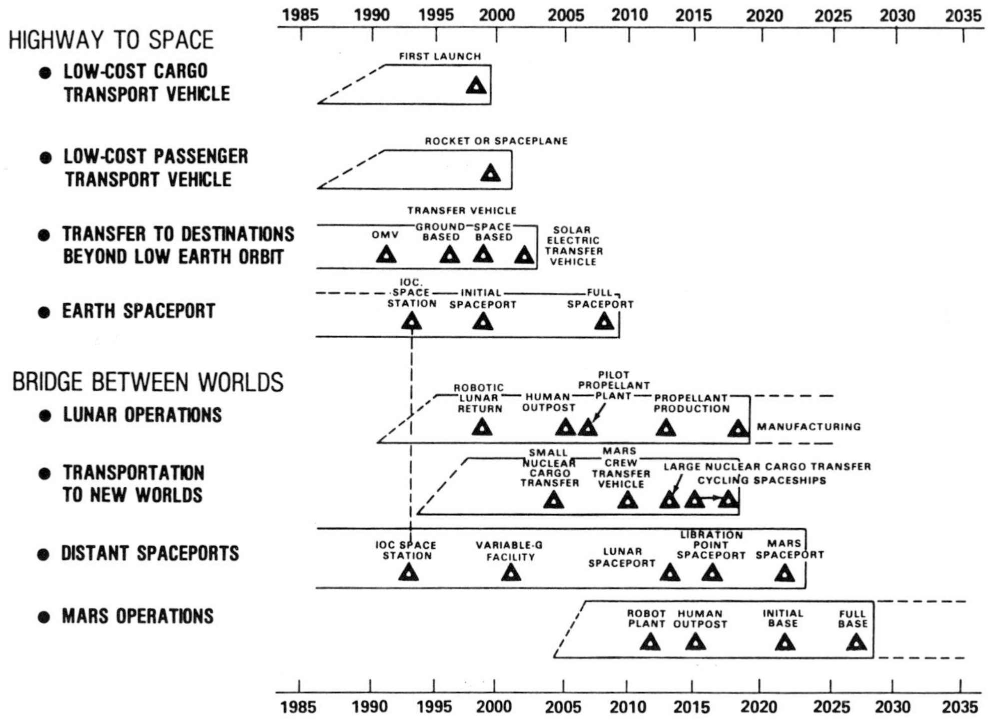

1985 1990 1995 2000 2005 2010 2015 2020 2025 2030 2035

HIGHWAY TO SPACE
- LOW-COST CARGO TRANSPORT VEHICLE — FIRST LAUNCH
- LOW-COST PASSENGER TRANSPORT VEHICLE — ROCKET OR SPACEPLANE
- TRANSFER TO DESTINATIONS BEYOND LOW EARTH ORBIT — TRANSFER VEHICLE: OMV, GROUND-BASED, SPACE-BASED, SOLAR ELECTRIC TRANSFER VEHICLE
- EARTH SPACEPORT — IOC SPACE STATION, INITIAL SPACEPORT, FULL SPACEPORT

BRIDGE BETWEEN WORLDS
- LUNAR OPERATIONS — ROBOTIC LUNAR RETURN, HUMAN OUTPOST, PILOT PROPELLANT PLANT, PROPELLANT PRODUCTION, MANUFACTURING
- TRANSPORTATION TO NEW WORLDS — SMALL NUCLEAR CARGO TRANSFER, MARS CREW TRANSFER VEHICLE, LARGE NUCLEAR CARGO TRANSFER, CYCLING SPACESHIPS
- DISTANT SPACEPORTS — IOC SPACE STATION, VARIABLE-G FACILITY, LUNAR SPACEPORT, LIBRATION POINT SPACEPORT, MARS SPACEPORT
- MARS OPERATIONS — ROBOT PLANT, HUMAN OUTPOST, INITIAL BASE, FULL BASE

1985 1990 1995 2000 2005 2010 2015 2020 2025 2030 2035

FIGURE 1

Product (GNP) for the past 25 years, and projects it forward for 50 years at an annual growth rate of 2.4 percent, as discussed in Part IV of our report. The estimated annual costs of the space advances that are outlined in Figure 1 are shown as an extension of the U.S. civilian space budgets of the past quarter century, assuming continuing international and commercial contributions to the program. Note that the percentage of the U.S. GNP invested in opening the space frontier would remain below one-half of the percentage spent on space during the peak Apollo years. We believe that these estimated levels of expenditure will prove to be affordable and reasonable in view of America's projected economic growth and the increasing significance of space development in the next century. We recognize, however, that this long-range program is a new challenge to the management of our Nation's space enterprise. For this reason we recommend that: **The Administration and the Congress continue to work together to set a new long-range direction and pace for America's civilian space program.** We sincerely hope that this Commission's report will contribute to a reexamination of and fresh approach to America's future in space. We see the need for longer-range vision, greater leadership, and more effective management of critical technological, financial, and institu-

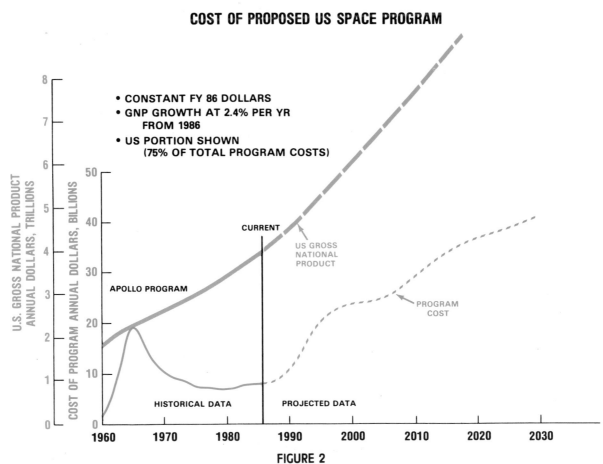

FIGURE 2

tional resources. This will also facilitate greater public understanding and participation, and more rewarding international partnerships.

The Commission's report has value only to the extent that its recommended space goals for 21st-century America are adopted and acted upon. If the decision is made to proceed along these lines, the detailed review, planning, and budget preparation should be carried out by NASA in consultation with NOAA and other agencies. The Commission therefore recommends that: **The President and the Congress direct the Administrator of NASA to review the Commission's findings and proposed space agenda, and by December 31, 1986, to recommend a long-range implementation plan, including a specific agenda for the next five years.**

Improved Oversight Through a Longer-Range Perspective

The President's Blue Ribbon Commission on Defense Management has recommended a number of reforms in defense systems acquisition that parallel our conclusions on improving the management of America's civilian space program. We recommend three specific changes similar to those proposed by the Packard Panel:

Twenty-year civilian space program and five-year budget planning to establish long-range goals and budgets for review and decision by the Administration and the Congress;

Multi-year procurements to replace year-by-year funding, with firm decisions that eliminate annual changes which have proven very costly to NASA and its contractors;

Two-year overall approval of civilian space budgets by the Office of Management and Budget and the appropriate Congressional committees to replace annual line-by-line auditing.

International Cooperation and Competition

This is discussed in detail in the section: *International Cooperation and Competition.* In proposing continuing American leadership on the space frontier, the Commission recommends that: **Vigorous steps be taken to attract other nations to work in partnership with us.** We must mobilize this planet's most creative minds to help us achieve our challenging goals. All of humankind will benefit from cooperation on the space frontier.

Twelve Technological Milestones in Space

The program we propose sets the stage for exciting achievements in pioneering the space frontier. A dozen challenging technological milestones would mark our progress:

- **Initial operation of a permanent Space Station;**
- **Initial operation of dramatically lower cost transport vehicles to and from low Earth orbit for cargo and passengers;**
- **Addition of modular transfer vehicles capable of moving cargoes and people from low Earth orbit to any destination in the inner Solar System;**

- **A spaceport in low Earth orbit;**
- **Operation of an initial lunar outpost and pilot production of rocket propellant;**
- **Initial operation of a nuclear electric vehicle for high-energy missions to the outer planets;**
- **First shipment of shielding mass from the Moon;**
- **Deployment of a Spaceport in lunar orbit to support expanding human operations on the Moon;**
- **Initial operation of an Earth-Mars transportation system for robotic precursor missions to Mars;**
- **First flight of a cycling spaceship to open continuing passenger transport between Earth orbit and Mars orbit;**
- **Human exploration and prospecting from astronaut outposts on Phobos, Deimos, and Mars; and**
- **Start-up of the first Martian resource development base to provide oxygen, water, food, construction materials, and rocket propellants.**

With these giant steps, America will lead a dynamic movement of humankind to new worlds in the 21st century.

BENEFITS

The new space program we propose for 21st-century America will return tangible benefits in three forms:

- **By "pulling-through" advances in science and technology** of critical importance to the Nation's future economic strength and national security;
- **By providing direct economic returns** from new space-based enterprises that capitalize upon broad, low-cost access to space; and
- **By opening new worlds on the space frontier,** with vast resources that can free humanity's aspirations from the limitations of our small planet of birth.

In the foreground is an aerospace plane and the Earth Spaceport. The Spaceport is receiving cargo from a cargo transport vehicle (lower left-hand corner). In the background, a two-stage transfer vehicle is returning to the Earth Spaceport from the Moon. (COURTESY ROBERT MCCALL)

"Pulling-Through" Technology

As we learned in World War II, government-academia-industry teams mobilized to accelerate advances in science and technology can build the foundations for new growth industries even though the original objectives were narrowly focused on military requirements. Wartime breakthroughs in jet propulsion, antibiotics, synthetic rubber, oil pipelines, nuclear energy, microwave radar, liquid-fueled rockets, radio guidance, electronic computers, and other systems led to America's high growth industries of the 1960s and 1970s in global jet transport, pharmaceuticals, synthetic materials, nuclear electric power, microwave communication, electronic computers, and many others. Technological advances from later Government programs made possible today's weather satellites, global marine communications, and the multibillion-dollar communications satellite industry that links together more than 100 nations on every continent. The space program has also initiated additional fledgling industries in remote sensing, direct broadcast, and navigation that appear likely to become future growth industries.

The program we recommend will motivate people, provide new standards of excellence, and stimulate many fields of science and technology, including those that we believe will be most critical to the economic growth of 21st century America. Specific examples include artificial intelligence, robotics, tele-operation, process automation, hypersonic flight, low-cost global and orbital transport, optical communication and data processing systems, ultra-high-strength and high-temperature materials, supercomputers, wireless power transmission, pollution-free vehicles (electric and hydrogen-oxygen fueled), orbital antenna farms, closed-ecology biosphere operation (which could revolutionize intensive agriculture)—and myriad others.

Return from Investment in Technology

In the last 50 years, Government-sponsored research and development created "enabling technologies" in aeronautics and in communications satellites. The needs of governmental agencies and of the public for new services attracted private capital to apply those technologies, leading to great new global industries. In the airmail contracts of the 1920s and 1930s, a public need for service played an additional vital role through the guarantee of markets to assist the growth of fledgling airline companies.

During the next 20 years, the Space Station may spark new industries by serving as a space laboratory for academic and industrial researchers. New processes of economic significance can be expected from applied materials and processes research in microgravity. Other new economic opportunities may come through laboratory environments isolated from Earth's biosphere, through the orbital global perspective for communications, navigation and observation of Earth, and through increased public access to space. Obtaining a return from new processes will require private investment in orbiting industrial parks established to provide common services to entrepreneurial companies carrying out independent operations in orbit.

New Space-Based Enterprises

In order to attract substantial private capital to build new space industries, the Government should create as early as possible the least expensive enabling technologies sufficient to open the energy and material resources of space. The private sector, especially its entrepreneurial part, is well situated and motivated to find the most rapid way to serve new markets. Companies are driven by the need to obtain returns on their investments, and financing is extremely difficult to obtain for high-risk ventures unless the returns occur quickly. This forces speed and concentration on specific opportunities.

We believe there will be such opportunities when the Highway to Space is extended via the Bridge between Worlds to high orbit and the Moon. The first products based upon materials found on the Moon include oxygen for rocket propellants and raw mass for shielding piloted orbital stations against cosmic and solar flare radiation. When the Highway to Space is extended to the Moon, an opportunity will be created to bring those products to Earth orbit at far less cost in energy than lifting them from Earth.

The transfer vehicle, capable of round-trip journeys from low orbit to the Moon and of piloted or remotely piloted operation, to which we give high priority in our recommendations, is the enabling technology needed to emplace experimental plants which could be operated by the private sector. When that second link in our space transport system is completed, the event will compare in significance to the driving of the Golden Spike in Utah more than a century ago that marked completion of the transcontinental railroad.

Private companies, driven by their need for rapid return on investment, could make use of the transfer vehicle to emplace economical pilot plants to provide lunar-derived shielding and oxygen. These plants would make strong use of robotics technology and would probably be tele-operated remotely from Earth. They would serve a highly valuable reinforcing role to the long-term space program by demonstrating soon the practical value of space resources. The Government could serve a vital role and reduce its own costs for space operations by committing to buy shielding and oxygen in Earth orbit.

We cannot foresee the ingenuity that companies, established or entrepreneurial, will bring to the building of new industries in the 21st century based upon the Highway to Space. Nor can we know the individuals whose names will rank with Douglas, Boeing, Sikorsky, and the other pioneers of the aeronautical industry. But looking back for analogies, we know that one of America's greatest heroes, Charles Lindbergh, practiced the skills of piloting in heavy weather, prior to his Atlantic crossing, by flying the U.S. mail.

New Worlds on the Space Frontier

The immediate benefits from advances in science and technology and from new economic enterprises in space are sufficient in our view to justify the civilian space agenda we propose. However, we believe that the longer-term benefits from the settling of new worlds and the economic development of the inner Solar System will prove even more rewarding to humanity. These returns are difficult to quantify. What was the true value of developing and settling North and South America, Australia, and New Zealand? Today more people speak English, Spanish, and Portuguese in the New World than in Europe, and they have built economies surpassing those of Europe. But the contributions to humanity from Columbus' "New World" are surely far beyond its material returns, impressive as they are. We believe that in removing terrestrial limits to human aspirations, the execution of our proposed space agenda for 21st-century America will prove of incalculable value to planet Earth and to the future of our species.

LUIS W. ALVAREZ

NEIL A. ARMSTRONG

PAUL J. COLEMAN

GEORGE B. FIELD

WILLIAM H. FITCH

CHARLES M. HERZFELD

JACK L. KERREBROCK

JEANE J. KIRKPATRICK

GERARD K. O'NEILL

THOMAS O. PAINE

BERNARD A. SCHRIEVER

KATHRYN D. SULLIVAN

DAVID C. WEBB

LAUREL L. WILKENING

CHARLES E. YEAGER

I

CIVILIAN SPACE GOALS
FOR 21ST-CENTURY AMERICA

Our nearest large galaxy: M31, Andromeda. If we were within this spiral galaxy, we would be near its outer edge. (COURTESY CALTECH AND CARNEGIE INSTITUTION)

No one can predict the dramatic scientific advances that will come in the next 20 to 50 years, but imagine what headlines might appear in the papers of the future as we expand our scientific activities in space (See page 29).

To answer all of our questions will take the efforts of generations of scientists in the United States and throughout the world, but current rapid progress in space science encourages the belief that one day the answers will be known. We believe that a well-planned, long-term program of space science along these lines will be a noble legacy for our descendants. New combinations of scientific disciplines, from theoretical physics to experimental biology, are needed to answer these complex questions. Coordination of these efforts across such a broad front may require new arrangements both in academia and in the Government. (See pages 149–151 for a description of the activities needed to realize our goals.)

Future Science in Space
The space science program of the United States has been guided since its inception by the Space Science Board. Their work, as cited in the bibliography, has laid out an excellent

SOME POTENTIAL SPACE SCIENCE HEADLINES

- IDENTIFICATION OF THE MISSING MATTER THAT MAKES UP 90 PERCENT OF THE UNIVERSE'S MASS.
- GRAVITATIONAL WAVES DETECTED.
- SOURCE OF HUGE ENERGIES IN EXPLODING GALAXIES DISCOVERED.
- IMAGE OF THE IMMEDIATE SURROUNDINGS OF A BLACK HOLE AT THE CENTER OF OUR GALAXY.
- AMINO ACIDS DISCOVERED IN THE URANIAN OCEAN.
- SUPERNOVA DEBRIS RECOVERED FROM COMET ICE.
- METHANE VOLCANOES DISCOVERED ON PLUTO.
- FIRST PLANET DISCOVERED OUTSIDE OF THE SOLAR SYSTEM.
- SIGNAL DETECTED FROM EXTRATERRESTRIAL INTELLIGENCE.
- MONTHLY SOLAR FLARE PREDICTIONS ACCURATE TO WITHIN HOURS.
- LINKS BETWEEN SOLAR ACTIVITY AND OUR WEATHER UNDERSTOOD.
- EARTH'S ENTIRE RADIATION BELT IMAGED.
- MONTHLY HURRICANE PREDICTIONS ACCURATE WITHIN 12 HOURS AND 100 MILES.
- THREE CONSECUTIVE EARTHQUAKES PREDICTED WITH 24-HOUR AND 50-MILE ACCURACY.
- SPACE STATION PROJECT TEAM CELEBRATES FIRST YEAR WITHIN A SYNTHETIC BIOSPHERE.
- BONE THINNING IN ASTRONAUTS HALTED WITH TREATMENT APPLICABLE TO PEOPLE ON EARTH.
- PERFECT GALLIUM ARSENIDE CRYSTALS PRODUCED IN SPACE STATION.
- THIRTY-DAY WEATHER FORECAST NOW 95% ACCURATE
- NEW STATE OF MATTER PRODUCED IN A SPACE LABORATORY.
- ICES DISCOVERED AT THE LUNAR POLES.
- FOSSILS FOUND IN ANCIENT MARTIAN RIVERBED.
- VENUS VOLCANOES VERIFIED.

program for the next decade. We have built upon their recommendations and those of other National Academy of Sciences committees. The SSB is currently preparing a study called *Major Directions for Space Sciences: 1995–2015* whose preliminary findings and recommendations were extremely helpful in plotting our course beyond the year 1995. The study delineates exciting new possibilities for fundamental research in every area of space science, using future space technology of the type described elsewhere in this report. This supports our recommendation that: **The United States launch a vigorous space science program aimed at (1) understanding the evolutionary processes in the Universe that led to its present characteristics (including those leading to the emergence and survival of life), and (2) using our new understanding to forecast future phenomena quantitatively, particularly those that affect or are affected by human activity.**

A Global Study of Planet Earth

For the first time in history we can observe the entire Earth as we would another planet, from its core to its outer atmosphere, both as it is now and as it has been over the eons. Advances in the technology of observing systems and computers promise to revolutionize terrestrial science. Moreover, advances in theoretical understanding and the availability of the supercomputer are providing detailed models that can be tested experimentally.

We propose that a long-range global study of planet Earth be undertaken. It is essential that studies of Earth be carried out in parallel with studies of other planets, for insights into the evolution of any planet throw light on the evolution of all. This study should be carried out with major international collaboration from 1995 to 2015 through a global satellite-based observing system, complementary measuring devices and surveys on Earth, computational facilities for modeling, and a system for archiving and disseminating data, all to be coordinated at the national level by the Federal agencies involved. Dynamic phenomena should be investigated over a wide range of time scales, with particular attention to processes that affect, or are affected by, human activities. Examples include continental drift, volcanic activity, earthquakes, ocean currents, events like El Niño, the response of the upper atmosphere to changes in radiation from the Sun, and potentially critical changes in the amounts of important gases such as carbon dioxide in Earth's atmosphere.

This global study of planet Earth will be based upon a strategy of observation, data handling, and research markedly different from that prevailing today, owing to new opportunities for an integrated approach and for increasing use of artificial intelligence techniques. Many, but not all, relevant measurements are best done from satellites. Simultaneous global coverage is essential to many observations, and the observing system must produce continuous and consistent records over long periods of time. This will require a number of geostationary satellites carrying a wide variety of instruments for long-term measurements. These satellites will be large high-powered spacecraft carrying improved versions of refurbishable or replaceable instruments currently in use or being developed.

Polar orbiting satellites will also be required to provide coverage of high latitudes and platforms for instruments that must operate at lower altitudes. Spacecraft now under development will increase our understanding of the "middle atmosphere," including the stratosphere, mesosphere, and lower thermosphere. These layers are just above the lower atmosphere, or troposphere, in which our weather is produced. Chemical changes like the production and

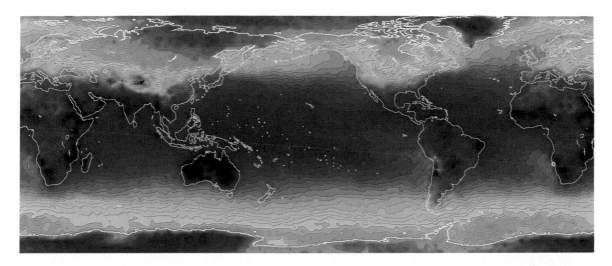

The mean surface temperature for November 1979—a mosaic of data taken by a NOAA satellite. (COURTESY M. CHAHINE AND J. SUSSKIND)

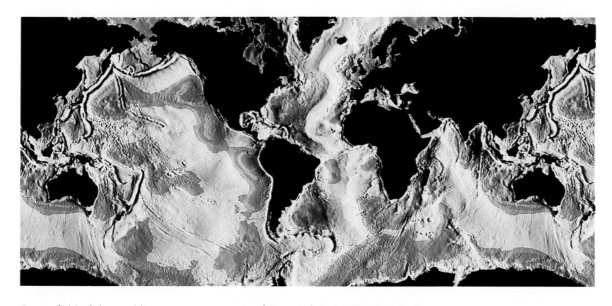

Gravity field of the world's oceans—a mosaic of Seasat data. (COURTESY W. HAXBY)

destruction of ozone take place in this middle atmosphere, with considerable consequences for living things on Earth. Other spacecraft in polar orbits will provide information on the differences between the northern and southern hemispheres and their responses to solar-terrestrial events. Starting in the 1990s, the Space Station and its co-orbiting and polar-orbiting platforms will provide even greater opportunities for probing the upper atmosphere. A tether system mounted on the Space Station will allow measurements at altitudes as low as 72 miles—a region only intermittently probed now by sounding rockets. Occasional special-purpose missions will require other orbits to test instruments and ideas for incorporation into the satellites described previously and to provide key one-time measurements. For example, "current buoys"—small satellites in selected orbits—will measure electrical currents with sufficient coverage to enable the construction of a global map of the currents that carry the ebb and flow of energy in Earth's magnetic field.

This global study of planet Earth is geared toward greater understanding of the physical and biological processes on our planet and their interactions. A vigorous and systematic study of the structure, dynamics, and evolution of the biosphere (i.e., living organisms and their

A false-color image obtained by the Einstein Observatory of the x-rays emitted by hot gas in the M87 galaxy. This gas, with a temperature of 10 million degrees, is invisible in optical pictures. The distribution of the gas enables astronomers to deduce that the galaxy has a mass of at least 3 trillion suns. (COURTESY D. FABRICANT AND P. GORENSTEIN)

interaction with the solid Earth, oceans, atmosphere, and polar ice caps) from the Space Station complex in low Earth orbit will be an essential component of the project. There is particular interest in the quantities that are changing rapidly, perhaps because of human activity, such as concentrations of ozone, methane, and carbon dioxide in the atmosphere.

To understand the early evolution of life on Earth requires the continued search for the oldest microfossils. This ground-based work should be supported by continued laboratory studies of the synthesis of key biological molecules under conditions approximating primitive Earth, as well as by further studies of meteorites and by the components of the space program that are concerned with studies of chemical processes on planets, asteroids, comets, and satellites. In view of the evidence that collisions with asteroids and/or comets have severe effects on Earth's biosphere, astronomical studies of such objects and continued geological studies of their effects are crucial.

The environment near Earth must also be studied carefully as part of the global attack. This requires not only major missions of the type described earlier, but also smaller-scale activities, including satellites, balloons, and sounding rockets.

Ground-based measurements will be a crucial part of the global study of Earth, since some effects cannot be detected by remote sensing from space. Ground-based surveys can provide high spatial resolution over limited areas and critically important calibrations, or "ground truth," for observations from space. Continuing studies of Earth's geological record are important to clarify long-term trends in geological processes, geochemical abundances, and climatic factors. From the global study of planet Earth, a rich harvest of knowledge will result, laying the groundwork for an increasing capability to observe and predict our terrestrial environment.

Human Biology in Space

The study of the response of organisms to conditions in space is vitally important if we are to undertake long-duration space flights by astronauts in Earth orbit and on missions to other bodies in the Solar System. The environment for living things in space differs from that on the ground, especially in the strength of gravitational fields, compositions and pressures of atmospheres, and radiation fluxes. Our knowledge of the effects of these factors is still primitive, owing to the paucity of experimental opportunities in the post-Apollo era. Substantial time and laboratory space must be made available for such experiments on the Space Station.

For the most effective experimentation, it is possible to simulate gravity from less than a hundred-thousandth to greater than one Earth gravity by using centrifugal force in a rotating system or by a gravity-gradient fixed tether. The atmospheric pressure should be variable from essentially zero to several times the pressure at sea level on Earth. We recommend **a new administrative entity, the National Space Laboratory as described on pages 149–151 and the development of a Variable-g Research Facility as discussed in Part II.**

Unshielded radiation fluxes pose potential problems both to the survival of organisms in space and to the interpretation of data. One concern requiring further study in this area is the high-energy high-charge component of the cosmic ray flux, which can damage non-dividing cells, including those of the central nervous system. Current practices regarding measurement of radiation doses should be reviewed, especially in view of the large range of particle energies encountered in space.

Of paramount practical importance are human safety and performance. Long-duration flights on the Space Station will increase our understanding of the effects of the space environment on people and other living systems. Problems of bone demineralization and loss of muscle mass persist, and effective empirical solutions are unlikely to be found soon. The impact of this problem becomes clear if we envision the response of a weakened skeletal structure to increased gravity when, for example, humans emerge on a planetary surface after a prolonged period of weightless flight. It is imperative that basic research on this problem continue, both on the ground and in space.

As opportunities for longer flights become available, new research should be undertaken with careful monitoring and evaluation of subjects. This will require more detailed monitoring of the environment than in the past, including gravity, radiation exposure, environmental toxicology, nutrition as it affects performance, microbial environment, epidemiology, functioning of the body's defense mechanisms, and dynamics of interpersonal interactions in a closed environment.

Remote health-care delivery in space must be developed as well. This will be a major issue as plans are made to send astronauts to the planets, since a rapid return to Earth will be virtually impossible. Little is known of the dynamics of drugs administered in a space environment, and the evaluation of even a small "space pharmacopoeia" will be a major undertaking; similar considerations apply to surgery under microgravity conditions. The importance of the latter is highlighted by recent estimates that one of a crew of seven astronauts selected from the general population for a Mars expedition would probably experience a medical problem normally requiring surgery. The selection process for astronauts must mitigate, but cannot completely eliminate, this problem.

The permanently occupied Space Station will, for the first time, permit relatively long-term laboratory experiments to be performed in the nearly weightless environment, or microgravity, of space and in controlled artificial gravity at levels between zero and one g (See page 35). A wide array of biological problems that have little direct bearing on human performance or safety can also be addressed by research in space. The vestibular system, for example, which is the part of the central nervous system concerned with bodily orientation, evolved over billions of years under Earth-gravity conditions. Studying its response in detail to microgravity should yield valuable new information about the central nervous system. This will require mammals (including primates) and facilities for their long-term care in space, as well as a centrifuge and, if possible, a sled to produce variable accelerations. Valuable experiments can also be undertaken on the long-term sensitivity of both plants and animals to gravity.

PHYSICS, CHEMISTRY, AND BIOLOGY IN SPACE

A Nobel Prize-winning theory predicts the change in heat capacity of liquid helium at uniform pressure as it makes a transition to the superfluid state. Although equipment has been developed to hold samples at a steady temperature within one part in 10 billion, the variation of pressure through the sample due to gravity is so large that experiments have yielded far less accurate results than desired. Reducing gravity by a factor of 100,000, as is possible in the Space Station, can provide a high-quality test of the theory.

Research is also proceeding on "fractal aggregates," structures that have the remarkable property that their mean density literally approaches zero the larger they become. Such structures are neither solid nor liquid, but represent an entirely new state of matter. So far, experiments on such structures are limited by the fact that the aggregates tend to collapse under their own weight as soon as they reach .0004 inches in size. In a microgravity environment, it should be possible to develop structures 100,000 times larger, or three feet across. Such sizes are essential if measurements of the physical properties of fractal structures are to be made.

Research on many other processes, including fractal gels, dendritic crystallization (the process that produces snowflakes), and combustion of clouds of particles, will profit substantially from the microgravity environment of the Space Station. It is not unlikely that novel applications will develop from basic research in these areas; just as the transistor grew out of basic research on the behavior of electrons in solids.

On Earth, laboratory experiments have shown that many of the biochemical compounds that are essential for life as we know it can be synthesized under conditions that we believe simulate those on primitive Earth. In space, we can investigate the effects of gravitational force on the behavior of these life-related compounds. Astronomers have found evidence for the existence of simple and complex compounds of carbon in interstellar space. In a microgravity laboratory in space we can investigate the apparently universal processes that form these compounds, which were no doubt present in the matter from which the Solar System was formed, and were probably the precursors to life on Earth.

To accomplish the goals of life science research in space will require Space Station facilities for growing plants, animal care and husbandry, for chemical and other types of analysis, and for neurobiological research focused initially upon the vestibular function. Since the Space Station's available volume, weight, and power will be limited, it is important that equipment be utilized for multiple purposes wherever possible, and that facilities essential for health-care delivery be adapted for basic biological research as well.

Fundamental Biology, Physics, and Chemistry in Earth Orbit

On Earth, the effects of gravitational forces on complex living systems are profound. We know this because of the so-called space sickness that strikes more than half the people who venture into space, apparently as a result of weightlessness. Experiments in space will allow us to identify and quantify the effects of gravity on the development, adaptation, and functions of plant and animal biological systems as well, on the biology of cells, and on the chemistry of complex biological molecules.

In the physical sciences, studies of the laws of gravitation are especially significant. For most purposes, the laws discovered by Newton are sufficiently accurate, but Einstein's more precise theory of general relativity predicts more subtle effects, including new states of matter, black holes, and a new form of energy called gravitational radiation. Although the general theory of relativity has passed all the experimental tests to which it has been subjected so far, more sensitive tests should now be carried out (See page 37).

We recommend that: **Flexible and rapid access be provided to a microgravity facility for researchers who will continue to devote the bulk of their effort to ground-based research in normal gravity; and new tests of general relativity be carried out wherever possible using facilities in space.**

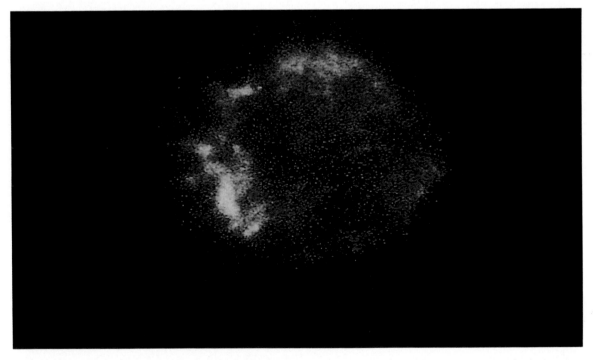

The orange dots are the positions where individual x-ray photons from the Cassiopeia A supernova remnant were recorded by the Einstein Observatory. The photons were emitted by a shock wave propagating into the interstellar medium from the supernova explosion. (COURTESY S. MURRAY)

WAS EINSTEIN RIGHT?

An especially promising avenue of research in space is the pursuit of new tests of Einstein's theory of general relativity. It has long been recognized that because deviations from the Newtonian theory of gravitation within the Solar System are minute, extremely sensitive equipment is required to detect them. Many experiments require the ultraquiet conditions of space. Because Einstein's theory is fundamental to our understanding of the cosmos—in particular, to the physics of black holes and the expanding Universe—it is important that it be experimentally verified with the highest possible accuracy.

Relativity predicts a small time delay of radio signals as they propagate in the Solar System; the accuracy in measuring this effect can be continuously improved by tracking future planetary probes. A Mercury orbiter would further improve the accuracy of measurement of changes in Newton's gravitational constant, already shown to be less than one part in 100 billion per year. An experiment in Earth orbit called Gravity Probe B will measure the precession of a gyroscope in Earth orbit with extreme precision, permitting verification of another relativistic effect.

Einstein's theory also predicts that a new type of radiation should be produced by masses in motion. There is great interest in detecting this so-called gravitational radiation, not only because it would test Einstein's theory in a fundamental way, but because it could open a new window through which astronomers could study phenomena in the Universe, particularly black holes. Gravitational radiation detectors are in operation, or are being built, on the ground, but they are sensitive only to wave periods less than 0.1 second because of Earth's seismic noise.

The radiation predicted from astronomical objects would have much longer periods if it is due to orbiting double stars and black holes with masses greater than 10,000 Suns, such as are believed to exist in the nuclei of galaxies. An attempt will be made to detect such radiation by ranging to the Galileo spacecraft en route to Jupiter. A more powerful approach for the future is to use a large baseline detector based upon optical laser ranging between three spacecraft in orbit about the Sun; detecting minute changes in their separations would indicate the passage of a gravitational wave.

Finally, instruments deployed for more general purposes can make measurements to test general relativity. For example, a 100-foot optical interferometer in Earth orbit designed for extremely accurate determination of stellar positions could measure the relativistic bending of light by the Sun with unprecedented precision. A spacecraft that plunges close to the Sun to study plasma in its vicinity could measure the gravitational red-shift of the Sun to high precision. In summary, a variety of space-based experiments on the shuttle and Space Station, in free flyers, and in orbit around the Sun and other planets have the capacity to test general relativity with a high degree of accuracy. Gravitational radiation from certain astronomical sources can be detected only in space. When that happens, astronomers will have an exciting new tool with which to study the Universe.

Solar and Space Physics

Our Sun is the only star that is near enough for detailed study. It is a complex and highly variable object whose variations cause changes on Earth. We need to understand how solar activity is produced, how this activity is linked to changes on Earth, especially to the changes that impact our environment. Space technology allows us to study the Sun and its effects on the rest of the Solar System, especially solar effects on Earth. Pluto, the most distant planet in the Solar System, orbits the Sun at a distance of about 3.5 billion miles, but the region affected by the Sun, called the heliosphere, may extend as far as 10 billion miles from the Sun. It is filled with an electrical plasma called the solar wind that flows from the Sun at about 300 miles per second.

A plasma, as the term is used here, consists of electrically charged particles, atomic nuclei and electrons, in electromagnetic fields. Nearly all of the matter found in the Universe exists as plasma in one or another state. Consequently, the study of plasmas has a number of branches, of which space physics is one. By using rockets and spacecraft, space physicists have learned that Earth's magnetic field extends far beyond our atmosphere, permeating a region of space referred to as Earth's magnetosphere. This region is filled with a complex mixture of space plasmas.

Understanding near-Earth space and the effects of solar activity is vital not only to the understanding of our weather and climate, but also to the safety of people in space. The effective operations of space-based facilities, especially electronic units and power systems, can also be adversely affected by the behavior of plasmas in their vicinity. Protecting humans from radiation outside the protective shield of the lower-altitude region of the magnetosphere requires that we develop sufficient understanding of the Sun and its effects to permit us to predict conditions in this region of space. Our recommendations for pursuing this area of space research are described on page 40.

Magnetospheres similar in many respects to those enveloping Earth and some of the other planets appear to exist in many other places in the Universe, from neutron stars to exploding galaxies. Consequently, studies of phenomena within our Solar System also increase our understanding of universal processes.

A program for solar and space physics from now until the mid-1990s has been developed in a number of studies under the auspices of the National Academy of Sciences and NASA. Beyond the initial operation of the Space Station, we recommend a program with four major components: (1) Spaceborne instruments to obtain observations from sets of orbits that are both closer to the Sun and global in their coverage; (2) Remote sensing of the plasmas in Earth's magnetosphere and the heliosphere using large-scale detectors in Earth orbit, at libration points, and on the surface of the Moon, in combination with directed energy sources as appropriate, and complemented by spacecraft to obtain direct measurements of the plasmas; (3) Active experiments designed to take advantage of the near vacuum of space in the study of the behavior of plasmas in the absence of confining walls that are

Image of the Aurora Borealis obtained by the *Dynamics Explorer* spacecraft as it orbited above the North Pole. (COURTESY NASA)

Photograph of an aurora in the southern hemisphere taken by the *Spacelab 3* crew in May 1984. (COURTESY NASA)

SOLAR AND SPACE PHYSICS

The objective of this field of study is to understand the physics of the Sun and the heliosphere, the vast region of space influenced by the Sun. Other regions of interest include the magnetospheres, ionospheres, and upper atmospheres of Earth, the planets, and other bodies of the Solar System. With this in mind, studies of the basic processes which generate solar energy of all kinds and transmit it to Earth should be emphasized, both because the physical mechanisms involved are of interest, and because there are potential benefits to life on Earth.

There are a number of sub-goals within this discipline: To understand the processes that link the interior of the Sun to its corona; the transport of energy, momentum, plasma, and magnetic fields through interplanetary space by means of the solar wind; the acceleration of energetic particles on the Sun and in the heliosphere; Earth's upper atmosphere as a single, dynamic, radiating, and chemically active fluid; the effects of the solar cycle, solar activity, and solar-wind disturbances upon Earth; the interactions of the solar wind with Solar System bodies other than Earth; and magnetospheres in general. Without assuming specific direct connection, the possible influence of solar-terrestrial interactions upon the weather and climate of Earth should be clarified.

A number of near-term activities are essential to the advancement of solar and space physics. Advanced solar observatories will study detailed energy production mechanisms in the solar atmosphere, while the European Space Agency's Ulysses spacecraft will make measurements of activity at the poles of the Sun. Spacecraft with sufficient velocity to leave the inner Solar System will make possible measurements in the outer heliosphere, including its transition to the interstellar medium of the Galaxy. The International Solar-Terrestrial Physics program, which will be carried out jointly by the United States, Japan, and Europe, will trace the flow of matter and energy from the solar wind through Earth's magnetosphere and into the upper atmosphere; investigate the entry, storage, and energization of plasma in Earth's neighborhood; and assess how time variations in the deposition of energy in the upper atmosphere affect the terrestrial environment. Interactions of solar plasma with other planets and with satellites and comets will be investigated by a number of planetary probes already in space or on the drawing boards.

Up to now, information about Earth's magnetosphere has been based upon measurements made continuously as various spacecraft move through the plasma and magnetic field in that region. An instantaneous global image of the entire magneto-sphere can be made using ultraviolet emissions from ionized helium in the magneto-sphere. It may also be possible to form an image of energetic particles by observing energetic neutral atoms as they propagate from various regions, having exchanged charge with other atoms there. Innovative experiments will be conducted from the shuttle to investigate the effects of waves, plasma beams, and neutral gases injected into Earth's magnetosphere.

To date, our knowledge of the outer atmosphere of the Sun has been based upon remote sensing from the distance of Earth. In a new concept, a spacecraft would be sent on a trajectory coming to within 4 solar radii of the surface of the Sun, only 1/50th of Earth's distance. The spacecraft would carry instruments to measure the density, velocity, and composition of the solar-wind plasma, together with its embed-ded magnetic field, in an attempt to discover where the solar wind is accelerated to the high velocities observed near Earth. Possible trajectories include a Jupiter swingby or a hypersonic flyby in the upper atmosphere of Venus. Such a mission would yield precise data on the gravitational field of the Sun with which to study its interior, and would test general relativity with higher precision. If a thruster were fired at the closest approach to the Sun, the energy change would be so great that the spacecraft would leave the Solar System with high velocity, reaching 100 times the distance of Earth in only nine years. This would provide measurements where the solar wind makes a transition to the local interstellar medium.

To acquire high-resolution information about the poles of the Sun over a long period, a solar polar orbiter should be flown. A network of four spacecraft at the distance of Earth, but positioned every 90 degrees around the Sun, would provide stereoscopic views of solar features which are otherwise difficult to locate in space, and would also monitor solar flare events over the whole Sun. Such a network would also give early warning to astronauts outside the protective shield of Earth's magnetic field.

Finally, plasmas in space should be studied for their own sake. Plasma is an inherently complex state of matter, involving many different modes of interaction among charged particles and their embedded magnetic fields. Our understanding of the plasma state is based upon theoretical research, numerical simulations, laboratory experiments, and observations of space plasmas. The synergy among these approaches should be developed and exploited. If neutral atoms and dust particles are present, as in planetary ring systems and in comets, novel interactions occur; they can be studied by injecting neutral gases and dust particles into space plasmas.

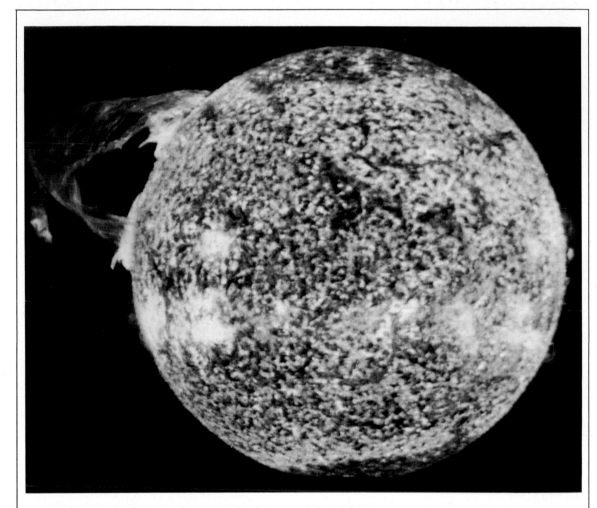

Photograph of a solar flare taken by the crew of the *Skylab 4* mission. (COURTESY NASA)

Voyager 2 flyby of Neptune in 1989. In the foreground is Neptune's moon, Triton. (COURTESY RON MILLER)

RETURNING SAMPLES FROM SOLAR SYSTEM BODIES

With the exception of the samples returned from the Moon by the Apollo astronauts and the Soviet robotic Luna spacecraft, and meteoritic materials that are believed to have fallen naturally on Earth from the asteroids, the Moon, and Mars, we have no samples of materials from bodies elsewhere in the Solar System for analysis in Earth-based laboratories.

Decades of study of meteoritic materials and lunar samples have demonstrated that vast amounts of information can be learned about the origin, evolution, and nature of the bodies from which samples are derived, using laboratory techniques which have progressed to the point where precise conclusions can be drawn from an analysis of even a microscopic sample.

The laboratory apparatus involved is heavy, complex, and requires the close involvement of people. Thus, given the substantial round-trip travel time for radio signals between Earth and these objects, it appears impractical to operate this equipment effectively under radio control on the bodies of greatest interest. The best method is to acquire and return samples, as was done by Apollo and Luna. Robot vehicles will be the most cost-effective approach to sample acquisition and return in the foreseeable future.

Unlike meteoritic materials, the samples will be obtained from known sites, whose location in an area which has been studied by remote sensing makes it possible to generalize the results to the body as a whole. Because of the variations among different provinces, samples are required from several sites in order to develop an adequate understanding of a specific object.

Considerable thought has been given to which targets are the most promising.

required in the laboratory; and (4) A long-life, high-velocity spacecraft to be sent out of the Solar System on a trajectory to the nearest star.

Study of the Solar System

The Solar System is of great interest not only because it is our extended home, but also because it represents a system, so far as we know unique, in which small solid bodies—the planets, satellites, comets, and asteroids—orbit a central star that interacts vigorously with them. In pursuing the question of the origin and evolution of the Sun and planets, we hope to discover other such systems and, by comparative studies, learn more about both.

Space techniques make it possible to make measurements throughout the Solar System using automated spacecraft. The overarching goal of planetary exploration enunciated by the

They must be reachable, and samples must be able to be returned with technology that can be developed in the near future. Their surfaces must be hospitable enough so that collecting devices can survive on them, and they must be well-enough understood that a complex sample-return mission can be planned and successfully executed. For these reasons, as well as others noted in the text, we recommend that a sample return from Mars be accomplished as soon as possible.

Though at present no individual comet meets the criteria discussed above, comets in general are promising targets for sample return. A start on the study of comets has been made by the 1985 encounter with Comet Giacobini-Zinner, and the 1986 encounters with Comet Halley. The proposed mission to a comet and an asteroid in the Solar System Exploration Committee's core program will yield much more information. Comets are probably composed of ices of methane, ammonia, and water, together with silicate dust and organic residues. The evidence suggests that these materials accumulated very early in the history of the Solar System. Because comets are very small (a few miles in diameter), any heat generated by radioactivity readily escaped, so they never melted, unlike the larger bodies in the Solar System. It is quite possible, therefore, that the primitive materials which accumulated to form the Sun, planets, moons, and asteroids are preserved in essentially their original form within comets. It is even possible that comets contain some dust particles identical to those astronomers have inferred to be present in interstellar clouds. If so, a comet could provide a sample of the interstellar matter that pervades our Galaxy. The Space Science Board has given high priority to determining the composition and physical state of a cometary nucleus. No mission short of a sample return will provide the range and detail of analyses needed to definitively characterize the composition and structure of a comet nucleus.

Space Science Board is to determine the origin, evolution, and present state of the Solar System. Two additional goals are to understand Earth better through comparative studies with the other planets and to understand the relationship between the chemical and physical evolution of the Solar System on the one hand, and the origin and evolution of life on the other. The SSB has developed a systematic strategy for this in which a program of reconnaissance of various types of objects in the Solar System is first carried out by telescopic observation and spacecraft which "fly by" the object. This is followed by more detailed exploration, for example by orbiters and landers. Finally, intensive studies are undertaken involving the return of a sample for analysis, and exploration by astronauts.

NASA's Solar System Exploration Committee (SSEC) has developed a plan to implement part of the strategy articulated by the SSB. The SSEC recommendations include an initial sequence of four missions: To Venus, to Mars, to a comet and an asteroid, and to

An automated spacecraft prepares to take a sample of the material on a comet's nucleus.
(COURTESY WILLIAM HARTMANN)

Saturn's moon, Titan. Later missions include a Mercury orbiter, additional probes to Mars, a probe into the atmosphere of Venus, a lunar orbiter, a mission to obtain a sample of debris from a comet, an asteroid mission, and missions to Saturn, Uranus, and their moons.

The missions mentioned here, like others in NASA's planetary exploration program, will provide measurements focused on critical questions about each target. For example, the Titan mission will focus on Titan's atmosphere, which is known to contain organic molecules of the type biologists believe played key roles in the origin of life on Earth. Measurements will be designed to tell us whether Titan's atmosphere has evolved so that primitive life is possible there, or whether lower temperatures or other factors on Titan have prevented the formation of life.

The attainment of many of the goals of the SSB will require new technology. Some of these requirements are discussed on pages 95–106. A highest-priority initiative is the returning of samples from various bodies in our Solar System, as described on page 44.

Mars is of particularly great scientific interest for a variety of reasons. It has experienced a complete range of geological and atmospheric processes, including vulcanism, the formation of canyons, dust storms, regional flooding, glaciation, and sedimentary deposition. Although some of these are similar to their Earth counterparts, there are important differences that can teach us much about our own planet. In contrast to Venus, which is highly inhospitable to life as we know it, we believe that Mars is an alternative home for humanity.

In keeping with our program and the recommendations of the Space Science Board for the study of Mars, a Mars sample return mission should be carried out early in the first decade of the 21st century. It is conceivable that Mars samples would include fossil evidence showing that life once existed on the planet; one can hardly imagine a more exciting discovery. In addition to their great scientific value, these samples can provide the basis for our initial steps in the development of Martian resources.

Asteroids and comets are of particular interest in our quest for knowledge about the origin of the planets. Because they may contain primitive materials that have been held in a deep freeze since the origin of the Solar System, they are accorded high priority for scientific investigation. These investigations will begin with flybys, and culminate with a sample return (See page 44).

The outer planets and their satellites, especially Uranus and Neptune, are difficult to explore because of their large distances from Earth. They are, nevertheless, of great scientific interest (See page 48). A long-term strategy for scientific study of the outer Solar System will depend upon the findings from missions to the outer planets in the Solar System Exploration Committee's core program, and upon technology developments recommended in this report (See pages 95–106).

EXPLORATION OF THE OUTER PLANETS

Beyond the asteroid belt lie four giant ringed planets (Jupiter, Saturn, Uranus, and Neptune), the curiously small world Pluto, more than 40 moons (two of which—Titan and Ganymede—are larger than the planet Mercury), and two planetary magnetospheres larger than the Sun itself. The center of gravity of our planetary system is here, since these worlds (chiefly Jupiter and Saturn) account for more than 99 percent of the mass in the Solar System outside of the Sun itself. The outer planets, especially Jupiter, can provide unique insights into the formation of the Solar System and the Universe. Because of their large masses, powerful gravitational fields, and low temperatures, these giant planets have retained the hydrogen and helium they collected from the primordial solar nebula.

The giant worlds of the outer Solar System differ greatly from the smaller terrestrial planets, so it is not surprising that different strategies have been developed to study them. The long-term exploration goal for terrestrial planets and small bodies is the return of samples to laboratories on Earth, but the basic technique for studying the giant planets is the direct analysis of their atmospheres and oceans by means of probes.

Atmospheric measurements, which will be undertaken for the first time by Galileo at Jupiter, provide the only compositional information that can be obtained from a body whose solid surface (if any) lies inaccessible under tens of thousands of miles of dense atmosphere. Atmospheric probe measurements, like measurements on returned samples, will provide critical information about cosmology and planetary evolution, and will permit fundamental distinctions to be made among the outer planets themselves.

The outer Solar System provides us with a special challenge, one that can be described as an embarrassment of scientific riches. It presents an overwhelming number of potential targets beyond the planets: The larger moons (Titan and Triton), the smaller moons (including the diverse Galilean satellites), the rings, and the magnetospheres.

Exciting possible missions include: (1) Deep atmospheric probes (to 500 bars) to reach the lower levels of the atmospheres of Jupiter and Saturn and measure the composition of these planets; (2) hard and soft landers for various moons, which could emplace a variety of seismic, heat-flow, and other instruments; (3) close-up equipment in low orbits; (4) detailed studies of Titan, carried out by balloons or surface landers; (5) on-site, long-term observations of Saturn's rings by a so-called "ring rover" spacecraft able to move within the ring system; and (6) a high-pressure oceanographic probe to image and study the newly-discovered Uranian Ocean.

Galileo probe descending into the atmosphere of Jupiter in the late 1980s. (COURTESY RON MILLER)

Astronomy and Astrophysics

Astronomy is based upon the collection of faint electromagnetic radiation from distant objects in the Universe, using sensitive telescopes operating at various wavelengths; cosmic-ray particles also yield important information. Answering the fundamental questions posed in this chapter requires the study of objects ranging from interstellar dust clouds, for which radio and infrared techniques are most appropriate, to extremely hot gas orbiting black holes in exploding galaxies, for which x-ray and gamma-ray telescopes are required.

Instruments must be launched into space to observe the complete spectrum of infrared sources, and ultraviolet, x-ray, and gamma-ray radiation from celestial sources, since these wavelengths do not penetrate Earth's atmosphere. Although optical and radio astronomy can be done from the ground, these disciplines also gain from space observations—optical astronomy by eliminating atmospheric blurring of the image that plagues ground-based observations and radio astronomy by providing extremely long baselines for ultra-high angular resolution.

Astronomical instruments in space can be located in low Earth orbit, geostationary orbit, solar orbit, or on the surface of the Moon. With a few notable exceptions, most of them have so far been in low Earth orbit, and in the near future will continue to be located there because of lower cost and direct support from the Space Station. As a lunar base is developed, astronomers will take advantage of the ability to build rigid telescope mounts, of the freedom from contamination by propellants, of the longer and colder nights, and of the shielding from Earth light and radio interference which are available on the far side of the Moon. If gravitational radiation is detected (See page 37), they will want to study the feasibility of locating gravitational radiation detectors on the Moon, where seismic noise is far lower than on Earth.

Virtually the whole electromagnetic spectrum has now been explored to some degree. Major new facilities, covering the gamma-ray, optical, ultraviolet, x-ray, and infrared bands of the spectrum, will permit exciting studies of faint and distant objects at wavelengths across the entire radiation spectrum. Orbiting astronomical observatories will remain in space for extended periods, with maintenance and refurbishment by astronauts on the space shuttle and Space Station. A program of "great observatories," which responds to the 1982 recommendations of the National Academy of Sciences, will address virtually all of the major questions now challenging astronomers and astrophysicists, with even more capable observatories now on the horizon (See page 52).

The stage is set for several decades of extraordinary accomplishments in space science. Using advanced technology, it will be possible to address the fundamental question of the origin of the Universe, the evolutionary steps which led to the galaxies, stars, planets, and life on Earth. We should be able to discover whether there is life elsewhere in the Universe. To bring about these accomplishments will require the dedicated effort of the world scientific community, continuing teamwork among university, industry, and government researchers,

Probe descending into the atmosphere of Titan, a moon of Saturn. (COURTESY RON MILLER)

FUTURE GREAT SPACE OBSERVATORIES

The size of the current generation of "great observatories" reflects the limitations on weight, size, and power of facilities that can be launched into low Earth orbit by the space shuttle. In the future, the permanently occupied Space Station will furnish a vitally important new capability for astronomical research—that of assembling and supporting facilities in space that are too large to be accommodated in a single shuttle launch.

Such large facilities will increase sensitivity by increasing the area over which radiation is collected, and will increase angular resolution using the principle of interferometry, in which the sharpness of the image is proportional to the largest physical dimension of the observing system. Though one or the other goal will usually drive the design of any particular instrument, it is possible to make improvements in both areas simultaneously. When we can construct very large observatories in space, these improvements will be achieved over the whole electromagnetic spectrum. Although the Moon will also offer advantages for astronomical facilities once a lunar base becomes available, we focus our remaining discussion upon facilities in low Earth orbit.

A large deployable reflector of 65 to 100 feet aperture for observations in the far infrared spectrum, that is, diffraction limited down to 30 microns wavelength (where it would produce images of a fraction of an arc second across), will permit angular resolutions approaching or exceeding that of the largest ground-based optical telescopes. This project would yield high-resolution infrared images of planets, stars, and galaxies rivaling those routinely available in other wavelength ranges. Assembly in Earth orbit is the key to this observatory.

A large space telescope array composed of several 25-foot-diameter telescopes would operate in the ultraviolet, visible, and infrared. The combination of larger diameter telescopes with a large number of telescopes would make this instrument 100 times more sensitive than Hubble Space Telescope. Because the image would be three times sharper, the limiting faintness for long exposures would increase more than 100 times. Such an instrument would with exquisite angular and spectral resolution enable detailed studies of the most distant galaxies and studies of planets.

A set of radio telescopes 100 feet or more in diameter could be constructed in Earth orbit by astronauts to provide a very long baseline array for observing radio sources, with the radio signals transmitted to a ground station. Such radio telescopes in space could greatly extend the power of the ground-based Very Long Baseline Array now under construction. The angular resolution of the latter, 0.3 milliarcseconds (the size of a person on the Moon as seen from Earth), could be improved 300-fold by putting telescopes in orbits ranging out as far as 600,000 miles. The resulting resolution of 1/1000th of a milliarcsecond—or one microarcsecond, would enable us to image activity in the center of our Galaxy—believed to be due to a black hole—very nearly down to the black hole itself. It would also provide images of larger, more massive black holes suspected to lie at the centers of several nearby galaxies.

A long-baseline optical space interferometer composed of two or more large telescopes separated by 300 miles would also provide resolution of 1 microarcsecond, although not complete information about the image. This resolution would permit us to detect a planet no larger than Earth in orbit around a nearby star (by means of its gravitational pull on the star) and to measure the gravitational deflection of light by the Sun as a high-precision test of general relativity.

A high-sensitivity x-ray facility, having about 100 times the collecting area of the planned Advanced X-ray Astrophysics Facility, could be assembled in orbit. A space station-serviced x-ray observatory would make possible the detection of very faint objects, such as stellar explosions in distant galaxies, as well as high-spectral resolution of brighter objects. This would make possible a study of x-ray signatures of the composition, temperature, and motion of emitted gases. For example, the theory that most heavy elements are produced in supernovae can be tested by studying the gaseous ejecta in supernova remnants. A hard x-ray imaging facility with a large (1,000 square feet) aperture is needed to study x-rays with energies in the range from 10 KeV to 2 MeV. Sources of such radiation are known, but are too faint for smaller-aperture instruments to analyze in detail. It is important to find out whether the known faint background radiation at these energies is coming from very distant objects, such as exploding galaxies, or from gas clouds heated by the stellar explosions that accompany galaxy formation.

The future development of gamma-ray astronomy will depend upon the results of a planned gamma-ray observatory, but it is anticipated that larger collecting areas and higher spectral and angular resolution will be needed to sort out the sources and carry out detailed spectroscopy. Cosmic-ray studies will require a superconducting magnet in space with 1,000 square feet of detectors to determine the trajectories of individual particles and hence their energy and charge.

The great observatories of the next century will push technology to its limits, including the capability to assemble large structures in orbit and on the Moon, the design of extremely rigid structures that can be tracked and moved with great precision, and the development of facilities on the Space Station for repairing and maintaining astronomical facilities in orbit. Because of the huge information rates anticipated from such observatories, great advances in computing will be required, especially massive data storage (up to 100 billion bits) accessible at high rates. The preliminary analysis of the data will be performed by supercomputers in orbit, transmitting only the results to the ground. The program will require a long-term commitment to education and support of young scientists, who will be the life blood of the program, as well as the implementation of high-priority precursor missions, including first-generation great observatories and moderate-scale projects.

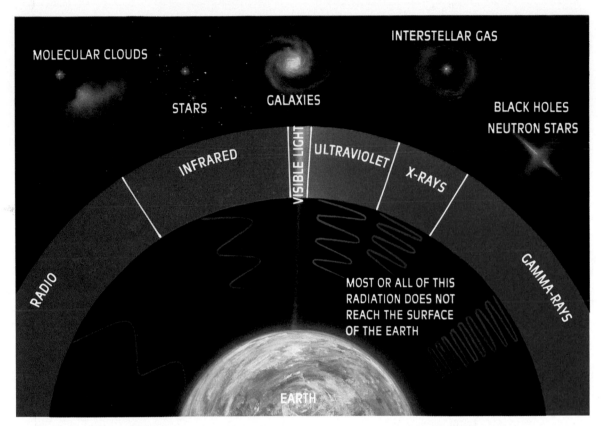

Astronomers use a variety of instruments to study events and objects in the universe. Some of these are visible to the naked eye, but many can be seen and understood only by studying images derived from other segments of the electromagnetic spectrum. (COURTESY RON MILLER)

and leadership at every level. The result will be a prize worthy of the ages—one which integrates the findings of many diverse disciplines of science into a comprehensive understanding of the cosmos which will provide humankind with a new perspective on our place in the Universe.

LIFE: EARTH AND THE UNIVERSE

The Evolution of Earth and Its Life Forms

Earth is the only one of our Solar System's nine planets that we know harbors life. Why is Earth different from the other planets? Life as we know it requires tepid liquid water, and Earth alone among the bodies of the Solar System has had that throughout most of its history.

Biologists have long pursued the hypothesis that living species emerge very gradually, as subtle changes in the environment give decisive advantages to organisms undergoing genetic mutations. The recent discovery that the extinction of the dinosaurs (and many other species as well) some 65 million years ago appears to have coincided with the collision of Earth with a large object from outer space—such as a comet or asteroid—has led to new interest in "punctuated equilibrium." According to this concept, a drastic change in environment, in this case the pall cast upon Earth by the giant cloud of dust that resulted from the collision, can destroy some branches of the tree of life in a short span of time, and thereby open up new opportunities for organisms that were only marginally competitive before. The story of the evolution of life on Earth—once the sole province of biology—thus depends in part upon astronomical studies of comets and asteroids which may collide with our planet, the physics of high-velocity impact, and the complex processes that govern the movement of dust in Earth's atmosphere.

Atmospheric scientists are finding that within such short times as decades or centuries the character of life on Earth may depend upon materials originating in the interior of the planet (including dust and gases from volcanoes), chemical changes in the oceans and the atmosphere (including the increase in carbon dioxide due to agricultural and industrial activity), and specific radiations reaching us from the Sun (such as the ultraviolet rays which affect the chemical composition of Earth's atmosphere). Through mechanisms still not understood, changes in Earth's climate may in turn depend upon the evolution of life. It has become apparent that life on Earth exists in a complex and delicate balance not only with its own diverse elements, but with Earth itself, the Sun, and probably even comets and asteroids. Interactions among climatology, geophysics, geochemistry, ecology, astronomy, and solar physics are all important as we contemplate the future of our species; space techniques are playing an increasing role in these sciences.

Space techniques are also valuable for studying Earth's geology. The concept of continental drift, according to which the continents change their relative positions as the dense rocks on which they rest slowly creep, is proving to be a key theory in unraveling the history of Earth as recorded in the layers of sediments laid down over millions of years.

The Possibility of Other Life in the Universe

Are we alone in the Universe? Virtually all stars are composed of the same chemical elements, and our current understanding of the process by which the Solar System formed suggests that all Sun-like stars are likely locales for planets. The search for life begins in our own Solar System, but based on the information we have gleaned from robotic excursions to Mercury, Venus, the Moon, Mars, Jupiter, Saturn, and Uranus, it now appears that Mars, and perhaps Titan, a moon of Saturn, are the most likely candidates for the existence of rudimentary life forms now or in the past.

The existence of water on Mars in small quantities of surface ice and in atmospheric water vapor, and perhaps in larger quantities frozen beneath the surface, leaves open the possibility that conditions on Mars may once have been favorable enough to support life in some areas. Samples returned from regions where floods have occurred may provide new clues to the question of life on Mars.

Titan has a thick atmosphere of nitrogen, along with methane and traces of hydrogen cyanide—one of the building blocks of biological molecules. Unfortunately, the oxygen atoms needed for other biological molecules are missing, apparently locked forever in the ice on Titan's surface.

How do we search for planets beyond our Solar System? The 1983 Infrared Astronomy Satellite discovered that dozens of stars have clouds of particles surrounding them emitting infrared radiation; astrophysicists believe that such clouds represent an early stage in the formation of planets. Another technique is to track the position of a star over a number of years. Although planets are much less massive than stars, they nevertheless exert a significant gravitational force upon them, causing them to wobble slightly. Through a principle called interferometry, which combines the outputs of two telescopes at some distance apart to yield very sharp images, it should be possible to detect planets—if they exist—by the perturbations they cause as they orbit nearby stars similar to our Sun. With sufficiently large arrays of telescopes in space we might obtain images of planets beyond the Solar System. By searching for evidence of water and atmospheric gases we might even detect the existence of life on those planets.

If life originated by the evolution of large molecules in the oceans of newly-formed planets, then other planets scattered throughout our Galaxy could be inhabited by living species, some of which may possess intelligence.

If intelligent life does exist beyond our Solar System, we might detect its messages. The Search for Extraterrestrial Intelligence, or SETI, is a rapidly advancing field. For several decades it has been technically possible to detect radio signals (if any) directed at Earth by alien civilizations on planets orbiting nearby stars. It is now possible to detect such signals from anywhere in our Galaxy, opening up the study of over 100 billion candidate stars. Such a detection, if it ever occurs, would have profound implications not only for physical and biological sciences, but also for anthropology, political science, philosophy, and religion. Are we alone? We still do not know.

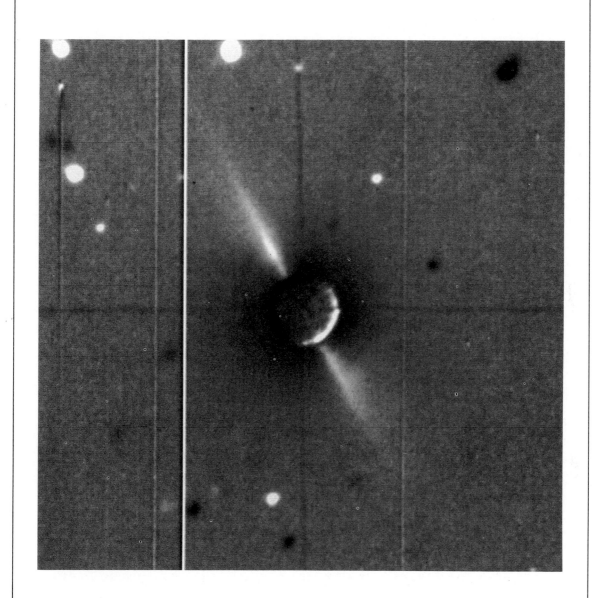

An optical image of the disk of dust around the nearby star Beta Pictoris. The disk may represent the first stage of the formation of a planetary system around the star. (COURTESY R. TERRILE AND B. SMITH)

EXPLORING, PROSPECTING, AND SETTLING THE SOLAR SYSTEM

Our drive to explore comes first from our human curiosity, a central attribute of intelligence. Closely following that urge to know, to understand, to see and touch with our own senses, there comes the practical desire to make use of what we learn.

Exploration, settlement, and enterprise are closely connected actions. Throughout the history of all three activities on Earth, we have explored both to search for scientific truth and to find valuable resources. We settled new territories not just to "be there," but to extend our presence on a permanent basis, generally to work at productive enterprises. In exploring and settling the inner Solar System, we expect the same close connections to prevail, because they make as much sense in space as they continue to do on Earth.

In the next section, *Space Enterprise,* we discuss commercial activities in space and the productive benefits of using the energy and material resources of space. This section focuses on discovery and exploration. We must keep in mind that space resources are already benefiting exploration and will do so even more in the future. Solar energy is a full-time resource everywhere in space except in the shadows of planets. Supplemented by nuclear generators when necessary, it powers the sensors, the computers, and the radio transmitters of the robotic spacecraft that we have sent ahead of us as our scouts to examine the planets and moons of our Solar System. Future research outposts, like today's major observatories in remote regions of Earth, will use local resources wherever possible to minimize costs. Once again by analogy to Earth's history, most of the people who pioneer the inner Solar System in the 21st century will do so to work at jobs based on the resources of space.

We must therefore transform the way that we operate in space both for science and for industry. The few short forays of humans beyond low Earth orbit repeated in method and spirit the early polar expeditions. Each was a quick dash, lasting only a few days, supported entirely by stores of food, water, air, and fuel lifted from the home base. As we move out farther, stay longer, and establish first outposts, then bases, then long-term settlements, some for scientific goals and others for production based upon space resources, we must "live off the land" for both energy and materials in order to reduce our costs of operation. In testimony before the Commission, there was remarkable unanimity on the need to develop indigenous resources to sustain the flow of settlement and enterprise stemming from initial periods of exploration. As phrased in one presentation to the Commission:

> The umbilical to Earth must be severed, or at least severely nicked. . . . This is best accomplished by the [on-site] utilization of extraterrestrial resources. . . . [We must] plot a future space strategy that "bootstraps" itself through the Solar System by the utilization of the resources found along the way.

For exploration and settlement, cutting the apron string to Mother Earth is necessary because we must otherwise support operations at the end of an increasingly long supply line. The logistics problem in space has its analog in the challenge of climbing Earth's highest mountains. Here on Earth, we live at the bottom of one of the deepest gravitational wells of the inner Solar System. Everything we hoist into space from Earth must be lifted out of a gravitational well 4,000 miles deep. By contrast, lifting materials from the Moon requires climbing a well only 180 miles deep. In recent years asteroids have been discovered which can be reached with even less cost in energy than traveling to the Moon. Finding them confirmed that the inner Solar System is a treasure trove of materials, available to support pioneers on the space frontier. Lunar, asteroidal, and planetary materials are valuable where they are found, and valuable also in "free space" which is the modern analog to the high seas (See page 61).

Exploration and settlement have an additional close connection because the distances we must traverse to reach all objects in space beyond our Moon are so great, and the times required to reach them are so long, that humans can best travel to them in ships that are much like movable settlements. What we learn about long-term life support in space will therefore be of value to us not only to support our exploration of the Solar System, but also for building the settlements necessary to support the space industrial activities of the 21st century.

Explorers throughout Earth's history could see only short distances ahead. The unknown, and with it often unknown dangers, lay just beyond the next headland or over the next mountain range. For that reason the charts of our nearly spherical Earth were built up only slowly and painfully over centuries, until flight was achieved. In space exploration we are already past that stage, because we can look outward in any direction through the transparent medium of space itself. There will be many surprises in detail, but we know in general which bodies are of potential interest. From the smallest to the largest, with some overlap of size, they are comets, asteroids, moons, and planets.

EARTH'S GRAVITY WELL

To lift payloads in Earth's gravitational field and place them in orbit, we must expend energy. We generate it first as the energy of motion—hence the great speeds our rockets must attain. As rockets coast upward after firing, their energy of motion converts, according to Newton's laws, to the energy of height. In graphic terms, to lift a payload entirely free of Earth's gravitational clutch, we must spend as much energy as if we were to haul that payload against the full force of gravity that we feel on Earth, to a height of 4,000 miles.

To reach the nearer goal of low Earth orbit, where rockets and their payloads achieve a balancing act, skimming above Earth's atmosphere, we must spend about half as much energy—still equivalent to climbing a mountain 2,000 miles high.

Once in "free space," the region far from planets and moons, we can travel many thousands of miles at small expenditure of energy.

INNER SOLAR SYSTEM GRAVITY WELLS

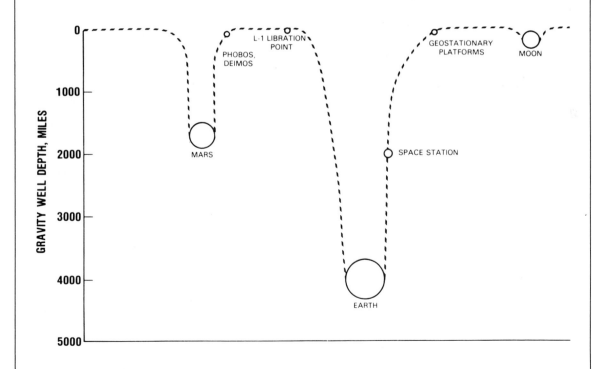

Astronaut Gene Cernan walking in the Taurus-Littrow region of the Moon in December 1972. (COURTESY NASA)

The Exploration of the Moon

To obtain a great value in knowledge from a small investment, we should send robotic explorer probes to the Moon equipped with sophisticated sensors. It is a first priority to search the permanently shadowed craters near the lunar poles, where ices containing carbon, nitrogen, and hydrogen may be found. We therefore recommend: **A robotic lunar polar prospector to examine the entire surface of the Moon from low orbit.** The prospector spacecraft should be equipped with remote sensors to examine the polar craters. We also recommend: **Probe missions to drive penetrators into the lunar surface, for on-site analysis at particularly interesting or valuable locales and missions to return samples for analysis from regions selected from prospector and probe data. It will then be time for people to return.**

Only 24 individuals have traveled as far from Earth as our nearest neighbor in space, and only 12 have landed upon it. The total time spent by humans on the lunar surface was less than two weeks, all of it in the Apollo years from 1969 to 1972. In those brief journeys a remarkable amount was learned: more than 800 pounds of soil and rock were returned to be analyzed on Earth; equipment was set up to measure heat flow from the Moon's interior, and to report Moonquakes and meteorite impacts. Laser reflectors were set up, which have allowed us to measure changes in the Earth-Moon distance to a few inches. Metal foils were stretched like sails to catch the wind of protons and heavier elements streaming from the Sun. And with electric roving vehicles, astronauts explored outward from their landing sites. But the 12 men who trod the lunar surface in the course of six Apollo missions could not venture more than five miles from their landed spacecraft. Quite literally, they could do no more than scratch the surface of the Moon. We therefore recommend that: **We return to the Moon, not only for brief expeditions, but for longer, systematic explorations; eventually, we should come to stay.**

As in the exploration of Earth, our exploration of the Moon can best proceed by a combination of visits to specific points, and the establishment of permanent outposts at locations of continuing interest. Separation of sites by purpose is more likely than the concentration of all activities at one "lunar base." Seismologists will need locations remote from mining, to achieve seismic quiet. Prospectors will need to make a series of land traverses, as is customary in resource exploration, and the promise of the lunar poles may draw prospectors at an early stage of lunar exploration. The first expeditions will make use of transfer vehicles as temporary camps on the Moon, just as the shuttle serves on each flight as a temporary space station. As more is learned and we find reasons to zero in on specific points, the temporary camps will be enlarged. Caches of food, fuel, water, and oxygen will be left there between visits and, finally, explorers will "overnight" at outposts through the lunar darkness that lasts 15 Earth days. We will return to the Moon for diverse reasons. As the first stage of the return to the Moon, we recommend: **Establishing human-tended lunar surface outposts, primarily for a variety of scientific studies.**

As revisits to the Moon become more frequent, the need will certainly grow for larger permanent "base camps," to serve as supply centers, local research laboratories, and medical centers for explorers taken ill or injured. One important facility will be located in lunar polar orbit. This will give excellent access to operations, particularly near the lunar poles or on the far side of the Moon, and good access to solar energy. Both before and after such facilities are established, we will have reason to visit specific points on the Moon for their scientific or resource interest. Volcanic features have been observed from Earth, and may yield vital

Lunar activities in the 21st century could include astronomy, both optical and radio wave, and the use of lunar material to manufacture products in space. In the foreground, a mass-driver is propelling baseball-size pieces of lunar material into space. (COURTESY ROBERT MCCALL)

information on the Moon's interior. The far side of the Moon offers locations for radio astronomy, shielded from the noise of earthly radio interference by 2,000 miles of rock.

In the development of technology for more distant travels, the Moon will serve as a laboratory. Because of its very slow rotation and consequent long nighttime, nuclear plants are likely to be necessary for power to provide life support on the lunar surface. They will be tested there before similar plants are sent as far as Mars. The movable space settlements which are likely to be used for journeys to Mars and the asteroids will be put through their proving voyages by trips around the Moon. All that we learn about long-term life support and medical service to astronauts in the relatively nearby environments of lunar orbit and the lunar surface will be put to good use when we venture farther into space.

Readily-accessible Asteroids

A special group of asteroids, almost unknown until the past decade, is particularly promising for exploration and resource utilization: the "Earth-crossing" group, whose orbits bring them closer to the Sun than Earth itself. About 40 such asteroids are now known, and we propose an intensive search for more members of what is believed to be a large family of these potentially valuable celestial bodies. The Earth-crossers are of more than academic interest. A considerable body of scientific evidence suggests that one such asteroid—or, perhaps, a comet—about five miles across, may have been responsible for our existence. About 65 million years ago that body, traveling perhaps 20 times faster than a bullet, is believed to have drilled through Earth's atmosphere and buried itself deep in Earth's surface. The resulting splash of material spread throughout the atmosphere in the form of finely powdered dust, cutting off sunlight to such a degree that, it is thought, plants died and the dominant fauna, the dinosaurs, were wiped out by starvation. That astronomical event allowed a tiny creature, the ancestral mammal, to grow, differentiate, and fill vacated ecological niches, giving rise eventually to *homo sapiens.*

A small number of the Earth-crossing asteroids have orbits that so nearly match Earth's that they can be reached more easily, in energy terms, than the lunar surface. Others are of interest for enterprise and settlement because they appear to contain the life-giving elements carbon, nitrogen, and hydrogen.

We have seen and tracked some of the Earth-crossers, but another group of asteroids, whose existence is still unproven, could be of even greater importance. Orbital theory suggests that asteroids may be trapped at other locations in Earth's own orbit, 600 million miles in circumference, around the Sun. Because of the unfavorable viewing angles from Earth, these "Earth-Trojan" asteroids are exceedingly difficult to spot. None has been seen. If they exist, material from them could be returned to the Earth-Moon system with almost no expenditure of energy. We therefore recommend: **Expanded Earth-based and space-based searches for readily accessible asteroids; continued telescopic characterization of their surfaces; and robotic prospector missions to particularly promising asteroids.**

The Exploration of Mars and Its Moons

After the accessible asteroids, the next easiest objects to reach in our Solar System are our neighboring planets Venus and Mars. Several decades of science fiction picturing Venus as a wet, steamy jungle planet were laid to rest when astronomical observations and Pioneer, Mariner, and Soviet Venera spacecraft confirmed that Venus has a poisonous atmosphere, a crushing pressure at the surface, and a temperature hot enough to melt lead. It is no place for humans. But Mars, our other nearest neighbor, is far more hospitable. Even more celebrated in science fiction than Venus, Mars turns out to be rich in surprises, mysteries, and promise.

The distance from Earth to Mars, averaging about 1,000 times as far as to our Moon, is great enough that we are more likely to visit the planet for exploration than for enterprise.

Olympus Mons, a mountain on Mars, is 15 miles high and 375 miles across at its base—the distance from Los Angeles to San Francisco (COURTESY JPL)

The exploration of Mars therefore offers an excellent potential for cooperation between nations. Discussions have occurred looking toward cooperative U.S.-Soviet Mars missions. In voyages to Mars orbit and to Mars itself, we can make good use of two techniques already proven in both piloted and unpiloted space travel: gravitational assists and aerobraking. A simple form of aerobraking was used for the safe return of Apollo astronauts, and the technique is also applied to reduce the orbital speed of shuttles before landing. Gravitational assists, in which the close passages of spacecraft around planets provide a "slingshot" effect to change directions and speeds, were used in the Apollo journeys and have been essential in the Voyager encounters with the outer planets. Mars has sufficient atmosphere to provide aerobraking, and the red planet is massive enough to provide useful gravitational assists.

Comparisons of the energy required to reach the Martian moons with that required to reach the surface suggest that Phobos and Deimos, the moons of Mars, should be investigated and some of their materials used before crews descend to the planetary surface. The Soviet Union plans to launch an international robotic prospector mission to Phobos and Deimos in 1988. Phobos, the larger moon, circles Mars at a distance of only 6,000 miles, closer than New York is to Australia. The period of time taken for one orbit of Mars by Phobos is correspondingly short, less than eight hours. Deimos orbits about three times as far away, with a period of 30 hours. Phobos is so close that it can become a natural space station, a potential location for an early base camp. Its color is very dark, suggesting that it may be a captured asteroid rich in carbon. Similar meteoritic material indicates that nitrogen and hydrogen are found with the carbon. If that is true in the case of Phobos, it could become an ideal refueling depot for descents to the planetary surface and for the return of spacecraft to the Earth-Moon system. Both moons are tiny, just 12.5 and 7 miles across; their gravities are weak and their shapes are lumpy and irregular. By contrast, Earth's Moon is about 250 times bigger than Phobos, with more than 15 million times its mass. A weak gravity can be an advantage: one need not "land" on Phobos or Deimos, but rather "dock" with them, as with an asteroid.

Mars has remarkable similarities to Earth, but in other respects is more like our Moon or Mercury. The Martian day is just over 24 hours long. Mars has polar caps of carbon dioxide (dry ice) and water ice which advance and retreat with the seasons, and its gravity is about one-third of Earth's, intermediate between our own and our Moon's. The U.S. Viking landers that set down on Mars in 1976 transmitted television images showing a pinkish sky, rolling hills covered by a reddish-gray soil, and a foreground scattered with numerous rocks. One could find in desert regions of the American Southwest, Australia, or North Africa, landscapes reminiscent of Mars.

The red planet retains a thin atmosphere with less than one percent of the density at Earth's surface. The atmosphere is mainly carbon dioxide, with traces of argon and nitrogen. Thin as it is, the Martian atmosphere supports winds powerful enough to carry dust and sand, and there are years when dust storms persist for months over much of the planet. Clouds, fog, and frost have been seen, and wisps of clouds frequently trail from the top of the highest Martian peak, giant Olympus Mons. Surface temperatures on the planet range from -184 degrees Fahrenheit in winter at the poles, to a summer record high of $+68$ degrees in an "oasis" near the equator, but at most places Martian temperatures are perpetually far below freezing.

Mars has impact craters, but it is also a world of immense canyons, volcanoes, sand dunes, and polar caps of water ice and dry ice. Television images from robot spacecraft orbiting Mars found vast erosional features, quite possibly formed by the swift flow of liquid water. If so, Mars must once have been far warmer and wetter than it is now. Its carbon dioxide atmosphere may have been much thicker in its early history, trapping the Sun's heat by "the greenhouse effect." There is evidence for the existence of permafrost and of liquid water about a mile below the surface at high latitudes, and water ice appears to underlie the northern dry ice polar cap.

The two Viking landers carried out chemical and biological experiments which detected no organic compounds. Although this tended to deny that life as we know it exists at those landing sites, the chemical reactions of the Martian soils resembled those which, it is now believed, may have been the precursors to life on Earth. As we learn more about Mars, we are likely to gain further insights to an important question: Is the origin of life commonplace in the Universe, and does it occur under a wide range of conditions? Or is it an extraordinarily rare event, which takes place only when everything about a planet is just right for it?

The distance of Mars, its gravity and atmosphere, and its tiny moons suggest a relatively complex plan for its exploration. The beginnings of that program have already been carried out by spacecraft in the 1960s and 1970s. A major step forward will be taken in 1989 when the Soviet space probe approaches Phobos and Deimos, firing laser beams at them to blast off tiny puffs of vapor for chemical analyses. Someday in the future, a new generation of robotic spacecraft, aerobraking in the Martian atmosphere to circularize their orbits, can return to Earth extremely detailed television images of the surface. Later, robotic hard landers can be targeted to potential Mars landing sites to carry out more detailed analyses of surface and subsurface soils in a search for water and other materials to support human habitation. It will be necessary to follow up these remote sensing missions by returning samples from Mars and its moons.

One of the most revealing exploration opportunities on Mars would be a journey by an automated rover vehicle down the length of one of the sinuous, water-carved channels that abound on the planet. Visual examination of the strata on the channel walls, or, even better, chemical examination, would yield information of a richness and complexity paralleling the data from an oil well drill core or the record of tree rings on Earth. This would be a particularly rich area in which to renew the search for evidence of life on Mars.

Sometime in the early decades of the 21st century we will establish permanent base camps either on the Martian surface or in orbit, possibly on Phobos. Exploratory journeys from Earth will then become routine, and will involve a series of cargo and crew transfers between vehicles considerably more complex than the maneuvers carried out for each Apollo mission. The people chosen for a mission will ride to an Earth-orbiting space station. From the space station they will move to a Libration Point Spaceport and then into a transfer vehicle capable of matching orbits with a cycling spaceship, repeatedly shuttling between the Earth and Mars systems. On the "cycler" they will experience a rotational gravity somewhere between that of Earth and Mars, possibly starting at an Earth-normal gravity and shifting to that of Mars in the last weeks before the cycler reaches its close encounter with the red planet.

Nearing Mars after a half-year voyage, the expedition will move into another transfer vehicle to make the transition to an orbiting spaceport or a base camp. There, after meeting and exchanging information with a crew that can provide current advice on Martian conditions, the expedition will transfer to a lander. The short trip to the surface will have as its destination either a major base camp or an outpost with a cache of supplies and equipment. Once on the surface, the expedition members may separate to carry out individual missions:

A Mars settlement in the 21st century with a Mars lander (in the foreground) arriving from the Mars Spaceport, and another Mars lander (in the background) departing. (COURTESY ROBERT MCCALL)

In the foreground, two astronauts are improving the capability of a large communications platform by installing a new dish antenna. Below them is a commercial space station in geostationary orbit. (COURTESY ROBERT MCCALL)

It is worth recalling that the "joint stock company," now the basis for most world commerce, was originally invented four centuries ago during the Age of Discovery to solve similar problems of high risks and delayed returns that were characteristic of early attempts to obtain value from the resources of the East Indies and the New World of the Americas. The Hudson Bay Company is still operating on the Canadian frontier.

Some of the largest corporations in the United States are involved in private satellite communications activities, exploiting a mature space technology with well-defined risks. Start-up firms are beginning to invest in developing their own space transportation, remote sensing, and microgravity materials processing systems. If current trends continue, the potential will exist for a wide array of privately financed space activities by the late 1990s. The United States should encourage these trends by maintaining an aggressive science and technology program to bolster U.S. competitiveness, by developing creative partnerships with the private sector that emphasize joint research programs and timely procurement practices, by ensuring that domestic and international regulatory approvals and other essential governmental decisions are processed rapidly, by transferring Government activities to the private sector wherever possible, and by striving to open international markets to U.S. space goods and services.

As the U.S. space program advances from Earth orbit to the Moon and then on to the planets, opportunities for the private sector will increase markedly. Like the early settlers who took advantage of wilderness forts to open the American West, we believe the private sector can make productive use of space infrastructure established by the Government.

At present, private space activities are limited to four general categories: satellite communications, space transportation, remote sensing, and microgravity materials processing. As we look forward to the 21st century, a broader definition of space enterprise will emerge. In the world of 2035, three categories of space enterprise will exist: supporting industries on Earth, space industries with markets on Earth, and space industries with markets in space.

Supporting Industries on Earth

In coming decades, privately owned and operated space vehicles may be departing on frequent flights from each of several terrestrial launch facilities to orbiting space stations and factories. The Earth launch facility will become a hub of private sector activity similar to that at today's major international airports. A full range of commercial services will be available to support launch operations.

As a result of the operational rather than research nature of future space vehicles, only small crews of specialized technicians will be required to support their launch and in-orbit operations. These services, along with vehicle maintenance and repair, may be performed by the companies that operate them. Other services and products like propellants, communications, and tracking may be provided by supporting industries. The same companies that

Landsat image of Death Valley, California. (COURTESY NASA)

The Commission is impressed with the power of a close partnership among Government, academia, and industry. In the case of remote sensing, the EOSAT Corporation represents a new private enterprise approach to managing the Nation's civilian remote sensing operation. We strongly believe, however, that America's success in this competitive arena will require continuing Government and academic support. We therefore recommend, **that NASA and NOAA continue a strong research and development program in the field of remote sensing, and that their budgets include funds for establishing five university centers to promote and support academic research in this critical field.** This support should encompass providing modern image analysis systems to develop new software, funding research projects to improve remote sensing systems, and establishing fellowships to encourage graduate students to enter the field.

Other Potential Industries

A third potential civilian growth industry, space-based navigation, will develop in the late 1980s and 1990s. In our highly mobile society, space-based navigation could be utilized by millions of travelers. It is possible that the growth rate of this industry will be limited only by price, product planning, and competition. The concept is a departure from the model of Government-funded technology and demonstrations preceding and leading to "commercialization." Today, while the Department of Defense is developing the NAVSTAR Global Positioning System of navigation satellites, commercial efforts are proceeding with entirely different system concepts, although the underlying principles are similar.

These early industries will be aided by advances in space transportation technology and on-orbit servicing, which will provide new options for advanced, more cost-effective designs for space hardware. It is difficult to determine today the direction that future orbital facility design may take. It is widely believed, however, that the ultimate configuration will consist of large platforms in orbit, of modular design to simplify maintenance, and with increased power to reduce the size of ground terminals.

In addition to communication, information, and navigation, which are virtual certainties for commercial growth, space may offer advantages for manufacturing unique new products. For example, some alloys cannot be produced on Earth because one metal is heavier than the other and gravity causes separation into two layers. These alloys could be manufactured in space, however, because the effects of gravity are reduced there a millionfold. Controlled gas bubbles could be dispersed throughout a heavy metal to produce a new or light weight material, or other new techniques developed. The future products of microgravity manufacturing are still difficult to visualize, but many ideas exist. High transportation costs may limit the opportunities to low volume, low weight, high value products initially, like drugs and pharmaceutical products, high-performance electronic chips, new composites and specialty alloys, and similar products.

A strong interest exists in the materials community for research and development using

REMOTE SENSING AND THE PRIVATE SECTOR

In the early 1960s, the Government, through NASA, developed and launched the first weather satellites. When the operation of weather satellites matured, they were turned over to the Department of Commerce's Environmental Science Services Administration, which became part of the newly-established National Oceanic and Atmospheric Administration (NOAA) in 1970. Today, NOAA continues to operate and manage the U.S. civilian weather satellite system, comprised of two polar-orbiting and two geostationary satellites.

The Landsat remote sensing system had similar origins. Developed initially by NASA, the first Landsat satellite was launched in 1972; the most recent spacecraft in the series, Landsat 5, was orbited in 1984.

So successful was the Landsat concept that a nationwide and worldwide group of users quickly grew, encouraged by NASA and the Agency for International Development (AID). A global network of ground stations now receives and processes Landsat-transmitted data, and many countries incorporate Earth remote sensing in their development projects. Over the years, Landsat has proven to be one of the most popular forms of American foreign aid.

Although remote sensing data are provided by the United States at relatively low cost, many user nations have installed expensive equipment to directly receive Landsat data. Their investments in Landsat provide a strong indication of the data's value.

Successive administrations and Congresses wrestled with the question of how

microgravity, but little space research has been focused on the development of commercial products. As a result, there is only a small data base of research results available to private companies. This will change as large corporations intensify their space research investment programs and as NASA and the private sector work together to make the space station effective as a research site.

The ideal space enterprise would have a stable, predictable, very large market on Earth, a potential for export sales, and once established, would not be dependent on Earth-to-orbit transportation costs to generate continuing revenues. The commercial satellite communications industry satisfies all those conditions except the first; its potential market size of several billion dollars per year is not large enough to make a substantial impact on the U.S. Gross National Product.

One highly speculative space enterprise would, if technically and economically feasible, satisfy all of the ideal conditions, including large market size. This enterprise would provide electric energy for Earth from satellites intercepting solar energy in geostationary orbit.

best to deal with a successful experimental system that had, in fact, become operational. Following exhaustive governmental review, President Carter decided in 1979 that Landsat would be transferred to NOAA with the eventual goal of private sector operation after 7 to 10 years. Following several years of transition between NASA and NOAA, the latter formally assumed responsibility for Landsat 4 in 1983. By that time, the Reagan Administration had decided to accelerate the privatization of Landsat, but despite the rapid growth in the demand for these services, no viable commercial entity appeared ready to take it over without some sort of Government subsidy. In 1984, Congress passed the Land Remote Sensing Commercialization Act to facilitate the process.

Seven qualified bidders responded to the Government's proposal to establish a commercial land remote sensing satellite system, and two were chosen by the Department of Commerce for final competition. One later withdrew after the Reagan Administration indicated that it would provide a considerably lower subsidy than anticipated. The remaining entrant, EOSAT, negotiated a contract that included a Government subsidy and requires them to build at least two more satellites in the series. In the fall of 1985, EOSAT, a joint venture between RCA Astro-Electronics and Hughes Santa Barbara Aerospace, assumed responsibility for Landsat.

The Government's capital assistance to EOSAT is in limbo at this time because of the current budget situation, even though EOSAT was contractually targeted for such financial support. It is, therefore, too soon to say whether the Landsat privatization process will provide a successful model for the transfer of a Government-developed space enterprise to the private sector.

The total market for electricity, at the prices now common for coal or nuclear power plants, is on the order of $400 billion per year worldwide. Capturing such a market would make a substantial impact on the U.S. GNP and balance of payments.

The basic concept of solar power satellites was studied in the 1970s. Space technologies that will become available within the next 20 years offer the potential to make these systems less difficult to achieve in the 21st century. These include improved space transportation systems, the use of lunar materials from the top of Earth's gravity well, and advanced robotics and tele-operation. There would, of course, be competition; the largest conference so far held on solar power satellites was held in Japan. The Soviet Union has announced the goal of building the first solar power satellite to supply energy to Earth in the 1990s. We feel that the United States would have sufficient technological skills and leadership to be able to dominate such a market if it develops, provided that U.S. research efforts continue.

From an environmental viewpoint, we suspect that the continued dumping of fossil fuel emissions into the atmosphere (particularly carbon dioxide) may have significant effects on

Earth's biosphere. If so, nuclear power and solar power satellites would become economic competitors. It is far too early to predict that solar power satellites can undersell nuclear power, but the possibility is significant enough that we endorse a strong continuing program of research.

Space Business with Markets in Space

Sometime in the next decades, space business will begin cutting its umbilical cord with Earth. The process may begin on a small scale, for example, with the production of lunar-derived oxygen to reduce the costs of operating chemical rockets beyond low Earth orbit. It will come to fruition when the first self-sustaining economy is established free of dependence on Earth for agricultural or principal industrial products. The transmission of information and entertainment, and the sale of small, complex high-value products, will link Earth to the space economies long beyond that time.

As we have noted, the Solar System is rich in raw materials, and we anticipate the eventual practicability of mining the Moon, asteroids, and the moons of Mars. This can provide future profitable opportunities for private enterprise. Non-terrestrial materials are attractive for use in space because on Earth we stand at the bottom of a gravity well 4,000 miles deep (See page 61).

If historical precedents for mining and materials purification are followed, the easiest and closest resources will be developed first, and the more sophisticated processing and distant sources developed later. The historical analog is terrestrial mining, in which minerals near the surface of the ground were used first, then deeper mines were dug. There is also a natural progression from simple processing of materials to more complex operations. In using materials found in space, at each stage of sophistication there will have to be a direct economic payback, if "enterprise" is to have real meaning.

In addition to these natural resources, there is a potentially valuable artificial space resource that is now going to waste: the shuttle's external tanks. At present, with each successful flight of a shuttle, an empty tank with mass greater than the full payload of the shuttle itself is brought to 99 percent of orbital speed and then discarded to burn up in the atmosphere. The shuttle fleet's flight schedule suggests that over a 10-year period about 10,000 tons of that tankage will be brought almost to orbit and then discarded. At standard shuttle rates, it would cost about $35 billion to lift that mass to orbit. There are reasonable arguments, involving potential hazards and the costs of maintaining tanks in orbit over time, against saving this resource, but we feel that so great a resource cannot be ignored, and propose that a new look be taken. We cannot set limits now on what uses could be made of shuttle tanks in orbit; ingenuity and the profit motive might produce useful ideas. One obvious use is as shielding against radiation; another possibility is mass for tether anchoring. We therefore recommend that: **The potential value, risks, and costs of stockpiling shuttle external tanks in orbit be reviewed again in light of increased orbital activities to determine whether preserving a large tonnage of fabricated aluminum, steel, and other materials is desirable in the next 10 to 15 years.**

Lunar Resources

Thanks to the priceless legacy of Apollo, we already know a great deal about the nearest source of materials on the "high ground" beyond Earth. The Moon is our partner in gravitational lock. To reach it we need no "launch opportunities"—it is always there waiting for us. Here, in rough order from the simplest and earliest to the most distant and complex, is one possible progression in our use of the lunar resources: first raw lunar soil, for shielding against radiation and as propellant for mass-driver engines in space; then oxygen for rocket propellant, as the main constituent of water and our "breath of life"; next raw lunar glasses, treated physically and thermally to become strong composites for structures; next iron, to be sintered (compressed in molds and heated) into precision products; and then silicon, for solar cell power arrays. Hydrogen is in low concentration on the Apollo sites, but its relatively higher concentration in the fine-grained lunar soils may allow its extraction. If so, it will be used both as rocket fuel and as a constituent of water. Finally there will be the separation of lunar soils into the full range of elements useful for industrial manufacturing and construction.

Apollo astronauts were the first prospectors of another world. All of the common elements they found on the Moon turn out to be useful. Oxygen is about 40 percent by weight in the lunar soils. Some have called the Moon a "tank farm in space" for that reason. Lunar oxygen solves 6/7ths of the problem of getting propellants from the top rather than the bottom of Earth's gravity well; our best rocket engines burn six pounds of oxygen for each pound of hydrogen they consume. When lunar oxygen is available for transfer vehicles operating to the Moon, the situation will be much like that of 19th-century railroad locomotives and steamships—"transfer vehicles" which refueled with local wood and water.

Next after oxygen, in order of richness in the lunar soils, is silicon, the "power element" useful for building solar energy arrays. The lunar surface soils are 20 percent silicon. Fortunately, techniques have now been developed on Earth for producing large solar arrays at low cost by the automated manufacture of thin films of amorphous silicon. Ranking behind silicon in abundance on the Moon are calcium and a number of metals. The ratios between various metals depend on the site (Mare, Highland, or other), but typical values are 14 percent aluminum and 4 percent iron, with smaller percentages of titanium, manganese, magnesium, and chromium.

Iron is abundant at every Apollo landing site. Much of it is in the form of fine powder deposited by meteorite bombardment over millions of years. Relatively pure metallic iron can, therefore, be readily recovered by simple magnetic separation of fine-grained lunar soils passing on a conveyor belt. The technology of powdered-iron metallurgy is well developed on Earth, where it is used regularly to manufacture strong, high-precision machinery parts such as gears. It lends itself well to automated manufacturing.

Hydrogen is in very low concentration in the bulk lunar soils, but as noted earlier, it is in higher concentration in the lunar "fines" (the portion of the bulk soil that passes through small-mesh sieves). The higher concentration of hydrogen was deposited in the lunar fines by millions of years of bombardment by the solar wind. Physical separation to concentrate the fines requires very little energy; heating the fines then releases small but usable amounts of hydrogen. For higher concentrations of hydrogen, and for carbon and nitrogen, we need to discover the lunar equivalent of Earth's concentrated ore deposits, if they exist. As noted previously, such deposits are most likely to be found in frigid craters, never exposed to sunlight, near the lunar North and South Poles.

The elements found on the Moon and on other bodies in space are familiar, but relatively little of our industrial experience on Earth is applicable to separating them from the lunar minerals in which they are found. To extract oxygen, several processes, both electrolytic and chemical, have been studied in the laboratory. The early results are promising enough to suggest that even a modest program of development would lead to satisfactory processes for oxygen extraction. We therefore recommend: **A continuing program to test, optimize, and demonstrate chemical engineering methods for separating materials found in space into pure elements suitable as raw materials for propellants and for manufacturing. Studies should also be carried out to allow choices to be made of the most cost-effective power sources for these processes at various locations in space and on selected bodies of the inner Solar System.**

The surface soils of the Moon and of many asteroids are mainly glass. Recent research indicates that those materials can be processed into structural composites—fibers in a softer matrix, analogous to fiberglass—without the need for chemical separation. Such processing would require far less energy than chemical separation processes for aluminum, titanium, or magnesium. We therefore also recommend: **Research to pioneer the use, in construction and manufacturing, of space materials that do not require chemical separation, for example, lunar glasses and metallic iron concentrated in the lunar fines.**

The Moon is not the only attractive site for extraterrestrial mining. Of all the material that could be found in space, the easiest to recover would be asteroids trapped in Earth's orbit around the Sun as discussed previously, but we do not yet know whether they exist. The next most accessible mineral lodes in space are probably the Earth-crossing asteroids. We know far less about the composition of those asteroids than we do about the soils of the Moon's equatorial region, but their reflected sunlight at different wavelengths leads us to suspect that many are stony or metallic. The most valuable would be the few thought to contain large amounts of carbon and hydrogen.

Phobos and Deimos are potential material resources of particular interest to resupply missions to Mars orbit or to the planetary surface. Tantalizing glimpses of the Martian moons were transmitted back to us from NASA's Viking spacecraft. The two moons seem to be quite different in composition, and Phobos, the larger, appears to be rich in water, carbon, and nitrogen. If so, there is an orbiting fuel depot just 6,000 miles above the red planet to top off the hydrogen and oxygen tanks of visiting spacecraft.

Main belt asteroids, in orbits between Mars and Jupiter, contain a rich variety of

Mining propellant on Phobos, a moon of Mars. (COURTESY ROBERT MCCALL)

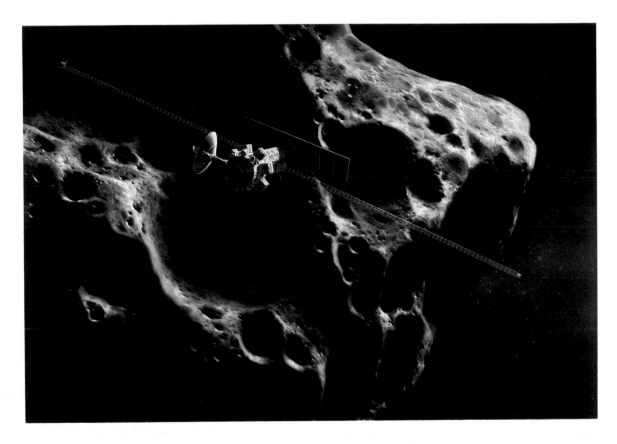

An automated spacecraft flys past an asteroid. (COURTESY PAUL HUDSON AND JPL)

winning opportunities will be those that can be developed most rapidly at lowest cost. Bootstrapping is almost surely a way to keep competitive.

Private industry is driven by its needs for return on investment to find opportunities for the fastest return. In a new business venture perceived by the financial community to be of high investment risk, future returns may be devalued by 50 percent or more for each year of interval between investment and returns. A venture which required five years from investment to returns must, in those conditions, be able to demonstrate future returns more than seven times the needed investment capital to get started at all.

That financial reality means that in practice, new business ventures can best achieve success by assembling technological building blocks industrially available at that time in novel ways rather than by investing in wholly new technologies. Such new ventures must carefully protect their proprietary rights, usually including patent protection. If protection for their contributions cannot be obtained, their financing sources will dry up. Making productive use of cast-off shuttle tankage in orbit or supplying lunar oxygen, hydrogen, or shielding mate-

An astronaut has departed a transfer vehicle for a close-up look at an asteroid. (COURTESY ROBERT MCCALL)

rials could provide future opportunities for entrepreneurial companies or for entrepreneurial divisions within large companies. They can do so only when the basic elements of space transportation to low orbit, and beyond to the Moon, have been developed to a reliable level under Government sponsorship.

The financial scale of new ventures has severe limits. Today a start-up requiring $10 million is large, a venture requiring $25 million is very large, and a new venture requiring over $50 million is so nearly impossible that there have been only two successful examples during the past 15 years. Yet, entrepreneurial drive tends to be found in just the small companies that face these odds and must work within such comparatively tiny resources.

These realistic limitations give us a useful insight into the new business ventures that are likely to succeed in space. They will probably make heavy use of existing robotic technology. They are almost certain to use tele-operation to reduce costs and liability. They will depend, if they are to be successful, on ingenious new short-cuts to reach their goals. They will, if they happen at all, happen quickly. And if they are successful, they will grow rapidly, draw imitators, serve as models for later ventures, and provide material for 21st-century business school textbooks. Every success will make it easier for future ventures to obtain financing; failures will reduce the chances for subsequent ventures. To reduce the risks to a level that will allow new ventures to attract investors, the Government could serve as a "pump-primer" as it did in the days of the early air mail contracts. NASA would gain substantially by reducing its costs for space operations, if through contracts for lunar materials or space services it drew in the talents of companies with entrepreneurial talents.

NASA has developed, and is now providing, a financial mechanism called the Modified Launch Services Agreement, which is effective in assisting the start-up of new space ventures without becoming a drain on Federal funds. In this Agreement, launch services are provided to the leading entrant in new commercial space services, and payments are deferred to a period following launch. We recommend that: **The NASA Modified Launch Services Agreement be extended, as space operations grow, to include interorbit transport services, base camp support services, and other services as appropriate.**

II

LOW-COST ACCESS TO THE SOLAR SYSTEM

BUILDING THE TECHNOLOGY BASE

American leadership on the space frontier requires aggressive programs in technology development. Indeed, our Nation's future requires that we lead in those technologies that have the greatest implications for 21st-century America's economic productivity, health, security, and national spirit.

Technological advance is critical to all three major elements of our recommended program: Science, Exploration, and Enterprise. Many valuable and exciting scientific investigations can be carried out in space with today's state-of-the-art technology, but major advances in optical resolutions and telescope pointing accuracy are required to allow us to detect Earth-like planets circling nearby stars. High-performance nuclear-electric power systems make possible exploration of the outer reaches of the Solar System, and are important for future spaceports and Moon bases. Our budding space enterprises must have lower-cost access to space through advancing technologies if "Made in Space" products are to succeed against Earthbound competitors in the next century.

The technologies needed for success in these ventures are many and varied. Some are rather specifically motivated by space needs, while many are of broad applicability. It is no exaggeration to say that applications in space are more technologically challenging than most terrestrial applications, in particular with respect to demands for reliability, low weight, and long life. Space needs, therefore, force technology developments which can later provide large benefits in terrestrial applications, though the latter might not by themselves have provided sufficient motivation for the research and development.

Space research and technology development is carried out by the Government, by industry, and by universities, with financial support derived from either direct funding by Government research agencies, or from the independent research and development expenditures of

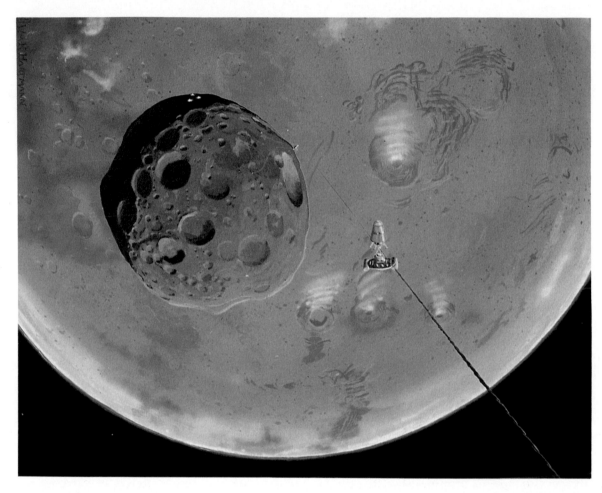

A very thin tether attached to the Mars moon Phobos could be used to transfer a space vehicle several hundred miles higher or lower in altitude without the use of any propellant. A small electric motor and a grappling device would be attached to the tether and would "capture" the space vehicle and transport it up or down the tether. (COURTESY WILLIAM HARTMANN)

industry. It ranges from very fundamental research carried out mainly in universities, to complex and expensive technology demonstrations, usually conducted by teams from Government and industry.

The character of basic research is such that, particularly in its early stages, its application cannot be reliably predicted. Research must be pursued on a broad front, to identify and quantify technical possibilities before their usefulness can be judged. Such a research and technology program is therefore properly conceived as *opportunity generating,* not directed to specific applications. When the technological opportunities have been identified, it is then

FUNDING OF SPACE RESEARCH AND TECHNOLOGY
AT NASA

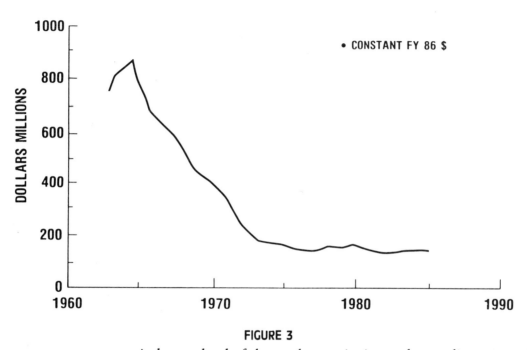

FIGURE 3

necessary to move aggressively to a level of thorough quantitative understanding to provide a basis for deciding whether and how to employ the new technology.

Our current space technology program is deficient in two regards: first, the scope and intensity of the base research and technology program is inadequate to provide the range of technical options we need for both the near and distant future; second, there are opportunities, now clearly identified, which we have not developed to the stage where they can be selected for application.

We believe the Nation's space technology effort must be substantially increased. Because of its critical role in generating technological opportunities, NASA's space research and technology program should be tripled, moving from its current two percent of NASA's budget to six percent. This increase should be accompanied by a major challenge to NASA's technology advisory committees to develop and recommend a bold new technology thrust for 21st-century America. These committees and boards, composed of the best technologists and managers from industry, Government, and academia, are well positioned to do this. We urge broadening and renewing their membership to cover new fields proposed in our program. The Commission also urges NASA to take full advantage of industry and academic inputs in structuring the technology base program.

There are, however, some specific areas of base technology which the Commission wishes to emphasize, and some areas in which it recommends special efforts to make technologies available for application.

Technology for Space Science

We know that even more distant and fainter celestial objects await detailed sensing through an entirely new class of space instrumentation. Very large and sensitive devices, constructed in space and situated singly or in groups at strategic points in Earth orbit and beyond, are essential to both Earth science and advanced astrophysics programs. The devices will range from radio antennas and area cosmic ray and gamma ray detectors, to Earth-scanning sensors and segmented visible light telescopes combined in pairs for interferometry, or in multi-element clusters for increased collecting area. Assembled at the low Earth orbit Space Station, these facilities will be transferred to their operational sites by a family of orbital maneuvering and transportation vehicles.

For these missions we must assure that structural techniques, such as on-orbit assembly, manipulators, and modular designs, are available at reasonable costs. Precise control of large structures is essential, especially in optical missions that call for the measurement of objects with high precision. Development of robotics, tele-operators, fluid transfer, and storage techniques can facilitate refurbishment and supply programs for large astrophysical observatories. Stationkeeping demands for interferometry missions with precise pointing requirements will necessitate highly efficient, small thrusters.

Large optical must remain clear of contaminants. Using these optics in space will challenge us to create the technologies for broad-band ultraviolet-optical coatings, reflection technology, precision surfaces, and lightweight mirrors. Autonomous systems, artificial intelligence, better time and motion studies, and improved computational paradigms will make possible smaller, more efficient ground crews to handle the expected floods of data relayed from space-based observatories.

As we fill near Earth space with instruments of great capability, studies suggest that the Moon is the preferred location for some future astronomy missions. The reasons include freedom from contaminants and the Moon's ability to provide a stable platform for astrophysical observations. A very cold view of space can be obtained at certain sites on the Moon, ideal for infrared systems. Far side radio telescopes could scan outward without radio interference from Earth. Gravitational wave astronomy could be implemented on the Moon, a body nine to ten times less active on a seismic scale than Earth. Precision instrumentation on Earth's Moon will yield new knowledge of our surrounding Universe, while challenging our technology base.

New propulsion technologies are needed to make advanced planetary sciences missions possible. Accordingly, major advancements in launch capability, and, most likely, in aerocapture/aeromaneuver capabilities as well, are essential if the exploration of the outer Solar System is to proceed beyond the Galileo level, or to examine in any detail the fascinating worlds beyond Saturn. These technologies are, in fact, generic requirements for all future advanced planetary missions; they are specifically required for sample return missions.

The necessary propulsion capabilities can be achieved in several different ways or perhaps by a combination of techniques: use of a space station for staging; development of solar electric or nuclear-electric propulsion; and the use of aerocapture/aeromaneuvering capabilities, as discussed in the next section.

Other technological developments required for future planetary missions in addition to propulsion and aerocapture techniques, include:

- Tethers able to move spacecraft electrically among the Jovian moons;
- Advances in Earth-observation sensors and data analysis;
- New communications techniques suitable for deep atmospheric probe missions;
- Radiation-hardened components and instruments that can operate for long periods of time in the hostile environments of the magnetospheres of Jupiter and Saturn;
- Robotic developments that will make possible long-lived autonomous spacecraft, landers, and rover systems;
- Atmospheric balloon technology applicable to balloon probes of Venus, Titan, and other worlds;
- Low-temperature technology for instruments needed to operate on Titan or in the colder environments of the worlds beyond Saturn; and
- High-temperature technology for deep atmospheres of the giant planets and surfaces of Mercury, Venus, and Io.

Technology for Piloted Spaceflight

We need an integration of humans and machines, each augmenting the other's capabilities, to meet future transportation needs. Enabling technologies include tools, life support and health maintenance, and astronaut selection and training.

Robotics is an extremely powerful tool, especially for extravehicular activity (EVA). The goal of our technology base in this area should be to replace EVA with robotics for routine satellite servicing and fueling operations. This is a repeatable and predictable activity and should take full advantage of robotics. For lunar distances, sensory-motor coordination of a space-situated robot's hands and eyes can be entirely within the brain of a human operator; for more remote operations, the robot itself must have this capability. NASA's robotic technology program should not follow U.S. industry, but should lead it, as industry thrusts will not produce the sensitive robotics needed for space operations.

Another tool needing support is a smart orbital maneuvering vehicle suitable for either tele-operation or piloted maneuvering and space-suited hands-on operation. Present-day space suits are not readily maintainable, do not permit ready reuse without servicing, and hamper their occupants by reduced dexterity, particularly in gloves and joints. Although we encourage development of new space suits, we believe that NASA should begin pursuit of technology leading to a non-suited astronaut capsule with appropriate arm-mounted end effectors. This "Alvin Submarine for Space" would contribute greatly to on-orbit repairs and construction duties.

A third class of tools is expert systems. We propose a goal of providing sufficient on-board capability for semi-autonomous spacecraft repair, maintenance, and replanning for those conditions with communication delays. Current systems are too inflexible and rule-based; they need to evolve into self-diagnosed model-based systems. We recommend that: **NASA explore the limits of expert systems, and tele-presence or tele-science for remote operations, including ties to spacecraft and ground laboratories. In working toward these goals, a broad examination of the non-space applications of tele-science should be included.**

In the category of life support, the goal must be to provide facilities and procedures to maintain crew fitness for long-duration missions. Soviet post-flight data suggest a comparatively long readaptation time is needed following prolonged spaceflights. The United States must begin to develop artificial gravity technology, including centrifuge, tether, and gravity-gradient techniques. As a related issue, provisions are needed for improved on-board detection of solar flare activity and for radiation protection to permit human travel beyond low Earth orbit.

Key to human journeys over long periods of time will be the development of reliable Closed-Ecology Life Support Systems (CELSS), leading to synthetic biospheres that close the air, water, and food loops. This will make possible low mass life support for large crews. Current systems require excessive use of expendables and, while the technology base for some advanced CELSSs exists, U.S. aspirations and research levels are unacceptably low. We recommend that: **NASA institute a major new effort to develop a space-qualified synthetic biosphere, building on current activities (See page 70).**

Astronaut selection and training does not require a great deal of technology development but does call for a continuing reassessment of the term "astronaut." As we move to the space-station era, the skills necessary to operate the facility are managerial, technical, and scientific. Many aspects of advanced missions in space involving humans will not require piloting skills. Our goal should now be the matching of astronaut selection and training to the needs of the mission. We must begin to secure mixes of people expert in their respective duties and capable of maintaining the Space Station as a highly productive workplace.

Technology for Nuclear Space Power

Nuclear power sources are critical for some future key missions, such as outer planetary ring exploration and human settlements on the Moon and Mars, and offer lower cost and higher reliability for others. They are able to provide large amounts of reliable energy output for 5- to 10-year durations, are lower in mass than competing solar power systems, are very compact and can survive severe radiation environments, and operate far from the Sun. However, to be acceptable to mission users, performance, reliability, schedule, and economy must be significantly upgraded.

There are four types of nuclear power sources available or under development: (1)

radioisotope thermoelectric generators in which a ball of plutonium-238 generates heat for long distance probes to planets like Jupiter—up to 1 kilowatt (kW); (2) dynamic power systems, now in use on Department of Defense (DOD) surveillance spacecraft—at the 1 kW electric (kWe) to 10 kWe level; (3) the SP-100 reactor power plant, with many possible uses envisioned, including the Strategic Defense Initiative, nuclear electric-propelled spacecraft and an evolutionary civilian space station—10 kWe to 1000 kWe; and (4) multi-megawatt reactors, seen as an important power source for lunar and Mars settlements—1000 kWe. In keeping with the promise of space nuclear power, we recommend: (1) conversion of the SP-100 nuclear reactor from a ground demonstration test in 1992 to a flight test in space; (2) expansion of the research and development effort on a multi-megawatt power system; (3) enhancement of the technology base of the radioisotope thermoelectric generator and dynamic isotope power system programs; (4) sustained commitment to an integrated space nuclear power program; (5) more active involvement by NASA and DOD in providing guidance and setting target requirements for the national space nuclear program; and (6) an increase in the level of effort in research and technology development on space nuclear power systems to decrease the technical risk of utilizing reactors in space.

Technology for Space Transportation

We believe that the Nation's advanced space transportation needs require: (1) significantly lowering the cost to achieve low Earth orbit; (2) safe, reliable, low cost transportation in space; and (3) increased propulsion performance to allow higher velocity changes in space to reach distant locations or difficult trajectories.

Earth-to-Orbit Transport

We discuss approaches to decreasing the cost of carrying cargo and passengers to low Earth orbit in the next section. Future space transportation to orbit will consist of unpiloted cargo transport vehicles and advanced technology passenger transport vehicles, or hybrid vehicles.

Our review of the space transportation area suggests that the technologies critical to achieving lower cost unpiloted launchers centers in the manufacturing of the principal components of the vehicle: materials, structures, engines, tanks, guidance, and control. A second critical need is to increase safety and reliability while reducing the "standing army" now needed to support launch operations. Launch vehicle checkout prior to lift-off must be increasingly automated, including built-in readiness tests coupled with hardware more tolerant to mishandling, and systems that correct their own failings.

To lower costs of passenger transport to low Earth orbit, we need reusable vehicles that are robust and reliable. Candidate propulsion systems with all stages recoverable, in order of increasing technological challenge, are: (1) two-stage rocket with separate hydrogen/oxygen and hydrocarbon/oxygen engines; (2) a single-stage vehicle whose engines can burn both hydrocarbon/oxygen and hydrogen/oxygen mixtures; (3) two-stage, airbreathing, liquid hydrogen first-stage, hydrogen/liquid oxygen rocket second-stage, horizontally launched; and (4) a single-stage, combined-cycle using hydrogen/oxygen, and capable of horizontal launch and airbreathing operation to orbit (aerospace plane).

The propulsion technology base must be vigorously extended for both rocket engines and airbreathing engines. Advances in durability of the thermal protection system and in light-weight materials and structures will pay off handsomely in lower operational costs, as will improvements in the information, guidance, and control systems. These vehicles can benefit from the major advances in computer technology that have taken place since the shuttle was designed if programs are initiated now to develop space-rated, fault-tolerant computers. All of these areas will require early technology demonstrations if the improvements are to be validated in time for vehicles to be operational by the late 1990s.

For the airbreathing option, extensive research and technology development is also needed, whether it is used in an airbreathing first stage, or in a single stage vehicle. Here the critical technologies are in the Supersonic Combustion Ramjet engine (SCRAMJET), a propulsion device that has been well understood conceptually since the early 1960s but has been experimentally validated only in ground experiments, and only up to Mach numbers of about 8. To be attractive for orbital launch, its Mach number must extend at least to 12, and preferably beyond 15.

The essential feature of the SCRAMJET is that the air is not slowed to low velocities before the fuel is added, as in all other airbreathing propulsion systems; rather, it is slowed only to a Mach number ranging from 3 to perhaps 8 relative to the vehicle, and the hydrogen fuel is injected into and burned in the supersonic flow before it is expanded in the nozzle. This minimizes two problems of high speed ramjets, namely the high pressure and temperature which the air reaches if slowed to subsonic speeds before combustion. One fundamental problem, however, remains. This is the fact that the amount of energy that is added to the air flow by the combustion of hydrogen fuel is very small compared to the kinetic energy of the incoming airflow at high Mach numbers, and also small compared to the kinetic energy of the combustion products flowing out the nozzle. Thus, the thrust, which results from conversion of the fuel's combustion heat to kinetic energy in the nozzle flow, results from a small difference between the nozzle flow velocity and the flight velocity. This difference can be less than one percent at a Mach number of 20.

It follows that the success of the SCRAMJET depends on extraordinary sophistication in fluid mechanical design. There is reason to believe that with modern supercomputer technology and experimental capabilities, a design can be achieved which will yield specific impulse values, averaged over the Mach number range from 0 to 23, as high as 1,000 to 1,500, which is two or three times that of a hydrogen-oxygen rocket. If these values can be achieved, the propellant mass fraction of the vehicle will be small enough to make single-stage-to-orbit practical. The critical step here is the validation of the propulsion system at high Mach numbers. Since no ground test capability is available at such Mach numbers, and indeed none seems feasible, the propulsion system must be validated experimentally in flight. This is the principal purpose of the national aerospace plane program, which the Commission strongly endorses.

For in-space transportation we need a transfer vehicle with aerobraking. The transfer vehicles, with attached aerobraking systems, will graze the Earth's upper atmosphere, dipping as low as 200,000 feet altitude in order to lose enough velocity to rendezvous with the Earth Spaceport. It is envisioned that ceramic fabric-coated trusses, inflatable balloon-parachutes, or other novel, lightweight high-temperature devices will be needed, with mass less than 15 percent of the transfer vehicle dry mass, and diameters of 50 feet or more. Adaptive fault-tolerant avionics will also be needed for precision guidance and control during the vehicle's critical pass through the upper atmosphere. An experimental program to fly an aerobrake launched from the shuttle is needed to characterize its aerothermodynamic design parameters and shock wave patterns. Data on non-equilibrium heating and reradiation from the shock cannot be obtained from previous Apollo and shuttle reentries, since they did not probe the relevant velocity-altitude profiles, and theoretical predictions are thus too uncertain for transfer vehicle aerobrake design. A modest investment in this technology can make possible major future reductions in space transportation costs.

Other critical technologies for transfer vehicle development include long-lived hydrogen/ oxygen rocket propulsion, reliable guidance and control systems, and orbital refueling capability. Flight demonstrations are badly needed to validate the combination of these technologies. These technologies can produce a potential doubling of payload for future mission planners.

Electric Propulsion

In an electric spaceship drive system, the energy needed to accelerate the propellant is provided electrically rather than from the chemical energy of the propellants themselves, as in a chemical rocket. Because the energy source is independent of the propellant, the propellant can be accelerated to an exhaust velocity optimized for a particular mission.

Electric propulsion holds great promise in at least two applications, involving two quite different technologies for the accelerator (See page 104). For demanding scientific missions to the outer planets, the appropriate technology is the "ion engine," in which ions of cesium, mercury, argon, or (possibly) oxygen are accelerated to high speeds by electrostatic fields. In such applications, the propulsion system produces a low vehicle acceleration, on the order of .001g to .0001g over the entire mission time, which may be years. Ion engine technology is highly developed, and ion engines have been used in space. The pacing item for their application to outer planet missions is the power source. For operation far from the Sun, a nuclear electric power source is almost certainly required, and it is, therefore, the pacing technology for the use of ion engines in the outer solar system.

The other electric propulsion accelerator technology is the "mass-driver," whose applications are quite different from those of ion engines. Mass-drivers have been developed to the level of successful laboratory demonstrations, and there is a rather high level of confidence in

ELECTROMAGNETIC ACCELERATORS

In an electromagnetic accelerator, electric or magnetic fields are used to accelerate material to high speeds. The power source can be solar or nuclear. There are two types of accelerators for use in space: the "ion engine" and the "mass-driver." The ion engine uses electric fields to accelerate ions (charged atoms). Ion engines are compact, relatively light in weight, and well-suited to missions requiring low thrust sustained for a very long time.

Mass-drivers are complementary to ion engines, developing much higher thrusts but not suited to extreme velocities. A mass-driver accelerates by magnetic rather than electric fields. It is a magnetic linear accelerator, designed for long service life, and able to launch payloads of any material at high efficiency. Mass-drivers should not be confused with "railguns," which are electromagnetic catapults now being designed for military applications.

A mass-driver consists of three parts: the accelerator, the payload carrier, and the payload. For long lifetime, the system is designed to operate without physical contact between the payload carrier and accelerator. The final portion of the machine operates as a decelerator, to slow down each payload carrier for its return and reuse.

A key difference between the mass-driver and the ion engine is that the mass-driver can accelerate any solid or liquid material without regard to its atomic properties. Used as a propulsion system, the mass-driver could use as propellant, raw lunar soil, powdered material from surplus shuttle tankage in orbit, or any material found on asteroids. Its characteristics make it suitable for load-carrying missions within the inner solar system.

Another potential application for a mass-driver is to launch payloads from a fixed site. The application studied in the most depth at this time is the launch of raw material from the Moon to a collection point in space, for example, one of the lunar Lagrange points. A mass-driver with the acceleration of present laboratory models, but mounted on the lunar surface, would be able to accelerate payloads to lunar escape speed in a distance of only 170 yards. Its efficiency would be about 70 percent, about the same as that of a medium-size electric motor. Loads accelerated by a mass-driver could range from a pound to several tons, depending on the application and available power supply.

their feasibility. However, their technology must be developed further to bring them to the same level of availability as ion engines. Mass-drivers must operate in a manner that will prevent their propellants from contributing to space debris.

Tethers

In space parlance a "tether" is a long thin wire which joins two orbiting masses to force them to orbit together at the same angular velocity (See page 126). Since the outer body is thus forced to orbit faster than it would if free, and the inner one slower, the tether is in tension. In another configuration, the two masses rotate about a common center of gravity.

Such tethers have myriad potential applications, from generating electric power by passage through a planet's magnetic field, to raising the orbits of satellites launched from vehicles like the shuttle, or the delivery of payloads to a space platform from a suborbital launch vehicle. In a spaceport application, tethers could conserve propellants by transferring momentum between upgoing and downgoing spacecraft. They have been extensively studied theoretically, but an in-space validation of these studies is needed soon so that the manifold advantages of tethers can be exploited. Such a demonstration is under development for flight on the shuttle. It should proceed forthwith. In addition, ultra-high strength materials, valuable for many applications, should be developed for higher-capability tethers.

Processing of Extraterrestrial Materials

Many of the potential cost savings for operations within the inner Solar System stem from reducing transportation needs by using materials available locally on moons, asteroids, and planetary surfaces. These range from shielding to the production of propellants, solar cells, and structural elements. In order to reduce the cost of future space operations, we recommend that: **The augmented technology program we propose for NASA specifically include vigorous development of the technologies for robotic and tele-operated production of shielding, building materials, and other products from locally-available raw materials.**

Research and Technology for Space Industry

Existing and emerging space industrial activities can be divided into four categories: communications, space transportation, remote sensing, and space manufacturing. Our civilian space program has investigated new frequencies and methods of improving communications satellite bandwidths; it has created meteorological satellites; it has stimulated use of and provided ready access to remotely-sensed data of Earth's surface, turning over the Landsat-series spacecraft to private industry; and it has provided the ability to perform experiments related to space manufacturing aboard such as the Skylab space station and the space shuttle. Such commercial uses of space have led to rather mature industries. Communications, navigation, and some aspects of Earth resource sensing are progressing well. Microgravity manufacturing, while still in its infancy, is inhibited by high launch-to-orbit costs, but has promise.

We encourage the Nation, with NASA as the focal point, to continue to stimulate a variety of potential commercial uses of space. In addition to the direct commercial returns, there will be benefits to the military sector, from the stimulation of the economy, from our ability to meet foreign competition, and from technology spinoffs. We support the augmentation of

NASA's space research and technology program, to more fully support the broad constituency of governmental space users. With such invigoration, NASA can reemerge as a developer of technology. NASA should have a role in space technology to support the space industry analogous to its role in aeronautics. In each case this is built on unique NASA aerospace facilities that others cannot afford to duplicate, and on the broad competence residing in NASA's scientific and technical personnel. As the Space Station becomes available in the 1990s and provides a central research and development facility in space, it will be analogous to NASA's terrestrial aeronautical facilities. This would clearly be in the tradition of the National Advisory Committee for Aeronautics that served as the basis for the creation of NASA in the National Aeronautics and Space Act (NASA Act) of 1958.

NACA was established by Congress in 1915 to supervise and direct the scientific study of the problems of flight, with a view to their practical solution, and to determine the problems that should be experimentally attacked, and discuss their solution and their application to practical questions. The cooperative nature of NACA was clearly indicated by its membership, representing the academic community, the military, and industry. It is clear from reading the NASA Act that in the field of space technology, NASA should follow in the footsteps of NACA, and play a role for the space industry analogous to that which it has had in aeronautics since its founding.

HIGHWAY TO SPACE

The recent tragic loss of shuttle Mission 51-L has created a temporary interruption in our Nation's primary launch system. Methods for dealing with this situation are under intensive examination by the executive and legislative branches of Government. The Commission's charter is to forge a long-term course for America in space. We are confident that the efforts now under way to resolve the short-term problem of meeting the Nation's launch needs will be successful, and our attention is therefore concentrated on next-generation launch vehicles.

The shuttle represents an effort to build one vehicle to serve many roles. Meeting the diverse requirements for human transport to and from orbit, for orbital stay times of a week, and for transport of large and heavy cargoes both to and from orbit, placed heavy demands on the technologies available at the time the shuttle was designed. The inevitable result was a very complex and somewhat fragile vehicle. A long and difficult development program has resulted in an orbital transport system that is both expensive and technically demanding to operate.

The capabilities of the shuttle's crew have introduced totally new space operations: satellite retrieval, refurbishment, repair, refueling, and reconfiguration. Scientific experimentation in a space laboratory environment is routinely available, and commercial product development can be tried in microgravity. The shuttle has given engineers access to experimental data on hypersonic flight over a wide range of Mach numbers applicable to future trans-atmospheric vehicles.

Nevertheless, the space shuttle is a technological triumph and a magnificent achievement both in pioneering winged flight into space and in providing a reusable vehicle for spaceflight. It is a visible symbol of United States leadership in technology and space accomplishment, and an important instrument of national and international policy. It has opened the Highway to Space.

Artist's illustration of the space shuttle launch in August 1983 (STS-8). (COURTESY ATTILA HEJJA AND NASA)

The Commission believes that cheaper, more reliable means for transporting both people and cargo to and from orbit must be achieved in the next 20 years. While all space programs would benefit from lower cost orbital transportation, it is especially important that the cost be dramatically reduced for free enterprise to flourish with commercialization of space operations. The Commission is confident that the cost of transportation can and should be reduced below $200 per pound (in 1986 dollars) by the year 2000. If the volume of cargo increases in the early 21st century as it is projected to do, further cost reductions should be achieved.

Should the United States choose not to undertake achievement of these economies in launch and recovery capability, then the Nation must face the probability that other nations will rapidly overtake our position as the world's leading spacefaring nation. The competition to get into space and to operate effectively there is real. **Above all, it is imperative that the United States maintain a continuous capability to put both humans and cargo into orbit; never again should the country experience the hiatus we endured from 1975 to 1981, when we were unable to launch astronauts into space.**

The Commission sees several elements that are critical to achieving more economical and reliable orbital transport. In the next-generation systems we must separate the functions of one-way cargo transport from the round-trip transport of humans and high value cargo to and from orbit. The extra costs associated with round-trip transport of people should not be imposed on vehicles optimized for cargo transport alone. Thus, for the next generation the Commission envisions two operational needs: cargo transport and passenger transport, which may or may not be met with the same family of vehicles.

For these vehicles, the Commission sees two essentially different but complementary means to cost reduction. One is the introduction of new concepts and technologies that lead to fundamentally more efficient systems; an example is the replacement of propellers by jets. The other is a process of systematic design improvement and evolutionary development directed at reliability and low operating cost; an example is the evolution of global jet transport into an extremely reliable and economical mode of transport over the last 30 years.

Both approaches must be followed in parallel if the United States is to retain preeminence in Earth-to-orbit transportation. To ensure that we are in a position to do so, it is essential that we continuously pursue a vigorous, systematic, and imaginative program of technology development, as has been outlined on pages 95–106. It is also essential that we develop new systems and make evolutionary improvements in existing systems at propitious times. We believe the time will be right to commit to the development of new Earth-to-orbit transport vehicles in the early 1990s, following an intensive exploration of advanced rocket and hypersonic airbreathing propulsion technologies. We also believe it is essential that the Nation continue in the meantime to pursue the evolutionary development of unpiloted orbital cargo transport systems.

Our view is consistent with that emerging from the joint NASA/DOD space transportation study, which indicates that the United States will need a mix of reusable launch vehicles in the future. These include unpiloted, automated cargo vehicles designed to carry spacecraft, propellants, bulk cargo, and other commodities; and passenger transport vehicles optimized for launch and return of crews, passengers, and compact, high-value cargo. The former may be logical derivatives of present launch vehicles, updated with technologies dictated by economic considerations, while the latter will constitute the follow-on to the present shuttle for two-way transport.

It is essential that from the outset the commercial sector be heavily involved in the design and development of these launch vehicles. This will ensure that the discipline of commercial feasibility will be applied to help reduce operating costs and make possible the earliest transfer of launch operations smoothly to the private sector. The Commission therefore recommends: **That next-generation cargo and passenger transport vehicles be designed and developed to be readily operable by commercial firms after the operational phase is reached. The sooner the private sector can assume responsibility for design, specification, development, fabrication, flight test, production, and operation of space vehicles and launch and landing facilities, the sooner the United States can begin to pattern Earth-to-orbit transportation after commercial airline operations.**

The Commission debated at length the critical issue: How and when can the private sector create a competitive U.S. launch service industry? In this, American enterprise will have to compete with national space transport systems developed and operated under substantial government subsidy in at least Europe, the Soviet Union, China, and Japan. The Commission sees no immediate solution to the dilemma of private versus Government launch services. Private operation of our first-generation shuttle fleet is not practicable. Prohibiting NASA from launching commercial satellites would not, in the face of strong competition from foreign governments, automatically create a private U.S. launch industry based upon existing military-developed rockets. We believe that this complex problem will be solved with next-generation launch vehicles, but we cannot propose a realistic early solution in this report.

The shuttle fleet will be reaching the end of its design life about the year 2000. While it may be possible to extend its usefulness, the prospects for drastically lowering transportation costs with these vehicles are not good. We believe, therefore, that the shuttle should be replaced by a new vehicle designed to meet all requirements for the transport of passengers and high-value cargo to and from orbiting spaceports. This vehicle, optimized for passenger transport, may be smaller than the shuttle.

Since the Space Station will have been operational five or more years before passenger transport vehicles (PTV) become operational, they will not need the capability for extended, independent stay times in orbit. The vehicles should be of modular design, insensitive to failure of individual systems, have autonomous system checks, and thus be capable of operating with a low level of logistical and operational support. While it is not realistic to think of operating these vehicles as autonomously as commercial aircraft, they should be far less dependent on ground support than the present shuttle. PTVs must be designed for reliable low-cost operations, even if this means increased development cost.

On its way to Earth orbit, the aerospace plane will take off like a conventional aircraft. (COURTESY ROBERT MCCALL)

AEROSPACE PLANE TECHNOLOGY

Technological advance across a broad spectrum is the key to fielding an aerospace plane. A highly innovative propulsion design can make possible horizontal takeoff and single-stage-to-orbit flight with high specific impulse (I_{sp}). The aerospace plane would use a unique supersonic combustion ramjet (SCRAMJET) engine which would breathe air up to the outer reaches of the atmosphere. This approach virtually eliminates the need to carry liquid oxygen, thus reducing propellant and vehicle weight. A small amount of liquid oxygen would be carried to provide rocket thrust for orbital maneuvering and for cabin atmosphere.

A ramjet, as its name implies, uses the ram air pressure resulting from the forward motion of the vehicle to provide compression. The normal ramjet inlet slows down incoming air while compressing it, then burns the fuel and air subsonically and exhausts the combustion products through a nozzle to produce thrust. To fly faster than Mach 6, the internal geometry of the engine must be varied in order to allow the air to remain at supersonic speeds through the combustor. This supersonic combustion ramjet could potentially attain speed capability of Mach 12 or higher.

Such a propulsion system must cover three different flight regimes: takeoff, hypersonic, and rocket. For takeoff and acceleration to Mach 4, it would utilize air-turbo-ramjets or cryojets. From Mach 4 to Mach 6, the engine would operate as a conventional subsonic combustion ramjet. From Mach 6 to maximum airbreathing speeds, the engine would employ a supersonic combustion SCRAMJET. At speeds of about Mach 12 and above, the SCRAMJET engine might have additional propellant added above the hydrogen flow rates needed for utilization of all air captured by the inlet. This additional flow would help cool the engine and provide additional thrust. Final orbital insertion could be achieved with an auxiliary rocket engine.

Such a system of propulsion engines must be carefully integrated with the airframe. Proper integration of the airbreathing inlets into the airframe is a critical design problem, since the shape of the aircraft itself determines in large part the performance of the engine. During SCRAMJET operation, the wing and forward

The Commission recognizes two competing technologies, each of which promises to drastically reduce the cost of achieving orbit: advanced rocket and aerospace plane technologies. An evaluation of these two approaches should be made in the early 1990s after five years of intensive research and development on both; one or both or a hybrid can then be selected for the Highway to Space.

The aerospace plane concept involves winged vehicles, fueled by liquid hydrogen, that can underbody of the vehicle would generate oblique shock waves which produce inlet air flow compression. The vehicle afterbody shape behind the engine would form a nozzle producing half the thrust near orbital speeds. Second-generation supercomputers can now provide the computational capability needed to efficiently calculate the flow fields at these extremely high Mach numbers. These advanced design tools provide the critical bridge between wind tunnels and piloted flight in regimes of speed and altitude that are unattainable in ground-based facilities. In addition, supercomputers permit the usual aircraft design and development time to be significantly shortened, thus permitting earlier introduction of the aerospace plane into service.

The potential performance of such an airframe-inlet-engine-nozzle combination is best described by a parameter known as the net "I_{sp}," which is the measure of the pounds of thrust, minus the drag from the engine, per pounds of fuel flowing through each second. The unit of measure is seconds; the larger the value, the more efficient the propulsion. For the aerospace plane over the speed range of Mach 0 to Mach 25, the engines should achieve an average I_{sp} in excess of 1,200 seconds burning liquid hydrogen. This compares with an I_{sp} of about 470 seconds for the best current hydrogen-oxygen rocket engines, such as the space shuttle main engine. It is the high I_{sp} of an airbreathing engine capable of operating over the range from takeoff to orbit that could make possible a single-stage, horizontal takeoff and landing aerospace plane. For "airliner" or "Orient Express" cruise at Mach 4 to Mach 12, the average I_{sp} is even larger, making the SCRAMJET attractive for future city-to-city transportation.

Another key technology is high strength-to-weight ratio materials capable of operating at very high temperatures while retaining the properties of reusability and long life. These can make possible low maintenance, rapid turnaround, reduced logistics, and low operational costs. Promising approaches to high-temperature materials include rapid-solidification-rate metals, carbon-carbon composites, and advanced metal matrix composites. In extremely hot areas, such as the nose, the use of active cooling with liquid hydrogen or the use of liquid metals to rapidly remove heat will also be employed. The use of these materials and cooling technologies with innovative structural concepts results in important vehicle weight reductions, a key to single-stage-to-orbit flight.

depart and land horizontally from conventional jet runways (See page 112). The configuration of principal interest here would be capable of flying to low Earth orbit using only a single stage. The critical technologies that must be advanced include airbreathing SCRAMJET engines, high-temperature materials, and hypersonic configuration aerodynamics (See pages 95–106).

In another possible configuration, an aerospace plane could rapidly transport passengers

reach the ground (See page 117). The capability to retrieve or repair satellites in orbit did not exist. With the advent of the space shuttle, this capability has been attained, and over the past three years we have begun to retrieve and repair satellites on an experimental basis. In April 1984, the Solar Maximum Mission spacecraft was retrieved and repaired in orbit and in November 1984, two communications satellites (Palapa and Westar) were retrieved and returned to Earth to be repaired and someday reflown. In August 1985, two astronauts "jump-started" the LEASAT 3 spacecraft, gladdening the hearts of its manufacturer, insurers, and customers.

Astronaut Dale Gardner, in a manned maneuvering unit (MMU), prepares to dock with the Westar communications satellite during space shuttle flight 51-A in November 1984. (COURTESY NASA)

Clearly our operational capability in orbit is rapidly expanding. Within the next decade we will be able to assemble, service, and repair in space structures of very large sizes. For example, the 24,000 pound Hubble Space Telescope will be placed in Earth orbit and serviced and repaired there. In the 1990s, NASA will assemble in orbit its first permanently-occupied space station, weighing about 150 tons, which will in turn facilitate increased orbital operations.

Space Station

In January 1984, President Reagan approved NASA's request for a permanently occupied space station in low Earth orbit, and asked that it be ready by 1994. The United States has launched only one space station, Skylab, which was successively occupied by three crews in 1973 and 1974. The final crew remained in space for 84 days, a record at that time. The new Space Station and its transportation link to Earth, the space shuttle, are twin elements that will make it possible for men and women to live and work in Earth orbit. The new space station will be built by NASA for multiple use with broad international participation (See page 120).

The introduction of the Space Station by 1994 will represent the end of our visitor status in space, signaling the beginning of the era of permanent occupancy of space for the United States and our partners. The primary functions of the Space Station crew will be servicing research and applications satellites, performing microgravity and other research, and learning to live and work productively in space for prolonged periods.

Many satellites whose final working locations are in low orbit will be checked out and then supported from the Space Station. At the checkout facility the antennas and solar panels of those satellites can be deployed, after which the satellites can be gently moved to their working locations. Spacecraft in this category include scientific telescopes, Earth-observation satellites, and unpiloted "long-duration pallets" on which microgravity processing and long-term experiments are mounted. To emplace and retrieve orbiting systems from the Space Station, NASA is developing an orbital maneuvering vehicle that is scheduled to be operational in 1991. It will be supported from the space shuttle until 1994, and then from the Space Station. In addition to moving satellites at low acceleration to their final locations in relatively low orbits, it will deliver expendable supplies to satellites and transport astronauts for satellite maintenance. The maneuvering vehicle will have remotely controlled manipulator arms to handle satellites under its care. Its role will resemble that of a "harbor tug" in a ship anchorage. Refueling operations for orbital maneuvering vehicles and other spacecraft require orbiting storage tanks for propellants. Shuttle external fuel tanks are too large and otherwise unsuitable for this application; specifically designed tankage will therefore be required.

The orbital maneuvering vehicle will be an indispensable tool for operations at future space stations and spaceports, and for other facilities in Earth, lunar, and Martian orbits. It will be mandatory for operations with cycling spaceships traveling between Earth and Mars.

SPACE STATION

In a purely physical sense, the Space Station will overshadow all preceding space facilities. Although often referred to as the "NASA" Space Station, it will actually be international in character; Europe, Canada, and Japan, in particular, plan to develop their own hardware components for the Station. As currently visualized, the initial Station will be a 350-foot by 300-foot structure containing four pressurized modules (two for living and two for working), assorted attached pallets for experiments and manufacturing, eight large solar panels for power, communications and propulsion systems, and a robotic manipulator system similar to the shuttle arm. When fully assembled, the initial Station will weigh about 300,000 pounds and carry a crew of six, with a replacement crew brought on board every 90 days.

To deliver and assemble the Station's components, 12 shuttle flights will be required over an 18-month period. The pressurized modules used by the Station will be about 14 feet in diameter and 40 feet long to fit in the shuttle's cargo bay. The Station will circle Earth every 90 minutes at 250-mile altitude and 28.5 degree orbital inclination. Thus the Station will travel only between 28.5 degrees north and south latitudes. Unoccupied associate platforms that can be serviced by crews will be in orbits similar to this, as well as in polar orbits circling Earth over the North and South Poles. Polar-orbiting platforms will carry instruments for systems that require a view of the entire globe.

The Station will provide a versatile, multifunctional facility. In addition to providing housing, food, air, and water for its inhabitants, it will be a science laboratory performing scientific studies in astronomy, space plasma physics, Earth sciences (including the ocean and atmosphere), materials research and development, and life sciences. The Station will also be used to improve our space technology capability, including electrical power generation, robotics and automation, life support systems, Earth observation sensors, and communications.

The Station will provide a transportation hub for shuttle missions to and from Earth. When the crew is rotated every 90 days, the shuttle will deliver food and water from Earth, as well as materials and equipment for the science laboratories and manufacturing facilities. Finished products and experiment results will be returned to Earth. The Station will be the originating point and destination for flights to nearby platforms and other Earth orbits. The orbital maneuvering vehicle used for these trips will be docked at the Station.

The Station will be a service and repair depot for satellites and platforms orbiting in formation with it. Robotic manipulator arms, much like those on the shuttle, will position satellites in hangars or special docking fixtures. "Smart" repair and servicing robots will gradually replace astronauts in space suits for maintenance work, as satellites become more standardized and modular in design.

Two transfer vehicles being slowed down by the upper atmosphere of Earth (aerobraked) during their return to a space station. A large, ceramic disc acts as the aerobrake. Behind the disc are six spherical propellant tanks and a cylindrical module containing several astronauts (COURTESY ROBERT MCCALL)

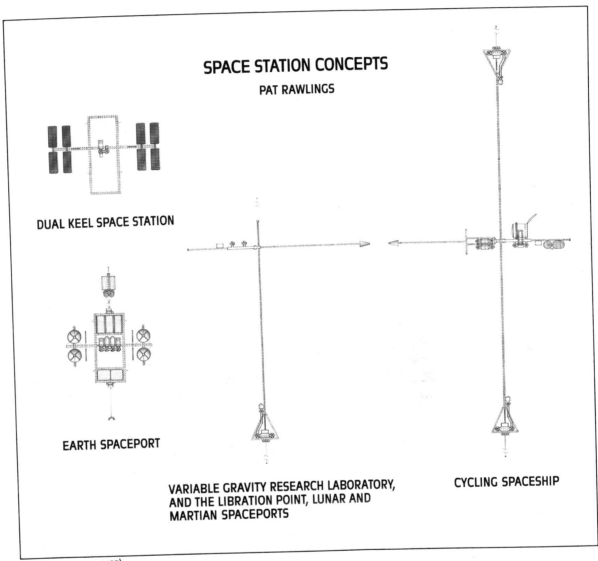

SPACE STATION CONCEPTS
PAT RAWLINGS

DUAL KEEL SPACE STATION

EARTH SPACEPORT

VARIABLE GRAVITY RESEARCH LABORATORY, AND THE LIBRATION POINT, LUNAR AND MARTIAN SPACEPORTS

CYCLING SPACESHIP

(COURTESY PAT RAWLINGS)

the Mars Run. The L1 Spaceport would facilitate a future intensive buildup of a Mars base. It would be a spaceborne combined motel/gas station/warehouse/restaurant/garage. It should have a closed-cycle life support system and some level of artificial g. The amount of g required will have been determined through experiments at the Variable-g Research Facility.

Mars Spaceport

The reach to Mars will tax our ingenuity in the 21st century, and will depend strongly on technology and experience acquired in working on the Moon and in Earth-Moon space. The leap of distance alone, from the relative proximity of the Moon's 240,000 miles from Earth out across the intervening void of up to 230 million miles separating Earth and Mars, will

The Libration Point (L1) Spaceport could serve as the jumping-off point for trips from Earth to Mars. Transfer vehicles, like the one shown in the foreground being serviced by astronauts, would travel from the Spaceport to the cycling spaceship which would continuously travel between Earth and Mars. (COURTESY ROBERT MCCALL)

of ilmenite (iron-titanium oxide), and electrolysis. In all chemical extraction processes the necessary reactive elements not found in high abundance on the Moon (such as fluorine and hydrogen) will be recirculated. Laboratory scale measurements of these recovery processes indicate that the trace amounts of these elements found in the lunar soils will be sufficient to make up losses in the recirculation process.

Energy costs will be important in determining which lunar elements can be delivered to their points of use at less cost than equivalent materials from Earth. Lunar mining is based on the premise that the energy required to lift material from the Moon to Earth orbit is less than five percent of the energy required to lift material from Earth to orbit. For shielding, in which no processing of the raw soil is required, the economic advantage may be significant. For oxygen and other pure elements, the energy cost of the processing plants will determine not only economic competition, but the best locations for processing. Much of the energy required for processing is thermal. That tends to favor locating processing plants in high orbit, where full-time solar energy is available. The alternative is location on the lunar surface. There, an economic trade-off is required for each processing application to determine whether it is less expensive to build a plant dependent on solar energy, and shut it down during the lunar night, or to emplace a nuclear generator to provide full-time power.

The resource development of the Moon would be altered drastically if volatile elements were found frozen in ices in permanently shadowed craters near the lunar poles. In principle, all of the propellant needs for hydrogen/oxygen rockets operating between the lunar surface and low Earth orbit could be met from lunar sources if such volatiles were found. The needs of lunar outposts, bases, and their biospheres for water could also be met from those sources. In earlier sections we have, therefore, set a very high priority on remote sensing and sample return missions to examine those special locations.

Initial lunar outposts can be built from the same modular components that will be employed in the Variable-g Research Facility and the spaceports. Their lineage will trace back to Apollo, Skylab, the shuttle, and the Space Station. The challenge is greater when the emphasis shifts, as it will, to the creation of a self-sufficient biosphere on the Moon, using local materials to replenish losses. But this challenge must be met in order to obtain the experience and the expertise to create equivalent biospheres, of high reliability, at the much greater distances of Mars and the asteroids, when those will be necessary. The proximity of the Moon, its inherent scientific interest, and its potential value for resources to be used in space all lead us to recommend: **Establishing the first lunar outpost within the next 20 years, and progressing to permanently-occupied lunar bases within the following decade.**

Mars Bases

Following unpiloted precursor missions, and drawing strongly on the experience gained in establishing one or more permanent bases on and in orbit over the Moon, people will visit Mars, first to establish Mars outposts, and later to develop Mars bases. The scientific justification for such missions was discussed in an earlier section. The methods required for the economical extension of the human reach to the distance of Mars are complex because of the times and distances involved, but also rich in possibilities because of the presence very close to Mars of its moons, Phobos and Deimos.

In our projection of a likely plan, the first humans to visit Mars will do so on the first trip of a cycling spaceship. They will visit the Martian moons, or descend directly to the surface of Mars, using a transfer vehicle with aerobraking.

If it is established that Phobos is rich in volatile elements, the first crew to visit Phobos will emplace a plant on Phobos to produce hydrogen, oxygen, and water. The propellants obtained from this plant will support future Mars operations, and greatly reduce the necessary cargoes transported over the long supply line from Earth.

On Mars, as earlier on the Moon, habitats and laboratories will be built out of standard spaceport modules. Again, both on the Moon and on Mars pressurized spaces will be shielded or constructed underground for protection from radiation.

There is a logical sequence of experience for the design of land-roving vehicles both for the Moon and for Mars, and that sequence has already begun with the exploration and permanent occupation of portions of Antarctica. For long-distance traverses of the surface, there will be enclosed vehicles, equipped with full life support systems, in which people can live and work in shirt-sleeve environments for many days. For short trips in the vicinity of outposts and bases, vehicles roughly similar to the lunar rover of the Apollo era will be used. To ride those vehicles, crew members will wear space suits with their own short-period life support systems. For observation, surveys, and checkout of changing conditions, remotely piloted Mars airplanes are likely to be useful. Those relatively small craft will draw on the design experience of low-speed aircraft operating in Earth's atmosphere, and on the extensive experience of remotely piloted military observation craft.

The great distance of Mars will dictate not only the development of complete and fully redundant biospheres for operation there, but also the establishment of two or more bases, for example, both on the planetary surface and in orbit, so that a serious problem occurring in one of the bases can be overcome by quickly transferring personnel from the affected base to another. Energy costs will determine what products can be derived economically from the Martian atmosphere. In principle, oxygen, hydrogen, water, nitrogen, fertilizer, and methane, as well as other compounds, could all be extracted from the atmosphere of Mars. As in the case of the Moon, the energy source to support a Mars Base could be solar or nuclear. Solar energy may be more usable on Mars than on the Moon, in spite of Mars' greater distance from the Sun, because the rotation rate of the red planet makes the intervals of darkness only about a thirtieth as long as on the lunar equator. A nuclear generator that powers life support systems must include redundant pairs or triplets of generators.

We project the growth of an initial Mars outpost to a Mars Base in about the third decade of the next century. While that seems far away now, many of the people who will live and work at that Mars Base have already been born. We see the Mars Base not as an end in itself, but as a logical step in the development of the inner Solar System. The discoveries in planetary science which are sure to be made as we explore the Moon, Mars, and nearby

FROM EARTH TO MARS

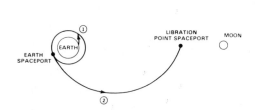

① THE CREW BOUND FOR MARS TRAVELS FROM EARTH TO THE EARTH SPACEPORT IN A PASSENGER TRANSPORT VEHICLE. ② AT THE EARTH SPACEPORT, THEY BOARD A TRANSFER VEHICLE TO TAKE THEM TO THE LIBRATION POINT TO ESCAPE EARTH'S GRAVITY AND REFUEL.

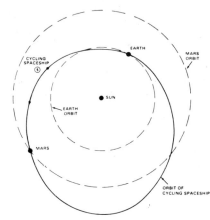

⑤ THE CREW TRAVELS IN THE CYCLING SPACESHIP FROM EARTH TO MARS IN 5–7 MONTHS. THE TRANSFER VEHICLE IS HANGARED AND REFUELED DURING THE TRIP.

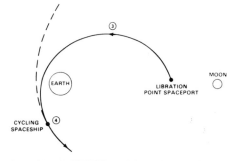

③ WITH A REFUELED TRANSFER VEHICLE, THE CREW DEPARTS THE LIBRATION POINT SPACEPORT AND HEADS FOR A RENDEZVOUS WITH A CYCLING SPACESHIP BOUND FOR MARS. ④

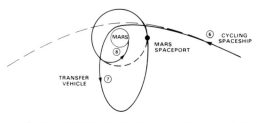

⑥ THE CREW BOARDS THE TRANSFER VEHICLE AND LEAVES THE CYCLING SPACESHIP. ⑦ AFTER AEROBRAKING THE TRANSFER VEHICLE IN THE MARTIAN ATMOSPHERE, THE CREW DOCKS AT THE MARS SPACEPORT. ⑧ THE CREW THEN BOARDS A MARS LANDER FOR THE JOURNEY TO THE SURFACE OF MARS.

asteroids, and the resource developments which will occur as the result both of resource exploration and further advances in processing systems, are likely to bring people to many locations in space. The habitats we build there and the experience we gain there will combine to be a springboard for human exploration still farther into our Solar System.

Communications Relays

The expansion of operations envisioned will require frequent communications contact with the orbital facilities and transfer vehicles throughout the inner Solar System. A number of tracking, navigation, communications, and data relay satellites will be needed. These will be located in geostationary Earth orbit, in orbit around Mars, and in libration points near the Moon.

With fully reusable rocket powered vehicles operating between Earth and the Moon, with a network of spaceports stationed near Earth, the Moon, and Mars, with high efficiency transport of raw materials into space for processing, and with cycling spaceships making the long voyage to Mars on a regular basis, the transportation network for the inner Solar System will be fully in place. That network will extend the reach of human aspiration, and will open the inner Solar System for continued research, productive enterprise, and human settlement.

III

OPENING THE SPACE FRONTIER: THE NEXT 20 YEARS

AN ECONOMICAL, PHASED APPROACH

Avigorous civilian space program will be an integral part of 21st-century America. This will extend productive industry into space, advance science, and maintain U.S. technological leadership in the face of increasingly skilled and ambitious rivals. Our program emphasizes the achievements and contributions of a forward-looking space program.

Our detailed program reaches out 20 years into the future, leading the way to U.S. leadership in space for 50 years. Financial realities will dictate the pace at which we proceed, but our mandate directed us to provide vision and policy recommendations rather than detailed budgets. Our proposals are technically reasonable and support increased private activities in space. They will return solid benefits to the Nation at every step—in the form of knowledge, productive technologies, economic returns, national security, motivation, inspiration, and international prestige. Bold leadership will be needed to pursue our visions, and national commitment to excellence will be essential for their achievement.

In developing our space agenda we recognized that the program must provide a real return to the American people. We have set three criteria which the program should meet:

- **Each element and increment of the program must be set in the context of a long-term plan.** Fragmented efforts and uncertainties as to future goals will only dilute accomplishments and increase costs. Our program for the next 20 years is complementary to and in anticipation of the space efforts that should occur over the next 50 years. Each segment builds on the previous step.
- **The program will be technically challenging, but feasible.** Our program requires significant technical progress and stresses the importance of continuing research and

technology advance. It does not depend on "spectacular" scientific or technological breakthroughs, although these may occur and our program would gain therefrom. Early emphasis on building a solid research and technology base in conjunction with careful advanced planning and analysis can effect major cost savings in the more expensive future operational phases; and

• **The program will be adequately funded.** We do not assume a sudden surge of resources in the years ahead. At the same time we recognize that world leadership in space will not be cheap, and that a reasonable fraction of national resources will be needed to maintain United States preeminence.

Our program assumes that the total NASA budget will grow modestly in constant dollars from 1987 to the end of the century, and that in the next century the civilian space program will remain below one-half percent of the Gross National Product (GNP), or half the peak percentage reached during the Apollo program in the 1960s.

We believe that the 20-year program summarized below can be carried out within these constraints and within the proposed schedule. In arriving at this conclusion we have drawn on NASA's experience and the Commission's best judgment. There is a distinct possibility that by taking advantage of the development of commercial activities in space, commercial launch and recovery services, innovative technologies and manufacturing methods, and mutually advantageous international arrangements, the cost to the U.S. taxpayer could be reduced, but the Commission has used conservative fiscal assumptions.

The Proposed 20-Year Program

The next 20 years should renew America's commitment to leadership on the space frontier. Our plan assumes continuation of NASA's present programs, recognizing funding constraints by assuming only modest budget increases, but we add over the next five years funds for the development of advanced technologies for cargo transport vehicles, passenger transport vehicles, and transfer vehicles. The Commission believes that NASA must significantly increase support of advanced research and technology. We propose a three-fold increase in this area, which in FY 1986 is funded at a nominal $158 million. In constant dollars, FY 1986 funding is approximately 10 percent of the research and technology funding levels in the peak Apollo years. NASA is still living on the investments made then, but cannot continue to do so if we are to maintain U.S. leadership in space.

Advanced planning for future systems must also be increased, like that now being done in the joint DOD/NASA study of advanced launch systems. With this sole exception, support of advanced planning and advanced technology development is far too low—only 10 percent of that in the Apollo days. This tiny budget should also be tripled. NASA should pursue the unknown and high/medium risk technology developments, while encouraging the private sector to move into routine standardized operations. Between 1990 and the year 2005, our program calls for significant advances toward each of the long-term goals outlined above, including:

- **Understanding the Universe.** Our cost projections require a significant increase in space science and applications funding over the next 20 years. During this period, bold space science programs would be initiated to ensure further major advances and extend our understanding of the Universe. This would provide the data needed for sound decisions in the development of programs to enable the United States within 50 years to establish a continuous presence on the Moon and Mars, and to utilize the resources of the Moon, Mars, Phobos, and asteroids in pioneering the inner Solar System.

- **Exploring, Prospecting, and Settling the Solar System.** Achieving these goals requires the development of the space systems needed for exploring and settling the Moon and sustained operations on Mars and Phobos. We also see a clear need for better scientific data in conjunction with a major research and technology effort directed at developing robotic systems and in designing biospheres and extraction and manufacturing processes for eventual use of the Moon, Mars, or elsewhere in space.

- **Space Enterprise.** Our program calls for aggressive actions over the next 20 years, starting immediately, to bring about a major expansion of commercial activity in space and related support functions. We believe that private industry should play an increasing role in the next family of space transportation vehicles, both automated and piloted. Properly challenging America's free enterprise system is a key element in reducing the cost of Opening the Space Frontier. We need to identify the economic opportunities and the role that Government should play in commercializing appropriate space activities.

- **Space Systems to Open the Space Frontier.** The Commission has identified three major space transport systems and three space facilities that require completion of development efforts during the next 20 years. These systems will provide the basic infrastructure to enable the United States to achieve the 21st-century goals that the Commission recommends. The three major space transport systems required are:

  - **Cargo transport vehicles;**
  - **Passenger transport vehicles; and**
  - **Transfer vehicles for round-trip travel beyond low Earth orbit.**

The Space Station should be maintained on schedule for initial operation in 1994. The next three critical space facilities required are:

- **Earth Spaceport;**
- **Variable-Gravity Research Facility; and**
- **Lunar Surface Outpost**

These facilities will be evolutionary versions of the Space Station that President Reagan has directed be operational by 1994. A geostationary orbit (GEO) space station is not included in our program; it is reasonable to believe that by the time it would be required, American industry can construct this with private financing and NASA's technical assistance. A GEO space station is an excellent candidate for the first major commercial services venture in space. An orbital maneuvering vehicle (a "space harbor tug") will be required in the early 1990s, and is already being developed by NASA. The Variable-Gravity Research Facility is required within the next 20 years in order to understand the required artificial gravity levels necessary for long-duration flights well in advance of human travel to Mars. As the program continues to evolve during the 21st century, there will be an evolutionary growth of the initial Space Station into the first spaceport. Future spaceports will be deployed beyond Earth orbit at the L1 Libration Point, in lunar orbit, and eventually in orbit around Mars. Outposts will be located as needed on the surface of the Moon and Mars and its moons.

CONDUCTING AN EFFECTIVE
SCIENCE PROGRAM

Science has benefited dramatically from our entry into space. Before the launch of Sputnik in 1957, the study of natural phenomena—including those occurring in space—was almost completely dependent upon measurements made on the surface of Earth or within its atmosphere. Today, spacecraft range from near Earth orbit to the realm of the outer planets. This enables scientists to monitor Earth's continents, oceans, and atmosphere on a global basis; its space environment from the outer reaches of its atmosphere to beyond the Moon; radiations from the Sun, planets, stars, and galaxies across the entire electromagnetic spectrum; and the planets and other bodies of the Solar System from close at hand. Scores of innovative experiments in physics, chemistry, and the life sciences have been conducted in the microgravity and near-vacuum conditions available aboard spacecraft. Thousands of bright young Americans, motivated by the excitement inherent in space research and often by the desire to fly in space themselves, have elected to pursue scientific careers. As a result of scientific activities in space, our quest to understand the Universe and the laws that govern it, as well as the processes that gave rise to the Solar System, Earth, and life, is vigorously expanding.

We have previously detailed our recommendations for advancing space science. Implementing those recommendations requires certain generic activities to support the various disciplines involved. For example, all elements of our recommended program are completely dependent upon the active involvement of creative scientists whose productivity requires generic types of support that apply to every subdiscipline of space science. Supporting research and technology funds are essential for maintaining laboratory facilities and providing a creative atmosphere in which new ideas can be tested.

Our space program has stimulated the development of new branches of science that barely existed before. As a result, the Nation now possesses a cadre of highly-trained scientists working in space science, almost all of whom interact with the space program to obtain meaningful data. They constitute a precious national resource that should be nurtured through continuing new opportunities for research. Government, industry, and academic scientists all play important roles in the space science program. Government scientists have a special responsibility to work with spacecraft designers and operations staffs to assure that the scientific objectives of a mission are attainable. Academic scientists conceive of many of the experiments carried out in space, and in the course of their research are responsible for training the young scientists who will be the backbone of the future program.

Because many space science programs take 5 to 10 years from inception to flight status, it is difficult for students to participate meaningfully in such projects during their relatively short period of research training. Opportunities to participate in projects of comparatively small scope, such as Spartan-class missions on the space shuttle, can ease these problems. On a larger scale, the development of the Space Station and its follow-on facilities will, for the first time, permit national space laboratories. Exciting research in physics, chemistry, and the life sciences will be carried out there.

For example, because certain physical and chemical processes occur differently under the microgravity conditions in Earth orbit than they do on Earth's surface, study of such processes could result in important scientific discoveries, some of which could later have substantial commercial applications. And as explained on pages 25–57, biological research on plants, animals, and humans under microgravity conditions is essential if we are to carry out the program of exploration and enterprise described in this report. It follows that state-of-the-art laboratory facilities must be available to carry out experiments in Earth orbit.

These facilities should have adequate volume and power available, with the capability to simulate various levels of artificial gravity. They should be accessible to technicians and scientists whose normal occupation is carrying out experiments in ground-based laboratories. They also should be equipped with state-of-the-art computational facilities for communicating with the ground and for storing and analyzing data. In some cases, it may be required to operate space experiments under the direct control of scientists on the ground. Because the leaders in the scientific fields involved are already heavily engaged in ground-based research, it is essential that the time and effort that they must expend to apply for laboratory space in Earth orbit, to conduct their experiments, and to obtain the experimental data in the form suitable for extended analysis on the ground be reduced to a minimum.

To achieve this goal, efforts should be directed not only to the optimum design of the physical facilities needed, but also to administrative and budgetary mechanisms that will provide ready access to laboratory facilities in space. Recognizing the considerable success the Nation has achieved in providing large experimental facilities for diverse user communities such as particle physics and astronomy, the Commission recommends that: **An administrative entity be established, known as the National Space Laboratory, to be responsible for planning the space-based laboratory facilities required by various scientific communities,** for selecting from applicants the scientists who are to be granted laboratory time, and for advising the managers of the relevant space-based facilities so as to maximize scientific productivity.

There is no reason that all the research conducted in space laboratory facilities should be funded by NASA. The Commission therefore recommends that: **The agencies that now fund research in related areas on the ground, such as the National Science Foundation (NSF), the Department of Energy (DOE), and the National Institutes of Health (NIH) be empowered to fund research coordinated by the National Space Laboratory as part of their normal programs; other sources of funding, such as universities and industry, should also be encouraged.**

The study of Earth and its environment is now funded by a number of different agencies of the Government, including NASA, NSF, DOE, National Oceanic and Atmospheric Administration (NOAA), United States Geological Survey (USGS), and others. As pointed out earlier, the time has come for a comprehensive study of planet Earth, including its interior, land surfaces, oceans, polar ice caps, and atmosphere. This offers the potential for an understanding of the processes which alter Earth on timescales varying from days to millions of years. Achieving the goals of such a global study requires the use of on-site measuring devices, remote sensing satellites, and computational facilities that can process an unprecedented flow of data. This global study will require the resources of the agencies now involved in studying Earth. We therefore recommend that: **The space-related activities of NASA, NSF, DOE, NOAA, USGS, and other agencies must be coordinated at both the programmatic and budgetary levels, beginning with an Earth-observing system now in early stages of planning.**

Other specific areas need to be addressed to accomplish our space science goals. Advances in detector technology can also vastly improve the ability to observe Earth and its environment, the Sun and planets, and remote stars and galaxies, so it is important to stress detector development in every area.

Often overlooked in the drive to develop more effective systems for gathering and analyzing data is the fact that theoretical work is essential to advance understanding and provide the conceptual framework needed to make the data intelligible. Rapid advances in supercomputers enable theorists to create much more sophisticated models and to test their models against the data rapidly and in detail. Because computational facilities are also such an important part of data gathering, storage, and analysis, funding should be provided to maintain computer facilities at a state-of-the-art level. An emerging need is for the conduct of space experiments under direct control of ground-based scientists using computer links to spacecraft. Well-planned development of this capability, especially in the context of the Space Station, has the potential to greatly improve productivity. We therefore recommend that: **Special emphasis be placed upon assuring that space scientists have available state-of-the-art computational facilities for communication, storage, analysis, and theoretical modeling of data.**

GOVERNMENT POLICY AND
THE PRIVATE SECTOR

I n the Presidential Commercial Space Policy Directive of July 1984, the Reagan Administration expressed its desire to support commercial development of space. Legislation alone is insufficient to bring about that goal, however; specific actions are required. These should be aimed at removing present barriers to commercialization (such as Government competition), reducing the cost of space operations, and encouraging the future provision of launch services by the private sector. We believe that it is in the national interest to press forward with the commercialization of space, and urge the Administration, the Congress, and all involved Government agencies to cooperate with the private sector in removing perceived barriers.

In response to the 1984 Presidential directive, NASA established an Office of Commercial Programs. Despite attempts by this office to foster industrial initiative in carrying out in-space research in materials processing, there have been only a few companies that have done so. Prominent among these is the McDonnell Douglas Company's decision to proceed with the development and operation of an electrophoresis experiment for test flight on the shuttle aimed at producing pharmaceutical products. NASA and university scientists are also carrying out a modest program in materials handling research using drop tubes, sounding rockets, and aircraft to gain a few seconds or minutes of microgravity; this work may spark future commercial interest. The 3M Corporation has expressed interest in flying on as many as 72 shuttle flights in order to obtain sufficient research results to develop new "Made in Space" products. They have signed a Memorandum of Understanding (MOU) with NASA regarding these flights, paralleling the MOUs of other corporations. Under these agreements NASA shares in the research findings, but agrees not to publish the data.

Another instrument used by NASA to promote private sector space activities is the Joint Endeavor Agreement (JEA). This allows a company to make a certain number of flights free of charge to ascertain whether a new business can be viable. The JEA has value because it enables small companies, which otherwise could not afford the costs involved, to carry out research in space. NASA carefully controls the number and type of these agreements and receives access to the data obtained. Should the company not continue with the processes within a specified time, NASA can use the information for its own purposes.

The Joint Endeavor Agreement is a powerful means of attracting research opportunities for space that otherwise would probably not be carried out. Unfortunately, no funding has been provided for JEAs. Therefore NASA's departments have been forced into a "zero-sum game," in which every successful JEA reduces their budgets accordingly. As a result, the Commission has found that some small start-up companies have been kept waiting for as long as a year. Since many of these companies are existing on venture capital, they do not have the resources to wait for a decision indefinitely. The Commission reminds NASA of its responsibility under the Presidential directive to assist companies seeking commercial opportunities in space, and suggests that JEAs be funded explicitly rather than charged to NASA departmental funds.

Developing National Space Policy

At the present time, responsibility for space policy within the Administration rests primarily with the Senior Interagency Group (Space). Referred to as "SIG-SPACE," this council is made up of representatives from the major Government agencies dealing with space matters, including NASA, the Departments of Defense, Commerce, State, Transportation, and Office of Science and Technology Policy. This group is responsible to the National Security Council, which has the power of veto over its decisions.

In addition to NASA, the Departments of Commerce and Transportation have significant roles in space commercialization. The Inter-agency Working Group on the commercial use of space was established under the President's National Space Strategy, issued in August 1984. The Department of Commerce chairs the working group, with NASA as Vice Chair. The group is responsible to the Economic Policy Council for the planning and initiation of the commercial development of space. The Department of Transportation has been directly involved in the space field since the Secretary of Transportation—acting on Executive Order 12435—established the Office of Commercial Space Transportation early in 1984. The new Office was given priority by being located within the Secretary's office. Under the Commercial Space Launch Act, enacted in October 1984, the Office of Commercial Space Transportation is responsible for encouraging, promoting, and facilitating commercial operation of expendable launch vehicles. The Office is also responsible for streamlining regulatory procedures that face the private operator of these vehicles, and for issuing licenses for commercial launches and launch sites to ensure compliance with international obligations and to protect the public health, safety of property and national security, and foreign policy interests. The Office and its licensing process are geared to fulfill two operational elements: Mission review and safety review.

The new Office takes this mandate seriously and has become an advocate within the Government for this constituency. This Office should play a vital role in ensuring that private operators have a fair opportunity to build and operate new launch vehicles for the Nation's benefit.

The Department of Transportation is responsibly carrying out its critical duties, and the Commission recommends that: **Space transportation regulatory and certification functions continue to receive high-level support.**

A National Aeronautics and Space Council

The new national space goals and the strategies to achieve them presented in this report will clearly involve many Government agencies and departments, the private sector, academic institutions, and international partnerships and treaties. To implement the strategies and subsequent plans in an effective and timely manner, a full-time space council at the Presidential level could make a major contribution to policy development and interagency coordination.

Reestablishment of a National Aeronautics and Space Council (as provided for by Congress in the NASA Act) could contribute professional advice on space policy issues, help ensure prompt and effective cooperation among Government agencies and departments, encourage an appropriate level of private sector involvement, make available high-level policy guidance on international cooperation and space treaties, and provide oversight on the overall progress of America's space programs.

The need for such a Council is further heightened at this time by the concurrence of five recent and important events which impact both near-term and long-term aeronautics and space programs. These are:

- The submission of our long-range recommendations to the President and to the Congress, calling for new national space goals and the strategies to achieve them;
- The President's initiation of a National Aero-Space Plane program, which has the potential to contribute to national security, next-generation commercial aircraft, and lower-cost transport to Earth orbit;
- Presidentially-directed studies now assessing near-term and long-term national launch needs. These studies will influence both the diversity and the extent of our launch capabilities into the next century;
- The development phase of the Space Station, planned to begin this year. The extent of its future role as a spaceport and in cooperative international programs is still evolving; and
- The Strategic Defense Initiative, a national defense program. SDI will have a growing, but as yet undetermined, impact on future space operations.

Based on the foregoing considerations, the Commission recommends that: **The President re-establish a small National Aeronautics and Space Council in the White House based on the NASA Act.**

INTERNATIONAL
COOPERATION AND COMPETITION

Since the early days of the Space Age, the United States has pursued a cooperative international approach to its programs and to the development of a legal framework for outer space. The United States has entered into over 1,000 agreements with 100 countries for cooperative endeavors in space. America led the way in drafting the principles that led in 1967 to the Outer Space Treaty (See page 158), and had earlier played a leading role in the formation of the United Nations Committee on the Peaceful Uses of Outer Space (COPUOS). The United States also initiated the formation of the International Telecommunication Satellite Organization (INTELSAT), and is an active participant in the International Maritime Satellite Organization (INMARSAT). The United States is a leader in the exchange of data from weather satellites and has encouraged and assisted many other nations in using its Landsat remote sensing system. We also have invited international participation in a large number of scientific projects in space, such as the Hubble Space Telescope, the Galileo probe to Jupiter, the Infrared Astronomy Satellite, and many others.

In 1975, the United States and the Soviet Union conducted the first international space mission involving human crews, the Apollo-Soyuz Test Project. Since then, the United States and the Soviet Union have carried crew members from 16 other nations on their spacecraft, including Bulgaria, Canada, Czechoslovakia, Cuba, Federal Republic of Germany, France, German Democratic Republic, Hungary, India, Mexico, Mongolia, Netherlands, Poland, Romania, Saudi Arabia, and Vietnam. Thus, people of many nationalities have observed our planet from the new perspective of space.

In 1984, the United States launched the largest cooperative international space project in history: a permanently occupied international space station. Our European, Japanese, and Canadian partners may contribute one-third of the cost, and key pieces of technology. The

OUTER SPACE AGREEMENTS

Five U.N. treaties are currently in force regarding activities in space: the Treaty on Principles Governing the Activities of States in the Exploration and Use of Outer Space, Including the Moon and other Celestial Bodies (1967); the Agreement on the Rescue of Astronauts, the Return of Astronauts, and the Return of Objects Launched into Outer Space (1968); the Convention on International Liability for Damage Caused by Space Objects (1972); the Convention on Registration of Objects Launched into Outer Space (1976); and the Treaty on Principles Governing Activities on the Moon and Other Celestial Bodies (1979). The major space nations, including the United States and Soviet Union, have ratified all but the last, which is more commonly referred to as the "Moon Treaty." Only five countries have signed and ratified that agreement.

In addition to deliberations at the United Nations, there is an organization called the International Institute of Space Law, which is part of the International Astronautical Federation that provides a forum for discussing space law at its annual meetings.

station is designed to grow and evolve, and is expected to remain in operation for 30 years. This enterprise is establishing an impressive new model for international cooperation in space.

Growing Competition in Space

For the first two decades of the Space Age, space exploration and utilization were conducted almost entirely by the United States and the Soviet Union. Space power is rapidly proliferating now as more and more nations achieve significant space capabilities; China, India, Japan, and the European Space Agency have the ability to launch satellites. Several European countries, especially France and Germany, have developed substantial aerospace industries to build launch vehicles, satellites, and the Spacelab module that flies in the cargo bay of our space shuttle. Canada, although it has no national launch capability, has a strong aerospace industry that has built communications satellites and the "robot arm" for the space shuttle. India has its own small launch vehicle and is developing its own remote sensing and communications satellites and more capable launch vehicles. Brazil is developing the capability to build and launch satellites by the end of this decade. Indonesia was the first of the less developed countries to establish its own domestic satellite communication system.

Although America's major political and exploratory competitor remains the Soviet Union, our major commercial competitors in space will be Western Europe and Japan. The Soviets and Chinese are offering competitive launch services, and the Europeans already are operating the Ariane, which competes with the U.S. space shuttle for launching satellites.

More capable versions of these systems are being developed, and Japan intends to have a similar launch vehicle in the 1990s. The French are now operating a remote sensing satellite system called SPOT, which will compete with the U.S. Landsat system. The Soviets, Germans, and Japanese have shown considerable interest in materials processing and energy supply from space, which will offer future competition for U.S. firms.

The United States will need to move forward steadily to meet these competitive challenges. In the non-commercial field, this will require sustained Government support for technology development and for exploratory and long-range developmental missions. In the commercial field, the United States will want to ensure that American firms are able to compete effectively in the provision of space-related products and services.

International Cooperation

International cooperation can help America realize its goals in space sooner and less expensively. Cooperation can also help us create the kind of international environment most conducive to an expansive space program conducted in accordance with American values. We greatly benefit from attracting the world's best minds to participate in our programs (See page 161). A good example is in the field of global remote sensing. By cooperating with more than 100 other nations in remote sensing systems, we have gained broad acceptance of the principle of freedom to observe Earth from space. Proving that this can be useful to all nations is our most effective policy. This has led to general acceptance of the U.S. position in international forums that it will not accept limitations on the rights of all nations to acquire data from space.

We solidly endorse American cooperation with other nations in selected space projects when such projects are mutually beneficial and technologically sound. For a few projects of lasting significance, we believe that the United States should lead coalitions of participating nations, as it did with INTELSAT and is now doing with the Space Station. In our approach to international cooperation, we must recognize differences among nations in terms of their technological capabilities. We must also recognize political realities, and distinctions between friends, neutrals, rivals, and adversaries. We recommend somewhat different approaches for three categories of nations: (1) the Soviet Union and its allies; (2) developed countries friendly to the United States; and (3) less developed countries.

The Soviet Union

The Soviet Union placed the first satellite, the first animal, the first man, and the first woman in space; launched the first space station (and now has its seventh successful station in orbit); returned the first pictures from the far side of the Moon and the first pictures from the surface of another planet (Venus). Clearly, the Soviets intend to expand their presence in low Earth orbit and then move out with piloted missions to Mars and possibly the Moon. The core of a large, new modular station was launched early in 1986. Two new rockets are

In 1988, the Soviet Union plans to send an automated spacecraft to Mars to get a close-up view of the moon Phobos. (COURTESY WILLIAM HARTMANN)

INTERNATIONAL SPACE YEAR

A specific opportunity for global space cooperation will occur in 1992. Called the International Space Year (ISY), it will take advantage of a confluence of anniversaries in 1992: the 500th anniversary of the discovery of America, the 75th anniversary of the founding of the Union of Soviet Socialist Republics, and the 35th anniversaries of the International Geophysical Year and the launch of the first artificial satellite, Sputnik 1. During this period, it is also expected that the International Geosphere/Biosphere Program will be in progress, setting the stage for other related space activities.

In 1985, Congress approved the ISY concept in a bill that authorizes funding for NASA. The legislation calls on the President to endorse the ISY and consider the possibility of discussing it with other foreign leaders, including the Soviet Union. It directs NASA to work with the State Department and other Government agencies to initiate interagency and international discussions exploring opportunities for international missions and related research and educational activities.

As stated by Senator Spark Matsunaga on the tenth anniversary of the historic Apollo-Soyuz Test Project, July 17, 1985, "An International Space Year won't change the world. But at the minimum, these activities help remind all peoples of their common humanity and their shared destiny aboard this beautiful spaceship we call Earth."

reported to be in development, one the equivalent of the giant Saturn V that carried American astronauts to the Moon. They also appear to be developing their own version of a space shuttle.

The Soviets have repeatedly alluded to the connection between their long-duration flights aboard the Salyut space stations (up to 237 days) and the need to obtain data about human physiological and psychological tolerance to weightlessness in case a decision is made to go to Mars. Although there are conflicting accounts by high-ranking Soviet scientists as to when such a mission might be attempted (some have said in the near future, others have indicated it will not be until after the turn of the century), it seems clear that they will visit Mars within the next 50 years.

In 1967, the Soviets created an organization called Interkosmos to facilitate cooperation with other countries; members include Bulgaria, Cuba, Czechoslovakia, German Democratic Republic, Hungary, Mongolia, Poland, Romania, and Vietnam. The Interkosmos organization has also been used as a mechanism for cooperating with other countries and organizations, including the United States, India, France, Sweden, Austria, Finland, and the European Space Agency.

Cooperation with the Soviet Union in space holds promise because of the substantial space capabilities it already possesses, but some cautionary principles should be observed. In addition to satisfying the general criteria for cooperative international space projects, U.S.-Soviet projects should be specifically designed to avoid ill-advised technology transfer, and to draw on the unique capabilities of each nation where possible. Coordinated parallel missions, rather than joint ones, will often provide the most feasible approach. The Commission recommends that: **Within these guidelines, selective cooperation should be actively sought with the Soviet Union.**

A good example of a possible cooperative project is the coordinated robotic exploration of Mars. The Soviets will carry out a 1988 automated mission to the Martian moons Phobos and Deimos with some international participation (including U.S. scientists), and the United States is planning to undertake a 1990 Mars polar orbiting mission. Exchanges of plans and data between these missions could be mutually beneficial.

On a more ambitious scale, it has been suggested that the United States send an automated surface rover to Mars while the Soviet Union sends a lander capable of returning samples of Martian material to Earth. The U.S. rover would roam the surface of the planet collecting a wide variety of documented samples, then bring them to the Soviet spacecraft for return to Earth. If either mission failed, or if either nation withdrew, the other nation would still have an extremely worthwhile project, but a successful joint U.S.-U.S.S.R. project would multiply the scientific rewards many times.

Friendly Developed Countries

Formed in 1975 by merging the European Launcher Development Organization and the European Space Research Organization, the European Space Agency (ESA) is a group of 11 European countries: Belgium, Denmark, France, Germany, Ireland, Italy, the Netherlands, Spain, Sweden, Switzerland, and the United Kingdom. Austria and Norway will exchange their associate status for full membership in ESA next year. All countries contribute to the organization's general operating budget which supports basic space activities. Special projects, such as the development of the Ariane launch vehicle, are selected separately and no country is forced to participate.

In addition to cooperating through ESA, several European countries have strong national space programs, especially France, Germany, Britain, and Italy. For example, France is the primary builder of the Ariane, and has also entered the Earth remote sensing business with the SPOT satellite. Germany, which was the prime developer of Spacelab for the shuttle, is very active in using that vehicle for research on materials processing in space, and is the lead country in the development of the Columbus space station module. Italy is one of the world's leaders in technology for communications satellites operating at very high frequencies (called the Ka band at 30/20 gigaHertz). As can be seen, these national space programs, combined with the ESA activities, make Europe a growing force in space.

The Japanese space program was founded in cooperation with the United States. Their N launch vehicle is manufactured from a U.S. design (the McDonnell Douglas Delta vehicle) and U.S. industry has built most of the satellites launched by the Japanese for meteorology and communications. While they are now trying to increase the percentage of parts in these satellites that are built in Japan, it seems clear that they will continue to want to cooperate with the United States. Japan is now building its own launch vehicle designated the H, which will use the higher efficiency liquid hydrogen/liquid oxygen fuels. The initial version of this vehicle will not have much lift capability, but it is probably the forerunner to larger capacity vehicles which could compete with other nations' systems.

Our relationships with Western Europe, Japan, Canada, and other friendly developed nations have additional dimensions. The growing space technology and science capabilities of these countries make them potentially valuable partners in a wide variety of space endeavors. At the same time we can expect them also to become vigorous commercial competitors. The Space Station project will require us to find the proper balance between these two considerations, and thereby establish a model for handling competitive and cooperative relationships. There will be many future opportunities for cooperation in space exploration and science missions, drawing on the knowledge and skills of these nations. The Commission recommends that: **Continued cooperative space ventures be pursued vigorously with friendly developed countries, with due regard for reciprocity and the protection of U.S. commercial interests.**

Less Developed Countries

The United States has a long history of cooperating with India in space activities. The 1975–76 SITE project, which involved Indian use of an American satellite for broadcasting educational television programs to 5,000 remote communities, is still cited as one of the most successful cooperative space programs in NASA's history. The success of this project was partially responsible for the Indian decision to procure its own satellite system, called INSAT, for communications and meteorology. These satellites are built by American firms to Indian specifications, and are launched by the United States.

A little-known fact outside the space community is that the Peoples Republic of China has been launching satellites since 1970. In 1984, China not only introduced a launch vehicle whose third stage uses high efficiency cryogenic fuels (liquid oxygen and liquid hydrogen), but also placed a communications satellite in geostationary orbit. These two feats were worthy of a major space power (the Soviets, for example, still do not have a launch vehicle that uses liquid hydrogen/liquid oxygen). The rocket, called the Long March 3, is now being marketed internationally by the Chinese, along with the less capable Long March 2; Sweden will be the first customer.

In the early 1980s, the Chinese announced that they had selected several individuals as astronaut-trainees, although they later disbanded the group, stating that a piloted spaceflight

Artist's concept of a possible joint U.S./Soviet Mars mission. The U.S. would provide a Mars prospector which would rove on the Martian surface collecting soil samples, and the Soviets would provide the spacecraft to return the soil samples to Earth. (COURTESY RON MILLER)

capability was not economically feasible at that time. Their interest in launching a person into space continues, however, and they have discussed with NASA the possibility of having a Chinese payload specialist fly on a future U.S. space shuttle mission.

Though India, China, and Brazil are potential space powers, most less developed countries do not now have the financial, technological, or industrial resources to become significant partners in major space enterprises. They can, however, benefit significantly from the application of space technologies such as satellite communications, remote sensing, and navigation, thus fostering economic growth, education, and institution-building. Cooperating with less developed nations in these fields can also advance broad U.S. foreign policy interests, provided that care is taken to prevent pass-through of sensitive information to third parties. We therefore recommend that: **The United States creatively seek broad opportunities to apply appropriate space technologies to meet the needs of less developed countries.**

The Future International Environment

America's space activities, as well as our cooperative ventures with others, are influenced by existing international institutions and agreements. The United States is party to four basic treaties concerning space that were negotiated within the United Nations Committee on the Peaceful Uses of Outer Space; it has not ratified a fifth, known informally as the "Moon Treaty." The United States also participates in COPUOS discussions of other issues and in specialized international organizations related to the uses of space, notably the International Telecommunication Union (ITU), INTELSAT, and INMARSAT. In addition, Americans participate in international non-governmental organizations such as the Committee on Space Research (COSPAR) and the International Astronautical Federation.

The open, cooperative international environment that the United States seeks to establish for space activity is threatened by a variety of pressures. Some international institutions, notably the ITU and United Nations organs such as the General Assembly and COPUOS, have become increasingly politicized. The one nation/one vote principle gives the controlling majority to countries that have no current capability for space exploration. The system of bloc politics that prevails in the United Nations results in extraneous issues such as the Arab/Israeli dispute, intra-African differences, and East/West rivalry intruding into space policy decisions. The strength of the Soviet Union in the United Nations (via its client states) gives it more influence on U.N. decisions than is enjoyed by the United States and other democracies. The Outer Space Affairs Division of the United Nations, which services COPUOS, suffers from politicization and bureaucratization, and includes no American representation at the professional level. These facts mean that actions by U.N. bodies can serve to hold back the exploration and utilization of space, particularly by the United States. The Commission therefore recommends that: **The United States avoid accepting international arrangements that give broad jurisdiction over American activities in space to international bodies in which adversaries have undue influence or in which decisions will be made by majorities with little current competence in the space field. In addition, we recommend against U.S. support for any global organization that purports to regulate broadly the utilization of outer space.**

There have been and continue to be pressures from less developed countries for guaranteed equitable access to the use of space and its resources. This has been particularly visible in meetings of the International Telecommunication Union devoted to allocating geostationary orbital positions and radio frequencies for commmunication satellites. Many less developed countries have pressed for long-term rigid planning to assure their access, while the United States has argued for a more flexible approach. We recommend that: **The United States maintain its positions favoring flexible rules for access to geostationary orbital positions and radio frequencies, and in support of the free gathering and dissemination of data to and from all countries. At the same time we urge NASA and the communications satellite industry to advance critical technologies that can expand access to orbit for all users, while minimizing electronic or other interference between satellites.**

Another example of pressures on the free use of space is the Moon Treaty negotiated in the United Nations, which would impose a generally more restrictive legal regime on the uses of space than existing agreements. In particular, the Treaty's provisions for the use of natural resources on other celestial bodies suggest a collectivized international regime analogous to the seabed mining regime in the Law of the Sea Treaty. Such a regime could seriously inhibit American enterprise in space. We therefore recommend that: **The United States not become a party to the Moon Treaty.**

Our Proposed Approach
In addressing the evolving international legal and institutional environment for outer space, the United States should support agreements that facilitate the constructive uses of outer space, and oppose those that restrict them. On Earth, American values flourish best under a regime of openness, without needless rules and regulations that limit freedom, inhibit diversity, and hamper innovation. The same is true in space. Our view is that the existing United Nations treaties that we have ratified provide a sufficient legal framework for the future uses of space.

We recognize that there may be specific areas of concern where additional, narrowly-focused agreements may be useful. Examples might include space rescue and standardized docking mechanisms, nuclear reactor safety, and the limitation of space debris. In some cases these may best be negotiated bilaterally and multinationally rather than through the United Nations.

The program we have proposed in this report will involve the international community, and can bring significant benefits to all nations in science, applications, access to space, the development of vast additional resources, and the creation of new human communities beyond Earth. Above all, it will open new options for humanity, eroding the notion that our future is limited and that international competition must be a "zero-sum game" in which one country's gain is another's loss.

We have recommended a global study of planet Earth with full international participation. Simultaneous coverage of Earth from satellites may evolve into an open global information system, in which all participating nations might operate their own ground stations. Scientists from all nations could thus participate freely in the analysis of global data. The results would lay the groundwork for an international system to observe and predict our terrestrial environment with ever-increasing accuracy, to the great benefit of all. Continuous observation of Earth from space could promote cooperative international management of the biosphere in which we all live.

Our suggested approach to technology development and lowering the cost of access to space will facilitate space applications of benefit to everyone. For most nations, space systems are still relatively expensive, so more capable satellites and cheaper launch services can bring space applications like communications satellites and remote sensing within the reach of developing countries. This would increase the demand for space transportation to the benefit of launch vehicle enterprises. The example that our program will set by lowering launch costs and opening access to space will stimulate other countries to pursue similar approaches, and thereby broaden entrance to space for all nations.

Space enterprises that draw on the mineral and energy resources of the Solar System will stimulate the growth of the human economy, to the long-term benefit of everyone. Primary industries in space will generate secondary and tertiary industries in which many countries can participate. The scale of primary mineral and resource industries in space may well require multinational consortia, perhaps along the lines of the Anglo-French Channel Tunnel now being proposed for construction across the English Channel. The precedent set by American leadership in space enterprises could provide a powerful model to be emulated by other nations. Above all, successful mineral and energy enterprises in space would signal that increasing abundance, rather than redistributing scarcity, is the wave of the future.

We believe that establishing new human communities beyond Earth is an implicitly international enterprise. Human settlements, not national colonies, should be the model. These new communities would allow a revival of cultural diversity that now seems threatened on Earth, broadening humanity's options for the future.

THE AMERICAN PEOPLE
AND THE SPACE PROGRAM

The support of the American public is the most critical resource of the U.S. civilian space program. It is the people who elect the leaders who, in turn, establish national priorities and allocate funds to each Government endeavor. Although our program calls for increased investment by the private sector, the Government remains the key to critical technological developments and overall implementation. Thus, the attitude of the American public toward space activities will determine whether or not our recommendations will be accepted. We firmly believe that the American people want a bold, imaginative civilian space effort. Such a program can inspire national excellence and challenge young people to pursue careers in science and technology.

Educating Our Children and Their Children
When Sputnik 1 penetrated the vacuum of space in October 1957, the reverberations shook the technological and educational underpinnings of the United States. A series of science education initiatives, including the National Defense Education Act of 1958, triggered a reformation of America's educational system.

This momentum has not been sustained; once again our Nation is confronted with the necessity to revitalize education. A healthy educational system emphasizing high standards is essential to U.S. technological and economic preeminence, national security, and our ability to advance scientific and technological frontiers, especially the space frontier. A citizenry able to understand and appreciate our Nation's space program is a key ingredient to the future of the program. The Commission believes that current weaknesses in our educational system must be corrected to ensure a vital 21st-century America.

In reviewing the promise of our future space program and the present status of our educational system, it seems appropriate to consider the warning posed by H. G. Wells that "human history becomes more and more a race between education and catastrophe."

According to the National Science Board's (NSB) 1985 "Science Indicators" report, recent studies found that high school graduates on the average took 2.2 years of science and 2.7 years of mathematics during their 4 years of high school. Except for basic courses, such as geometry, first year algebra, and biology, enrollment in science and mathematics courses was generally low. Furthermore, the NSB reports that the 10th grade is the last time most high school students in the United States are exposed to science. Less than one-half of the juniors and only one-third of the seniors take a science course. A substantial drop in the percentage of students taking pre-college science courses from the late 1940s to the early 1980s has been tallied.

These statistics, when held against similar data regarding students in other countries, are even more disturbing. American high school students take substantially less coursework in science and mathematics than pupils in countries such as Japan, West Germany, East Germany, China, and the Soviet Union. While national educational systems vary widely in structure and goals, therefore making comparisons difficult, it appears that United States students spend only one-half to one-third as much time learning science as their counterparts in these other five countries.

In summary, as revealed in a recent national survey of student achievement, an estimated 90 percent of America's high school graduates may not be capable of accomplishing even the most routine high-technology tasks in the future. While up to 90 percent of high school graduates in other countries enjoy a proficiency in math and science, a mere 6 percent of U.S. graduates attain the same aptitudes. Faced with a growing teacher shortage and a poverty of supplies and equipment to expose students to classroom science demonstration and laboratory experimentation, the United States must counter the surge of scientific illiteracy now epidemic within our country. This challenge exists at every level from elementary through graduate education.

Our space program plays important, but different, roles within our elementary schools, high schools, colleges, and universities. At the elementary through high school levels the space program provides incentive and inspiration. It is here that our next generation of engineers and scientists must be motivated.

Future managers, scientists, engineers, social scientists, doctors, and technicians for tomorrow's space endeavors must be attracted to these fields while attending the elementary and high schools of the Nation. It is essential to expose bright students at an early age to science and mathematics, and to offer them a solid program throughout their formative school years. Although many of our youth will not pursue scientific careers, a basic understanding of science and mathematics is essential in our increasingly technological world for tomorrow's lawyers, Government officials, business experts, and financiers. Indeed, our whole society must attain a higher level of scientific literacy.

In our deliberations and public forums, we have found many educational initiatives centered upon the space program. For example, the privately sponsored Young Astronaut Program is effectively reaching out to elementary and junior high school students to ignite their enthusiasm for studying science, mathematics, and high technology. The highly success-ful "Space Camps" grow in attendance each year as young people (and even adults) gain valuable "hands on" experience with space hardware. We encourage public and private programs that translate the space program into motivational activities for students in kinder-garten through 12th grade. In simple terms, as the United States signals a commitment to the exciting civilian space agenda we are proposing, young talent will follow enthusiastically.

At the university level the issues are less of motivation and more of providing substantive education and training. At the undergraduate level, issues of concern to the Commission have been raised by many groups, including quality training in basic disciplines, loss of the best students from research oriented disciplines to applied disciplines or non-technical disciplines for financial reasons, loss of faculty in high technology disciplines through inadequate budgets, and so on. These issues must be addressed for America's future health and competi-tiveness. Our future in space will involve a broad range of skills beyond astronautics. Strong basic education will provide the foundation on which these specialties can be built.

Universities are and will continue to be a vital component of the U.S. space science program. University scientists perform basic space research: They develop and build instru-ments, analyze data, develop new theoretical models, and they pose scientific questions that can be answered only by space missions. Universities train the next generation of space scientists and engineers. The interaction at universities between scientists who are in the space program and those who are not provides a source of new ideas for the space program, and speeds the incorporation of the space program's results into the mainstream of the Nation's scientific and technological base.

NASA's research and analysis and research and technology base programs have provided the underpinning for most space research and graduate education efforts at universities. These programs support the development of new instruments and mission concepts, the analysis of data from ongoing missions, the analysis of data from completed missions, the development of theoretical models, and the education of graduate students. We concur with studies that have emphasized strongly that the quality of NASA's scientific program and the return that the country receives from its investment in space missions directly depends on the effective-ness, the health, and the vitality of the research and analysis and research and technology base programs within NASA, and on similar university-oriented programs in other agencies.

The training of graduate students and postdoctoral fellows is an integral part of univer-sity research programs directed toward the increase of fundamental knowledge in the various scientific and engineering disciplines. The long-term vitality of the space program depends on the infusion of new talent, ideas, and innovation through the participation of young graduate students in the relevant disciplines. Equally important, however, is the transfer of knowledge and technology that occurs when students trained in these disciplines work in other areas in industry and in the national laboratories, bringing to these new areas the skills and the familiarity with advanced technology that are characteristic of space science and technology.

The provision of fellowships to graduate students studying in fields related to space science and engineering has been intermittent. We recommend that: **Congress authorize NASA to create a fellowship program in space science and engineering. This will help attract the best students to pursue careers in these disciplines and permit access to space careers by highly qualified young people regardless of their financial situation.**

Universities educate more than just specialists, however. As results from space sciences are distilled and incorporated into the coherent bodies of knowledge associated with the appropriate disciplines, they become part of the general education of a much larger number of students, eventually becoming woven into the fabric of society.

University laboratory equipment for space research is increasingly out of date. With declining funding and the reduced purchasing power of research funds, new equipment could not be, and was not, purchased. The next generation of students is being trained on the old equipment used to train their teachers. New generations of computing, analytical, and other equipment have become too costly for universities and colleges to purchase. The need to improve university laboratory equipment has been recognized by the National Science Foundation and the Departments of Energy and Defense which have established programs to meet those needs. NASA should also be funded to undertake similar programs to upgrade university space research equipment.

Involving students in flight research requires frequent, readily accessible flight opportunities. New instruments need to be tested on short shuttle flights and on suborbital flights before being placed on expensive, long-duration missions. Graduate students need the "hands on" experience of designing, building, and then flying a low-cost payload during the short term of a graduate education career.

The shuttle is supposed to provide frequent flight opportunities through "get-away specials," "hitchhikers," and free-flying Spartans, but this potential of the shuttle program has yet to be fully realized. Further steps are necessary to increase and simplify flight opportunities for science and technology. The reduction in the cost of space transportation advocated by the Commission would address one aspect of this problem.

The suborbital flight program includes aircraft, sounding rockets, and balloons which provide low-cost, low risk, and quick-turnaround flight opportunities. This program has been the mainstay of instrument development and graduate student participation in the space program since its inception, and will continue in this role for the foreseeable future. This low-cost, high leverage component of the NASA effort should receive continuing support.

In the future the National Space Laboratory, which we advocate for scientific research, should also be accessible to graduate students. A "space semester" at the National Space Laboratory would enable highly qualified students to carry out experiments in orbit as part of their educational program. Our hope is that such a laboratory would provide an environment in which a wide range of disciplines could flourish and in which cross-fertilization and a confluence of creative activity would stimulate innovation—an environment comparable to the traditional Earth-based university laboratories.

In summary, we recommend the following five actions:

That public and private educational initiatives centered on the space program be encouraged to motivate and inspire young people toward science and technology from elementary through high school;

That Congress authorize the creation of a vigorous graduate fellowship program to be administered by NASA;

That funding in the Research and Analysis and Technology Base programs within NASA and similar university-oriented research programs in other agencies be increased;

That NASA undertake a program to upgrade university space research equipment; and

That the suborbital program and shuttle programs provide more frequent flight opportunities for researchers.

Our Sampling of Public Attitudes

Over the course of several months, we sought public comment on the future of the U.S. civilian space program through a series of country-wide Public Forums, various electronic surveys, and direct mail solicitation of opinions. In addition, an article published in a widely distributed Sunday supplement suggested that readers contact us. The thousands of people who responded to these calls for participation in shaping the Nation's future in space are listed at the end of this report; the Commission is extremely grateful to all.

The 15 Public Forums were carried out from September 13, 1985 to January 17, 1986, in cities that were chosen for their geographical representation and to seek a wide diversity of opinion from the general public (as well as from industry and academia). The first Forum, in Los Angeles, heralded the elegant remarks, visions, and criticisms of space activity that were to follow throughout the United States: views from social scientists, concepts from the aerospace industry, caveats from lawyers, visions from authors, deep misgivings about the perceived militarization of space from the general public, and a potpourri of views on the wheres, whens, whys, and hows of space activity from a supportive public.

In some cities, such as Seattle, the public shared the excitement of participation in space tourism. Grass-roots enthusiasm in Houston amplified the commercial prospects of space. Salt Lake City sent a strong message that the future of the space program lies in educating and stimulating the imaginations of young people, even to the point of including them on space journeys.

Tallahassee, Ann Arbor, and Iowa City witnesses brought out the concerns of academia, emphasizing the risks of displacing basic research with inflexible programs. Albuquerque and Boulder participants expressed eagerness for participation in the Nation's aerospace research programs and roles in space for diverse professionals from chefs to philosophers. Citizens in San Francisco advocated something for everybody, from fanciful space sports, a "feminine frontier," and serious technology in nuclear pulse engines, to orbiting cities and bolstering the search for extraterrestrial life.

The older cities of space activity, Cleveland with NASA's Lewis Research Center and Huntsville with NASA's Marshall Space Flight Center, produced individuals worried about the decline in research dollars, enthusiasm, and career potentials in space. Speakers asserted that only an aggressive space program with an international flavor would rectify the U.S. space enthusiasm deficit.

The District of Columbia Forum was a collage of presentations on "space infrastructure" policy and strategy. Testimony in Boston on revolutionary technologies, the grass-roots movements of the "space generation," colonies in space, and private sector expansion, all had special relevance for a Public Forum held in historic Faneuil Hall.

Witnesses at the Forums consisted of invited individuals, those who contacted us prior to a specific Forum requesting time to speak, and unscheduled individuals making use of our "open microphone." Over 1,800 people attended the Forums, with a large percentage of this total actually making presentations.

Disciplines represented at the Forums included theology, philosophy, and teaching from elementary, high school, and college levels. Former astronauts, folk singers, lawyers, and congressional leaders also showed up. The bulk of those attending our Forums had no direct link to the space program. We were overwhelmed by the high caliber of comments obtained, and duly impressed by the commitment of the citizens in attendance to respond intellectually to the call for participation.

A young laborer from Salt Lake City, inspired by the attendance of Commission member Chuck Yeager, expressed his aspirations to go into space during his lifetime. During an open microphone session he advocated the commercialization of space: "People are motivated by profit and the technological advancement that comes from that," he stated. "Our future is in the almost unlimited resources and energy in space. Private access to space would allow someone like Pan Am to shuttle people back and forth to manufacturing facilities in space." But in a note of caution, he warned: "Be careful not to monopolize any one aspect of that commercialization so that they cannot control the advancement and retard our growth."

A philosopher in Boulder started his presentation with "I would like to thank the National Commission on Space for this opportunity to voice my excitement and reservations concerning the development of an aggressive civilian space agenda." Later in the Forum, a 12-year-old warned that the "big people here today are talking budgets and spending. A lot of big words that I don't understand. We kids today have incredible dreams and goals. Mine is to use space as a resource to help solve the problems we have today and create a firm foundation for kids like me and the ones coming behind me. You are not making these decisions for just your generation.''

A nine-year-old San Franciscan countered that testimony with "space is neat. It's a good idea to go there because Earth is getting crowded." A housewife from Seattle, in an emotional, podium-pounding, impromptu testimony, stated: "This room ought to be filled with people. Where are they?" Her response to spending too much money on the Apollo lunar landing effort: "We didn't spend a dime on the Moon, we spent it right here on Earth, to promote space, peace, and a new way of life. Now we are seeing a new frontier, a frontier that belongs to our young generation. How are we going to educate those children if we, the older generation, don't understand what is going on out there?" Continuing, she remarked: "We need to have a bigger vision. We don't need to be like people standing on the banks watching Robert Fulton and his steamboat saying he will never make it up the river. Take our tax dollars and give it to the people who can promote a new vision for our young people. They must have the God-given right to dream and have the opportunity to be educated to make that dream become a possibility."

A farmer from western Iowa took time from a busy harvest schedule to share his vision of a piloted mission to Mars by 2010, and added: "I would prefer to see free men and women be the first to set foot on the red planet," and voted for increasing the NASA budget for space research via taxes.

A Colorado cowboy proudly displaying a large American flag said: "There is an opportunity to solve a great many problems by going into space if we cooperate with the Russians and Chinese. If we do, then we stand a chance to repair some of the damage that has been done in the last 5,000 years on this globe. To do otherwise is 'cowboy mentality' . . ."

Only one presentation denigrated our efforts, expressing a view of being "extremely disconcerted" by our stress on "exploitation" of a space frontier.

Visions of future space activity were not as numerous as the reasons for exploring space. One Albuquerque participant, noting that her testimony was being given on the 28th anniversary of the launch of Sputnik 1, observed: "We do not spend billions of dollars voyaging into space so we can build a better frying pan or computer. As wonderful as our technological achievements are, they are not the reason we go. We are driven to go. Driven by that same necessity that drove early humans outward until their descendants covered the globe. It is a biological imperative. We must do all we can to be certain our existence as a species is continued."

Capping off the Public Forum series was our visit to Hawaii, the destination of ancient Polynesian explorers and settlers. There we were apprised of a number of potential cooperative ventures in space with other countries, including the prospects for the establishment of a "Pacific Space Center"—an international spaceport that would promote space-related educational and business activities for the Pacific Basin in the 21st century. Others commented on the need to develop innovative approaches to small closed ecological systems, a prerequisite for establishing human settlements in space and on planetary bodies, and the importance of striking a balance between piloted and robotic space pursuits.

We were repeatedly thanked by individuals for creating the Public Forum concept and coming to their city. In essence, our activity was viewed as "bringing the space program to the people." In doing so, the Forums took a major step in addressing a frequent desire expressed by the public—to personally participate in the future of the space program.

Although it is impossible to list the total scope of comments heard during the Forums, several themes were brought forward repeatedly:

- A desire to learn more regarding the scope and direction of the civilian space effort and to assist in shaping the fate of the program. A perceived lack of information on current and projected space goals was heard throughout the Forums;

- A desire for creation of a lottery in which the prize would be a ride aboard the shuttle to galvanize public interest in the spaceflight experience and initiate a space travel industry;

- A cautionary sentiment that our final report not be too conservative, and that it not highlight "one item gimmicks," but promote the entire concept of space exploration—the movement of humans from Earth into space. "Give us a space program we can really count on" was the comment frequently heard;

- A strong wish that our next goal for piloted space activity not be another Apollo—a one-shot foray or a political stunt. Some supported establishment of a lunar base because of the Moon's closeness, potential economic payback, and scientific merit. Others argued that Mars remains untouched by humans and therefore would offer a more exciting challenge and technology driver. Any new push into space must supplement living on Earth. "Don't abandon our home planet";

- Tremendous support for the role of international cooperation in space and belief that space offers an avenue through which to seek peace on Earth. New initiatives to establish bases on the Moon and Mars were seen by many as prods for international cooperation, as well as a method to decrease the cost of the project to the United States;

- A desire that NASA avoid the routine operation of space systems, and instead pursue bold research, development, and exploration objectives. This position was heard in strong measure from the space science community. The future of NASA as an organizational entity was not discussed to any great degree, but incentives to strengthen private sector space involvement were expressed on a number of occasions; and

- The fear that the intellectual capital of the Nation is ebbing away. A shoring up of the U.S. educational system and our ability to conduct basic research is urgently required if the country is to truly move outward into space and remain competitive on Earth. Also, the youth of the Nation needs to be stimulated to consider careers on the frontiers of human activity, including the space program. Many who testified argued for better career guidance for those interested in space futures. "We need to be able to excite our most promising young investigators . . . and let them know the opportunity will be there."

The Public Forum series polled a representative cross-section of concerned America. Some individuals came forth with bold visions of the 21st century, but for the majority, the Forums provided an outlet for constructive public criticism of today's civilian space program; no unified vision for the future emerged. By and large, the general public apparently feels inadequately informed to offer substantive guidance for our civilian space program's future direction. Although most of the general public feels the program is not under their direct control, they all are eagerly awaiting a new roster of civilian space challenges. The Public Forums strongly reinforced the Commission's perception of the citizen interest in a broad space program and handsomely repaid the effort on the part of the Commission and public.

In addition to the Public Forum series, several surveys were conducted on behalf of the Commission. Along with solicited responses from selected individuals, we also received public views on future civilian space objectives through electronic computer networks, consisting of the CompuServe Information Service, Terra Nova Communications, the Astronet Network of the Young Astronauts organization, and the Space Network Services of the Boulder Center for Science and Policy. We also received the output from membership surveys prepared by the L-5 Society and Spacepac. The poll taken by the L-5 Society indicated, among other items, strong support for the development of the prerequisite space systems that would enable future space pioneering to be carried out. Spacepac's member tabulation concluded that a top priority of the country is a move toward long-range space goals and planning. We also received, by way of a "Space Outreach '85" program of the National Space Society, ideas from the public on innovative uses of space, such as a site for space tourism, space hospitals, and disposing toxic wastes.

Individuals from all walks of life were solicited for comment by letter and via electronic survey networks and were requested to respond to the following set of questions:

(1) The kind of life you would like the average U.S. citizen to have in the 21st century, and how the space program might play a role in providing it;

(2) Whether the private sector should play a larger role in space in the future and, if so, how;

(3) Whether the United States should begin to colonize space, first by permanent occupancy of an Earth-orbiting space station and later by establishing bases on the Moon and Mars.

Our letters and electronic network survey techniques inspired hundreds of individuals to respond to our set of queries. It would be impossible to list the many substantive comments we have received, other than a select few. Former Skylab astronaut Edward Gibson saw the space program as the "custodian of much of the new technology" of the 21st century. In addition, Gibson stated that "each human, regardless of his or her station in life, has an internal eye that responds to images of human evolution that lead us away from our planet. The images of space colonization and exploration will always motivate, inspire, and unify."

Wrote author Tom Wolfe: "The purpose of the space program should be pointed and singleminded: namely, the exploration, by men and women, of the rest of the Universe—and the establishment of extraterrestrial colonies." Seconding that position was writer James Michener: "I vote a strong yes in favor of continued study with a target of getting men and women to Mars as soon as practical." Added the novelist, "I cannot visualize mankind stopping at our present thresholds, either physically or mentally, and I am convinced that if we Americans do not do the exploring and the rationalizing of our data, someone else will, and I do not necessarily mean the Russians. France, Great Britain, Germany, India, China, and Japan either have the capacity now to forge ahead or will soon have it. The job will be done and it seems to me that we have a national obligation to help or even lead."

IBM Vice President and Chief Scientist Lewis Branscomb expressed his personal view that it is difficult to imagine "a scientific or economic justification for large colonies of people living in space or on the Moon." He further stated, "I would like to think that the public's extraordinary excitement over the space achievements of the 1960s and 1970s would continue. The scientific revolution that extra-atmospheric astronomy and unmanned planetary exploration can provide is unimaginable, but the extent of it will be limited by affordability. I suspect that the glamour field will be something else by then, probably biological and having to do with enhancements of human brain power and physical well-being. Space will be a familiar, trusted, and useful field of engineering. It will have to earn its way without as much help as it received from Jules Verne in the past."

Of those individuals who expressed their skepticism of the Nation's space program, perhaps the viewpoint espoused by Mitch Snyder of the Community for Creative Non-Violence rings a general sound: "I do believe that we are a Nation of technological giants, and moral, ethical, and spiritual midgets. We can travel to the Moon and back. We can even create and 'freeze-dry' life. Yet, we are incapable of creating a reasonable and rational and livable world. We presume too much. We reach too high. Personally, I wish that we were more concerned about our inner spaces than we are about our outer spaces."

The space program represents different things to different people. By and large, through the many public survey techniques we used, and from unsolicited surveys as well, we found minimal opposition to America's space program commitment. It is clear, however, that the public is hungering for the enunciation of goals and objectives that constitute the Nation's civilian space program.

Need for Continuing Public Involvement

As the United States nears three decades of national commitment to a space program, sustained public support for continued progress is paramount if our recommendations are to be pursued and realized. Today, we sense that the public is confused regarding the Nation's civilian space program, its purpose, objectives, and goals. We hope to influence the national posture concerning our space program by focusing on a new, far-reaching agenda.

According to a wide variety of public opinion polls, the American space program has "earned its keep." Nevertheless, statistics also show that space exploration is not a pressing topic to a majority of Americans despite a reasonably healthy level of public interest in the topic. These same surveys state that the number of Americans who believe too much money is being spent on civilian space activity has decreased in the past years, with most now feeling the level is "just about right." In short, a core group of the public is committed to supporting and advancing space objectives, although at a reasonable budgetary pace. This core segment represents a large enough constituency to have a voice in the political process that will ultimately guide our future space objectives.

In considering the scope and magnitude of our recommendations, we recognized that attention must be given to nurturing citizen interest and support for space exploration. The polls show clearly the diversity of public interests that support national space objectives. For the entrepreneur, the commercialization of space is a new, attractive arena for investment. For the explorer, the opening of new worlds stirs the soul. Space as the "high ground" promotes interest for a military strategist. For other citizens, space represents an opportunity to establish new societies that can provide a fresh start for Earth-bound humanity. For many, the Nation's space program is a stimulant to technology developments that enhance our quality of life here on Earth—the so-called "spinoff benefit."

In order to reinforce public appreciation and support for the space program, all of these interests need to be cultivated. NASA was widely criticized in our Public Forum series for a lack of effective communication. As one witness testified, "NASA has great management skill. They've managed to make the space program absolutely boring." Many specifically singled out the need for distributing more widely NASA's collection of well-produced special publications. In short, an immediate problem is augmenting the space agency's ability to disseminate information regarding present-day programs.

Many citizens who have an interest in space express this by joining space interest groups. These groups constitute a national resource of enthusiasm, knowledge, and expertise that NASA should take greater advantage of; hence we propose that NASA increase communications with existing space interest organizations.

One way to annually revisit our space heritage, and hence our space future, is to declare July 20, the day men first set foot on the Moon, as "National Space Day," without establishing it as a legal holiday. This would provide an opportunity for the Nation to reflect on space-related activities and our on-going civilian program.

We should develop a strategy for preserving our space program's heritage. Already, unique structures from our premier space program days lie in decay—forgotten and rusty mementos of great technological triumphs. For future generations, we laud and endorse the efforts of the Smithsonian Institution to save what will be then considered the Wright Brother-like technologies of our space effort: the orbiters, astronaut training simulators, etc. In addition, we urge the Department of the Interior to complete its Congressionally-mandated *Man in Space Study,* which concerns the deterioration of historic resources associated with the American space program and their possible preservation and interpretation for future generations.

Finally, we strongly urge that NASA stress that any future unpiloted scientific missions to the Moon, Mars, or the asteroids are important precursors to eventual human visits. This policy should be pursued in the context of the Mars Observer. By stating that this probe will address questions important for eventual human occupancy of the planet, the public would become much more aware of current activities and informed on future long-term plans. It would cost NASA nothing, and would instill in the public mind a better feeling for the more advanced programs that will follow in the future.

In summary, if the Nation is to support a more vibrant civilian space program, increased public appreciation and involvement will be required. After 29 years of spectacular achievements in space, the American public has become uncertain as to our national space objectives. We must strengthen and deepen public understanding of the challenges and significance the space frontier holds for 21st-century America if we are to capitalize on the human and financial investments of the first quarter century, and attain the bright future we envision.

IV

AMERICAN LEADERSHIP ON THE SPACE FRONTIER: THE NEXT 50 YEARS

21st-CENTURY AMERICA

The Commission was charged to recommend a civilian space program that will advance the broader goals of American society in the next century. We have therefore considered the United States in terms of its heritage, its likely future goals, and its potential impact on world history. We have also considered our planet's changing social, technological, economic, and political environments over the next 50 years, and how these will affect America.

Simple extrapolations of current trends are clearly inadequate. We must stretch our minds to evaluate such factors as expected population growth, technological progress, geopolitical stability, changing national values, and the strength and vitality of the U.S. economy. For example, will tomorrow's leaders represent an outward-oriented America that welcomes change as opportunity, or an inward-looking Nation that reacts to change as a threat? Will the United States accord high priority and sustained support to preeminence in science, technology, and exploration? Will rising productivity and competitive strength in world markets still motivate America? Or will zero-growth, increased leisure, and risk avoidance replace America's traditional expansiveness?

To address these questions, Commission members drew on their knowledge of broad-based projections, weighed the opinions received from citizens in Forums across the country (particularly from the many young people who participated), took testimony from experts in critical technical fields, initiated a historical review of two centuries of national and world economic growth by Herbert Block, and met with a group of U.S. futurists to discuss their views of the 21st century. From these activities a vision of the next 50 years emerged that provided a basis for our recommendations.

Dispassionate studies of the future environment are rare. Like the proverbial blind men groping to describe an elephant, studies of 21st-century America produce divergent views reflecting the perspectives of the authors. Complex computer models simply compound the confusion. In *The Two Cultures,* Lord Snow observes that non-technical writers often project a pessimistic view of the future, based on their suspicion of human irrationality and dehumanizing bureaucracy (e.g., *1984, Brave New World*), while technically-oriented writers often paint a rosy picture of advancing science and technology rationally applied for human benefit in a global enterprise (e.g., *2001, The World, the Flesh and the Devil*). To us, history demonstrates that while human nature changes very little, technological advances can initiate revolutionary social change. Not surprisingly, our technically-oriented perspective leads us to envision a progressive 21st-century America boldly leading humanity outward on the space frontier.

Planet Earth in Transition

We live in an era of remarkable change. A 1976 study by the late Herman Kahn and staff members of Hudson Institute presents alternative views of our planet's next two centuries, ranging from pessimism to technocratic optimism. Their book, *The Next 200 Years,* is based in large part on an analysis of the technical, economic, and social changes that have taken place in the developed countries since the start of the Industrial Revolution in late 18th-century Europe. A more recent study reviews comparative world and national growth rates for population and economic output since 1800. Because comparing different eras and national economies involves complex problems of concept and methodology, results can be ambiguous. Taking this into account, we estimate that in 1800 our planet's total population was about 900 million people, 10 percent urbanized, producing a Gross World Product (GWP) of about $350 billion, or $390 per capita (all monetary units in this section are in 1985 U.S. dollars). We estimate today's world population at 4,845 million people, averaging around 40 percent urbanized, producing a GWP of about $17,300 billion, or $3,510 per capita (almost the U.S. per capita income of 1900). In other words, after many centuries of relative stability, the first 200 years of the Industrial Revolution have seen the population of the world multiplied about 5.4 times, Gross World Product about 50 times, and GWP per capita about 9 times. Since 1950 the world's population has almost doubled from about 2,549 million to 4,845 million people, while the Gross World Product has quadrupled from $4,028 billion to $17,300 billion, and GWP per capita has multiplied two and one quarter times from $1,590 to $3,510. This momentum promises to continue through the next 50 years, but with uneven progress in different economies.

Figure 4 provides a sense of historical perspective by depicting comparative real economic growth rates over the last 50 years for 12 nations across the development spectrum in terms of Gross Domestic Product per capita. As the figure shows, some countries, such as West Germany, Japan, and Singapore, are achieving relatively rapid rates of economic growth, surpassing the per capita incomes of other countries with long histories of higher ranking positions. Virtually no one looks on such statistics as ends in themselves, but they do

REAL GROWTH OF GROSS DOMESTIC PRODUCT PER PERSON: 1935 TO 1985

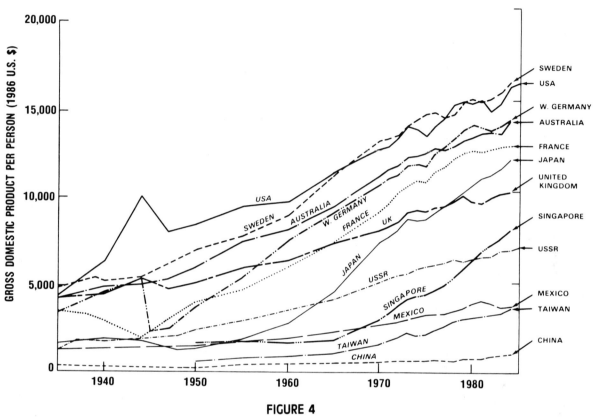

FIGURE 4

correlate with other social measures to indicate nations whose citizens will enjoy greater opportunities and higher standards of living.

One quarter of Earth's population now lives in the 80 percent urbanized and industrialized nations of Europe, North America, Australasia, and Japan. This group enjoys a Gross Domestic Product per capita of more than $10,000 and a life expectancy 50 percent greater than that prevailing in the least developed nations. The uneven progress of economic development is reflected in a roughly 50:1 disparity in productivity and wealth between modern and traditional economies. In spite of this gap, the impact of science and technology is felt in every nation. Witness, for example, the unprecedented global medical campaign that has completely eradicated smallpox from our planet, and the proliferating "Green Revolution" that in the space of two decades has made possible a grain surplus for a third of the human race in Asia.

Because many of the new nations that gained their independence after World War II are smaller than previously industrialized nations, international trade is critical for their economic growth. Developing nations need ready access to the technology, capital, and markets of industrialized nations. With good management sustained growth can then be achieved, as demonstrated by Japan and more recently by the four newly industrializing economies of East Asia: South Korea, Taiwan, Hong Kong, and Singapore. Indeed, the most significant socio-economic trend of our times may be the interaction of Western industrialization with Asian culture. The success of combining Eastern drive with Western technology may spur greater economic growth for the whole planet, if other nations regard the recent gains of Asian economies not as a threat but as an example and encouragement to raise global standards of living. Moreover, if Beijing's new leadership, which began in 1978 to emphasize economic development as a pre-eminent goal of national policy, can implement its flexible market policies, China may be able to follow the development path of its East Asian neighbors. This would improve prospects for global economic growth by bringing another quarter of the human race into productive trading and investment relationships with Europe, North America, Australasia, and Japan.

Many problems will occur as the widening impact of the industrial revolution continues to transform our planet, but five fundamental factors suggest favorable prospects for global cooperation and economic growth in the 21st century:

- Forty years in the shadow of nuclear weapons without a third world war;
- Accelerating technical progress across a broad spectrum that will improve public health and continue productivity gains in agriculture, industry, and services;
- The availability of capital investment to update the planet's industrial, agricultural, communication, and transportation infrastructure;
- New synthetic substitutes for scarce materials and effective pollution control techniques; and
- The demonstrated rapid growth of national output in well-managed, globally-oriented, market economies.

In the next 50 years an increasing percentage of humanity will have the advanced technology, the economic resources, the trained people, and the future-oriented leaders that will enable them to participate in opening the space frontier.

GROWTH OF THE UNITED STATES: 1800 TO 1985

To provide further historical perspective for envisioning America's next 50 years, Table 1 summarizes America's population and real economic growth since 1800.

In the past 186 years, America's population has multiplied by about 45 times, Gross Domestic Product about 770 times, and GDP per capita about 17 times. Although this history of expansion is impressive, it had its critics at the time; zero-growth is not a new slogan. For example, in 1803 Senator Samuel White, deriding Thomas Jefferson's proposal to purchase the Louisiana Territory (which more than doubled U.S. land area), declared:

TABLE 1
U.S. REAL ECONOMIC GROWTH: 1800 TO 1985

YEAR	MID-YEAR POPULATION (1000)	GROSS DOMESTIC PRODUCT (GDP)	
		TOTAL GDP (1985 $ BILLIONS)	PER PERSON (1985 $)
1800	5,297	$ 4.9	$ 923
1855	27,386	48.3	1,762
1885	56,658	156.4	2,761
1900	76,094	277.7	3,650
1933	125,579	517.3	4,120
1950	152,271	1,245.7	8,181
1965	194,303	2,157.6	11,104
1985	238,631	3,769.4	15,796

". . . as to the Louisiana, this new immense unbounded world, if it should ever be incorporated into this union . . . I believe it will be the greatest curse that could at present befall us. . . . We have already territory enough . . . I would rather see it given to France, to Spain, or to any other nation. . . ."

Similarly, opponents of Secretary of State Seward's purchase of Alaska from Czarist Russia in 1867 sneered at the transaction, calling the vast territory "Seward's Ice Box." Despite such criticisms, a majority of Americans accepted the challenge of the frontier and thrived on it. Indeed, it was the promise of the frontier that brought many of our forefathers to the expanding United States.

The half century of U.S. economic growth between 1885 and 1935 was stimulated by a remarkable age of science and invention. During this period advances in medicine and public health reduced infant mortality and lengthened life spans, while scientific agriculture and farm mechanization continuously raised agricultural productivity, releasing labor for better-paying factory jobs created by the invention of new machines. The rapid growth of the electrical, chemical, metallurgical, telephone, automobile, entertainment, petroleum, and other industries transformed the U.S. economic landscape, giving Americans increasing freedom of choice and the highest national product and standard of living in world history.

The economic growth that accompanied America's expanding physical, technological, and institutional horizons demonstrates the long-term flexibility and vitality of the U.S. political and economic system. As Table 1 shows, the U.S. national product grew throughout the 19th century and up to World War I by slightly more than 4 percent annually, and from then to 1929 by close to 3 percent. After a steep decline in the Great Depression, the average growth rate from 1939 to 1986 was 2.7 percent, reaching 4 percent between 1959 and 1973.

America's Next 50 Years: 1985 to 2035

As we project our thinking 50 years into the future, we should bear in mind that even the most visionary science fiction writer of 50 years ago completely missed the scale of the technical, financial, and managerial resources that would be needed to open the space frontier, and none imagined that these resources would become available by 1960. The Air Age was as young in 1935 as the Space Age is today. "You'll never get me up in one of those things!" was a familiar cry. The non-fiction best seller that year was *North to the Orient,* Anne Lindbergh's account of a pioneering survey of future intercontinental air routes. When the first DC-3 was ordered by American Airways, Director Richard W. Millar asked Chairman Donald Douglas how many he expected to sell, and was told "I'll be happy if we sell ten!" More than 14,000 were finally produced (including some 2,000 in the Soviet Union and 487 in wartime Japan). With 1935 gross federal receipts of about $35 billion (in 1985 dollars), the most ardent Buck Rogers fan could never have dreamed that within 30 years America would launch Apollo astronauts to explore the Moon, and that the $75 billion cost would represent less than one percent of the U.S. Gross National Product of the decade of the 1960s. The Depression obscured America's outlook in the 1930s, just as budget deficit headlines can cloud our vision now.

America faces critical issues in economic policy today, including the federal budget deficit, exchange value of the dollar, trade barriers and imbalances, Third World debt, unstable oil prices, high levels of corporate and consumer debt, tax policies, and the health of existing loans to farmers, energy companies, real estate projects, and foreign countries. From our 50-year perspective, however, these problems appear manageable in light of the demonstrated long-term vitality and adaptability of the U.S. economic system. We are impressed with the growth prospects of the economy in coming decades based upon the underlying promise of advancing science and technology.

According to economist Edward F. Denison, about 30 percent of the growth in U.S. gross national product can be traced to advances in knowledge. The Commission believes that the potential for significant breakthroughs in science and technology has never been greater, from molecular biology and plasma physics to supercomputers and robotic factories. Applying these myriad opportunities to achieve economic growth will require cooperative interactions between the investment community and research and development innovators in Government, university, and industrial laboratories. It will also require entrepreneurs eager to invest in risky growth industries, a tax policy that encourages savings and investment, and a national acceptance of the social change accompanying rising productivity. The robotics revolution, for example, promises to reduce the percent of the labor force working as factory operators toward the low level now employed in agriculture. This shift will tilt the job market even more toward high-technology industry and services, with major environmental impact on the U.S. educational system. We are confident that American institutions will have the flexibility and resilience to adapt to the changing conditions of the 21st century, and that leadership in pioneering the space frontier will "pull through" technologies critical to future

U.S. economic growth, as World War II military developments set the stage for major post-war growth industries.

How bright are the 50-year prospects for the American economy? Will 21st-century America be able to afford investment on the space frontier? Will it choose to do so? These questions are as difficult to answer in 1986 as they were in 1935, but we must nonetheless seek reasonable estimates for planning purposes. From our consideration of potential technology advances and the environment of the next century, we believe that an average two to three percent annual real growth in the U.S. Gross Domestic Product through 2035 is a realistic assumption, and we have selected a 2.4 percent annual economic growth rate for our projections. This is probably on the low side; it could well be surpassed if our leadership remains realistic and firm, if U.S. military strength is strong enough to deter threats to international stability (maintaining global tensions within post-World War II limits), if immigration continues, if regulatory and tax reforms move forward, if world trade continues to grow, and if major science and technology advances are pulled through by challenging programs on the space frontier. We therefore believe it reasonable to project a 21st-century America with a 2035 population of 320 million people, a Gross Domestic Product of $12,900 billion, and a GDP per capita close to $40,000 in today's dollars. Even at our low 2.4 percent annual growth assumption, 21st-century America should be able to afford to lead the world on the space frontier. Our pioneering heritage should certainly encourage us to do so. With the vast resources of the inner Solar System opening for exploration and development, the growth potential for humankind beyond the next century is incalculable.

Summary of Proposed Steps and Estimated Costs

As stated in our opening section, Figure 5 outlines on one page the program we recommend to achieve low-cost access to the Solar System. The Highway to Space between Earth and low Earth orbit starts with economical cargo and passenger transports, adding an orbit transfer vehicle for destinations beyond low Earth orbit. These three systems would be operational in conjunction with an orbital spaceport by the year 2000. Beyond low Earth orbit is the Bridge between Worlds to support initial robotic lunar surface operations, followed by outposts for human operations on the Moon starting about 2005. Extension of the Bridge between Worlds would initiate robotic exploration of Mars, followed by outposts to support human activities starting about 2015. This phased growth of an economical space transportation infrastructure starts with simple components for early results, but evolves over time into a powerful network of spaceports, bases, and connecting transport systems that open the space frontier for exploration, science prospecting, initial economic development, and eventual settlement. The three hallmarks of this program are: (1) economy through technological advances that reduce costs, (2) sustained investment to extend capabilities step-by-step, and (3) robotic processing of local resources to "live off the land," rather than bringing everything from Earth.

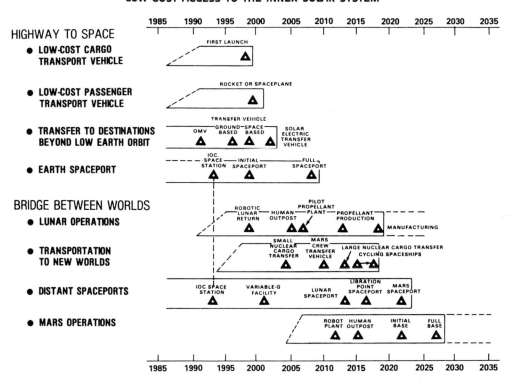

FIGURE 5

As pointed out previously, civilian space budgets since 1960 and the estimated cost of our recommended program projected out to 2035 are shown in Figure 6. Allowances have been made for commercial and international participation. The growth of the U.S. Gross National Product for the past 25 years is also shown, with a projection to 2035 at our assumed annual growth rate of 2.4 percent. Note that the percentage of the U.S. Gross National Product invested on the space frontier would remain below half of the peak percentages spent on the civilian space program during the peak Apollo years. In view of the increasing significance of space and the critical economic importance of U.S. scientific and technological preeminence in the next century, we believe that these estimated levels of expenditure are reasonable in relation to the expected benefits to our Nation and the world. The enormous human and economic potential of opening vast reaches of the inner Solar System for settlement in the 21st century can be realized within these budget limits, but an early national decision on the long-range direction and pace of our civilian space program is required.

COST OF PROPOSED US SPACE PROGRAM

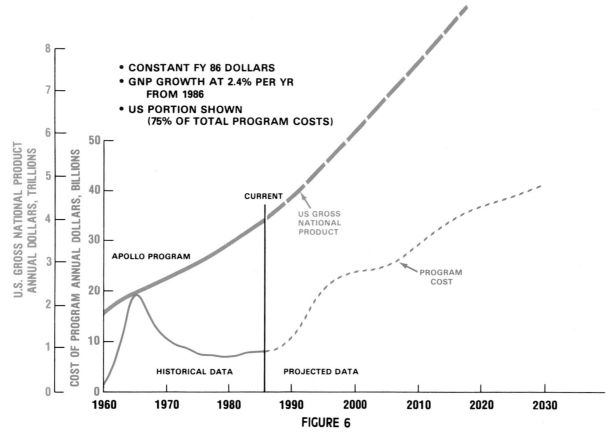

FIGURE 6

Is our expansive view of America's future realistic? Are the technical advances we project achievable? Will people accept risks and discomforts to work on other worlds? We believe that the answer to all three questions is "Yes!" Few Americans in the early days of the Air Age ever expected to fly the Atlantic, let alone in jumbo jets or supersonic transports, yet nearly 75,000 people now fly the Atlantic daily. The result of 50 years of cumulative technological progress was impossible to foresee. It is equally difficult for Americans this early in the Space Age to visualize the 21st-century technologies that will enable the average citizen to soar into orbit at low cost, to fly to new worlds beyond Earth, and to work and live on the space frontier in closed-ecology biospheres using robotically-processed local resources. Continuing technological progress in astronautics, robotics, and closed-ecology biospherics will make this possible.

Our proposed civilian space agenda for 21st-century America can achieve our recommended long-range goal of exploring, developing, and settling the inner Solar System with reasonable milestone dates. The emphasis is upon the creation of new wealth rather than the management of scarcity. We are not proposing to flee mother Earth, but to improve it by removing limits to human growth. The pace of advance we propose on the space frontier is consistent with reasonable budget levels in an expanding U.S. economy. The final decision will, of course, be made by the American people. We should therefore emphasize that: **The Commission is not prophesying; it is describing what the United States can make happen through vigorous leadership in pioneering the space frontier.**

WHAT OUR RECOMMENDED PROGRAM WILL DO

The Commission believes that 21st-century America will still be a vigorous, expansive society, its citizens inquisitive and adventurous, eager for new challenges in the forefront of humanity. If we are right, the bold space agenda and goals we have recommended will channel a small fraction of this restless energy into extending life outward from our home planet Earth. The required technical, economic, and managerial resources will certainly be available in a prospering America, and increasingly also in other nations.

Throughout this report we have emphasized a few key themes:

- The new **scientific knowledge** that space exploration will produce about the Universe, the Solar System, our planet and, indeed, the origin and destiny of life;
- The major **technology advances** that will be pulled through to strengthen 21st-century America's civilian economy and national security;
- The **leadership** that the United States should continue to provide in the development of critical technologies, and in building a Highway to Space and Bridge between Worlds;
- The **new opportunities** that we can create by opening the space frontier for personal fulfillment, for enterprise, and for human settlement; and
- The **hopes and dreams** inspired by removing terrestrial limits to human aspiration, and the relevance of these hopes and dreams to America's pioneer heritage.

Long-Range Space Policy: Setting Direction and Pace
These themes and the broad principles outlined in our opening Declaration for Space can provide a new rationale and direction for our civilian space program. However much the space

policies of the past 15 years may have accomplished, we feel that declining budgets allocated annually to competing individual projects without an overall context are inadequate. Longer-range, more visionary leadership is demanded. We urge the Administration and the Congress to work in concert to raise American aspirations and to set new goals for civilian space activities in which planned programs are carefully phased to achieve a well-understood, sustained national purpose.

We specifically suggest that the Congressional authorization committees work closely with the Administration to develop a new long-term direction and pace for America's civilian space program, while the appropriations committees and the Office of Management and Budget concentrate on annual budget reviews and watchdog activities within the resulting agenda and policy framework. We believe that long-range goals established by strong leadership will lead to a better-informed public, improved management of major national assets, accelerated technical progress, more economical operations, and greater private and international participation. We hope that our report will contribute to this longer-range management perspective.

NASA's Long-Range Planning

Since the 1960s, NASA's programmatic emphasis has been on the development of the shuttle, and major scientific observatories and planetary missions. While this has unquestionably led to spectacular achievements, NASA has placed such low priority on long-range planning that internal planning work is no longer adequate. We note that the budget for this area has shrunk by a factor of 10, while the agency as a whole decreased by a factor of 3 (See Figure 6).

The Commission therefore recommends that: **NASA substantially upgrade its emphasis on long-range spaceflight planning studies. We urge NASA to raise the visibility and organizational stature of planning to ensure that the programs we recommend receive continuing and adequate attention; and that NASA operate on the basis of an annually updated five-year budget plan and a 20-year space plan.**

Conclusion

In the increasingly competitive world of the future, it is clear that maintaining America's preeminence in science and technology will once again test our Nation's technical vision, resolution, and institutional strengths. To meet this challenge, we must initiate challenging programs that will attract and motivate the best minds of the 21st century. We must stimulate advances across a broad spectrum of scientific fields and technologies critical to America's future. With the lessons of history in mind, and with a vision of humanity moving outward from Earth, the Commission recommends a new direction for our civilian space program that we believe will advance the broader goals of 21st-century America: **To lead the exploration and development of the space frontier, advancing science, technology, and enterprise, and building institutions and systems that make accessible vast new resources and support human settlements beyond Earth orbit, from the highlands of the Moon to the plains of Mars.**

THE NATIONAL COMMISSION ON SPACE (NCOS)

DR. LUIS W. ALVAREZ
Nobel Laureate Physicist—Lawrence Berkeley Laboratory; Professor Emeritus—UC at Berkeley.

MR. NEIL A. ARMSTRONG
Chairman—CTA, Inc.; Former Astronaut; Commander—Gemini 8 and Apollo 11; First Man to walk on the Moon.

DR. PAUL J. COLEMAN
President—Universities Space Research Association; Assistant Director—Los Alamos National Laboratory; Professor—UCLA.

DR. GEORGE B. FIELD
Senior Physicist—Smithsonian Astrophysical Observatory; Professor—Harvard University.

LT. GEN. WILLIAM H. FITCH, USMC (RET.)
Defense Consultant; Former Head of Marine Corps Aviation.

DR. CHARLES M. HERZFELD
Vice Chairman—Peterson, Jacobs, Ramo & Co.; Former Vice President—ITT Corporation; Former Director—Advanced Research Projects Agency.

DR. JACK L. KERREBROCK
Associate Dean of Engineering—MIT; Former Associate Administrator—NASA.

AMB. JEANE J. KIRKPATRICK
Professor—Georgetown University; Senior Fellow—American Enterprise Institute; Former Representative of the United States to the United Nations.

DR. GERARD K. O'NEILL
President—Space Studies Institute; CEO—Geostar Corporation.

DR. THOMAS O. PAINE
Chairman—NCOS: Former President—Northrop Corporation; Former Administrator—NASA.

GEN. BERNARD A. SCHRIEVER, USAF (RET.)
Management Consultant—Schriever & McKee Inc.; Former Commander—Air Force Systems Command; Former Director—Air Force Ballistic Missile Program.

DR. KATHRYN D. SULLIVAN
Shuttle Astronaut; First American Woman to walk in space; Adjunct Professor of Geology, Rice University.

DR. DAVID C. WEBB
Consultant in the field of Space Development; Chairman—National Coordinating Committee for Space.

DR. LAUREL L. WILKENING
Vice Chairman—NCOS; Vice President of Research and Dean of the Graduate School—University of Arizona; Planetary Scientist.

BRIG. GEN. CHARLES E. YEAGER, USAF (RET.)
Test Pilot; First man to break the sound barrier.

NON-VOTING MEMBERS OF THE NATIONAL COMMISSION ON SPACE

CONGRESSIONAL ADVISERS

SENATOR SLADE GORTON

REPRESENTATIVE DON FUQUA

SENATOR JOHN GLENN

REPRESENTATIVE MANUEL LUJAN

EX-OFFICIO MEMBERS

DR. ORVILLE BENTLEY
Department of Agriculture

MR. ERICH BLOCH
National Science Foundation

AMBASSADOR JOHN NEGROPONTE
Department of State

MR. RICHARD SHAY
MR. ROBERT BRUMLEY
Department of Commerce

DR. GEORGE KEYWORTH
DR. JOHN McTAGUE
Office of Science and Technology Policy

MS. JENNIFER DORN
MS. MADELINE JOHNSON
Department of Transportation

STAFF OF THE NATIONAL COMMISSION ON SPACE

MS. MARCIA SMITH
Executive Director

MR. THEODORE SIMPSON
Director of Planning

MS. LINDA BILLINGS
Research Associate

MS. JULIA SHISLER
Executive Assistant

MR. LEONARD DAVID
Director of Research

MR. RICHARD DALBELLO
Research Associate

MS. ELIZABETH PEASE
Administrative Assistant

ADMINISTRATIVE STAFF DETAILED FROM THE NATIONAL AERONAUTICS AND SPACE ADMINISTRATION

MS. MECHTHILD PETERSON
Director of Administration

MS. THERESIA WISE
Secretary

MS. DAWN MOORE
Student Aide

MR. STEVEN HARTMAN
Presidential Management Intern

MS. MICHELLE THOMPSON
Secretary

CONTRACTORS

MR. S. NEIL HOSENBALL
General Counsel

MR. CLAYTON DURR
Research Associate

MR. WILLIS SHAPLEY
Research Associate

MS. MARY WARD
Secretary

GLOSSARY

Aerobrake: An "air brake" used to slow a spaceship with the upper layers of a planet's atmosphere to conserve the spaceship's propellants.

Artificial Intelligence (AI): The discipline of developing and applying computer systems to produce characteristics usually associated with intelligent behavior, e.g., understanding language, learning from experience, logical reasoning, problem solving, and explaining its own behavior.

Automation: The use of electronic or mechanical machines to perform routine functions with minimal human intervention.

Base: A permanently occupied center for people on the Moon, Mars, or in space that provides life support and work facilities; bases would evolve from outposts (See Outpost).

Biosphere: The total environment of Earth that supports self-sustaining and self-regulating human, plant, and animal life, or an artificial closed-ecology system in which biological systems provide mutual support and recycling of air, water, and food.

Carbonaceous: A type of meteorite or asteroid containing significant percentages of water, carbon and nitrogen—essential elements, when processed, that would permit humankind to increase its independence from Earth.

Closed-Ecology Life Support System (CELSS): A mechanical or biological system that recycles the air, water, and food needed to sustain human life on a space station or base.

Cycling Spaceship: A space station designed for human habitation that permanently cycles back and forth between the orbits of Earth and Mars.

Ecosystem: A community of humans, plants, and animals together with their physical environment.

Galaxy: An irregular, elliptic, disk- or spiral-shaped system containing billions of stars. Earth is situated in a spiral-shaped galaxy called the Milky Way, one of billions of galaxies in the Universe.

Geostationary Earth Orbit: A circular orbit approximately 22,300 miles above Earth's surface in the plane of the equator. An object in such an orbit rotates at the same rate as the planet and therefore appears to be stationary with regard to any point on Earth's surface. It is a specific type of geosynchronous orbit.

Heliosphere: The large region of space influenced by the Sun's solar wind and the interplanetary magnetic field. This vast sea of electrical plasma activity may extend as far as 10 billion miles from the Sun, affecting the magnetospheres, ionospheres, and upper atmospheres of Earth and other Solar System bodies.

Inner Solar System: The part of the Solar System between the Sun and the main asteroid belt. It includes the planets Mercury, Venus, Earth, and Mars—distinct from the outer planets, Jupiter, Saturn, Uranus, Neptune, and Pluto.

Libration Points: Unique points in space, influenced by gravitational forces of neighboring bodies, in which objects with the correct initial location and velocity remain fixed without significant expenditure of propellant. They are also called Lagrange points, after the French mathematician who calculated their existence.

Magnetosphere: A region surrounding a planet, extending out thousands of miles and dominated by the planet's magnetic field so that charged particles are trapped in it.

Mass-Driver: An electromagnetic accelerating device for propelling solid or liquid material, for example, from Earth's Moon into space, or for providing propulsion by ejecting raw lunar soil or asteroidal material as reaction mass.

Microgravity: An extremely low level of gravity. As experienced by shuttle crews, for example, one-millionth the level of gravity on Earth's surface.

Orbital Maneuvering Vehicle: A device used much like a "harbor tug" in ship operations, with remotely controlled manipulator arms to handle spacecraft and refueling operations with great care.

Outpost: An initial location to provide shelter for a few people on the Moon or Mars; it may not be permanently occupied.

Robotics: The use of automated machines to replace human effort, although they may not perform functions in a humanlike manner.

SCRAMJET: A supersonic combustion ramjet engine which can operate in the hypersonic region of flight.

Settlement: A permanent community of humans in space, or on the surface of the Moon or Mars with life support, living quarters and work facilities; it will evolve from a base (See Base).

Spaceport: A transportation center in space which acts like an airport on Earth. It provides a transport node where passengers or cargo can switch from one spaceship to another, and a facility where spaceships can be berthed, serviced, and repaired.

Specific Impulse: A measurement of engine performance. It is the ratio of the pounds of thrust produced by the engine, minus the drag from the engine, per pounds of fuel flowing through the engine each second.

Tele-operator: A system equipped with its own propulsion system, television camera, and equipment that can be remotely operated (See Orbital Maneuvering Vehicle).

Telepresence: The use of real-time video communications coupled with remote control techniques which would provide an operator on Earth's surface or other location with the capability to carry out complex operations in space or on the surface of a planet or moon.

Telescience: Conducting scientific operations in remote locations by tele-operation.

Unpiloted: A spacecraft without human operators.

ACKNOWLEDGMENTS

Listed below are the hundreds of individuals who spoke at one of the 15 Public Forums we held across the country, communicated with us via letter or computer network, or testified at one of our full Commission meetings. Through these avenues, we have gleaned an idea of what many Americans believe about the U.S. civilian space program and its future for the next 50 years, and we have been briefed by the very best minds in the country about what is and may be possible.

We have benefited immensely from hearing these many and varied points of view. While they do not represent a scientific sampling of the country, we are certain that they are the opinions of a substantial cross section of the United States, and thus are of great value when considering what this Nation should pursue in its future civilian space program. We wish that we could publish all their comments, but it would take thousands of pages to do so. The letters, papers, testimony, and tape recordings that contain these views will be retained for historical purposes by the National Archives, however, and are available to anyone who wishes to see them.

We are extremely grateful to all who shared with us their dreams and concerns, and to each we express our deepest thanks.

PUBLIC FORUMS: Sandra Adamson, Tucson, AZ * Larry Ahearn, Ann Arbor, MI * Buzz Aldrin, Grand Forks, ND * Joseph Allen, Houston, TX * Dale Amon, Pittsburgh, PA * Deborah Anderson, Seattle, WA * Hugh Anderson, Bellevue, WA * Roger Anderson, Iowa City, IA * Rep. Michael A. Andrews, Houston, TX * Peter Apo, Honolulu, HI * James Arnold, La Jolla, CA * Robert Arnold, Alexandria, VA * Donald F. Baer, Rancho Palos Verdes, CA * Von Bailey, Tarpon Springs, FL * James Baird, Huntsville, AL * Rex Baker, Boulder, CO * Robert Barnes, Tallahassee, FL * Jim Banke, Daytona Beach, FL * John Barainca, Salt Lake City, UT * Jimmy Bartholemew, West Newbury, MA * David Baxter, Salt Lake City, UT* Lorie Beeman, Boulder, CO * George Belken, Des Moines, IA * Richard Berendzen, Washington, DC * Norman Bergrun, Los Altos, CA * Gregg Berman, Cambridge, MA * Robert Berry, Palo Alto, CA * Michael Best, Plymouth, MI * Gregory Biestek, Detroit, MI * Peter Bishop, Houston, TX * Frank Bittinger, Houston, TX * Bob Blackledge, Colorado Springs, CO * Ed Blaylock, Honolulu, HI * Paul Bohannon, Los Angeles, CA * Charles Bonsall, Sandy, UT * Art Boslick, Huntsville AL * Penelope Boston, Boulder, CO * S. James Boumil, Lowell, MA * Amy Bouska, Columbus, OH * Ben Bova, West Hartford, CT * David Bowen, Huntsville, AL * Jim Bowery, La Jolla, CA * Paul Bowman, Tallahassee, FL * Peter Boyce, Washington, DC * Kevin L. Boyens, Manilla, IL * Ray Bradbury, Los Angeles, CA * Michael Bradley, Salt Lake City, UT * Aviva Brecher, Boston, MA * Mark Brender, Washington, DC * Jack Brisbin, Plymouth, MI * Steve Brody, League City, TX * Lou Brogna, Tallahassee, FL * Rep. George E. Brown, Jr., Riverside, CA * Mark Brown, Iowa City, IA * Michael Brown, Richland, WA * Donald Brownlee, Seattle, WA * Robert Bruccoleri, North Billerica, MA * Jessica Bruggeman, Honolulu, HI * Liliana Bruggemann, Aiea, HI * David Buden, Albuquerque, NM * Steve Bullock, Trussville, AL * Harm Buning, Ann Arbor, MI * Eric Burgess, Sebastopol, CA * Kurt Burmann, Ann Arbor, MI * Jim Burns, Detroit, MI * T.J. Burnside, Boston, MA * David Burwassser, Cleveland, OH * Jim Byler, Los Angeles, CA * Charles R. Caillovet, Jr., Houston, TX * Steven D. Calahan, Seattle, WA * Michael Campbell, Iowa City, IA * Bobby Caraway, Huntsville, AL * Colleen Carey, Ann Arbor, MI * Clifford Carley, Houston, TX * Rachael Carmody, Honolulu, HI * Chuck Carpenter, Providence, Rhode Island * Gerald Carr, Houston, TX * Michael Carr, Palo Alto, CA * Robert Carson, Pearl City, HI * William Carswell, Santa Clara, CA * Robert Carter, Dearborn Heights, MI * Henry Casso, Albuquerque, NM * Rocky Castleman, Cleveland, OH * Ned Chapin, Menlo Park, CA * Philip K. Chapman, Acton, MA * Mike Charles, Albuquerque, NM * Mark Chartrand, Aurora, CO * Gloria Chester, Cleveland, OH * Alan Chuculate, Honolulu, HI * Joseph Ciotti, Honolulu, HI * Robert Citron, Seattle, WA * Stephen Claeys, Ypsilanti, MI * Benton Clark, Boulder, CO * John Clark, Ann Arbor, MI * Sophia Clifford, Birmingham, AL * J.E.D. Cline, Woodland Hills, CA * Harold Close, San Francisco, CA * Ken Conry, Huntsville, AL * Lisa Cornelius, Renton, WA * Patrick Cornelius, Renton, WA * Tom Cottle, Boston, MA * Dave Covington, Vail, CO * Andrew Cox, Albuquerque, NM * Maureen Cragg, Arlington, VA * Mary Ellen Craig, Arlington, MA * Blake Crary, San Jose, CA * Thomas Cravens, Ann Arbor, MI * Tom Cremins, Washington, DC * Robin Crews, Boulder, CO * Jim Crisafulli, Honolulu, HI * Dave Criswell, La Jolla, CA * Chris Croswhite, Brighton, UT * Attila Csanyi, Albuquerque, NM * Eric Dahlstrom, Washington, DC * George Dalton, Boston, MA * Konrad Dannenberg, Huntsville, AL * Frank Davidson, Concord, MA * Merton Davies, Santa Monica, CA * Mike Davis, College Station, TX * Stewart G. Dawson, Redondo Beach, CA * Philip Dean, East Lansing, MI * Dan Delong, Huntsville, AL * Richard DeMeis, Needham, MA * George Demico, Cleveland, OH * Hamilton Desaussure, Akron, OH * Jim Dewitt, Ann Arbor, MI * Peter Diamandis, Cambridge, MA * John Dickel, Los Alamos, NM * Charles Divine, Trenton, NJ * Robert Dixon, Columbus, OH * Paul Doerr, Suisun, CA * Thomas Donahue, Ann Arbor, MI * Guy Donaruma, Huntsville, AL * David Dooling, Huntsville, AL * Melody DosSantos, West Newbury, MA * Becky Dow, West Newbury, MA * Art Dula, Houston, TX * H.M. Dumas, Albuquerque, NM * Joe Durocher, Cleveland, OH * Neil Dutcher, Denver, CO * Richard T. Dykema, Laurel, MD (on behalf of Rep. Herbert Bateman) * David Easton, Murray, UT * Julia Ecklar, North Huntington, PA * Dani Eder, Kent, WA * Jeff Edwards, Magna, UT * S. David Eisenberg, Cambridge, MA * R.D. Ekers, Socorro, NM * Frank Eldridge, Honolulu, HI * Margaret Ellis, Salt Lake City, UT * Ty Ellis, Roy, UT * Mark Ely, Tarpon Springs, FL * Richard C. Ensign, Detroit, MI * Bob Eramia, Seattle, WA * C.A. Erickson, Bremerton, WA * Doyle Evans, Los Alamos, NM * Marty Extington, Houston, TX * Louis Falgoust, Provo, UT * Larry Fannin, Tallahassee, FL * Ed Fausel, Tallahassee, FL * Kay Fausel, Tallahassee, FL * Chuck Filley, Houston, TX * Patricia Filley, Houston, TX * Ben Finney, Honolulu, HI * John Fisher, Carpinteria, CA * James Fitzsimmons, Honolulu, HI * Mark Fleming, West Newbury, MA * Wesley Fleming, Cleveland, OH * Clair Folsome, Honolulu, HI * Robert Forward, Malibu, CA * Georgia Franklin, Seattle, WA * John Freeman, Houston, TX * Tom Frieling, Bainbridge, GA * Larry Friesen, League City, TX * John C. Fuechsel, Washington, DC * Charles Fuller, Davis, CA * Rep. Don Fuqua, Altha, FL * Keith Gale, Emeryville, CA * Eilene Galloway, Washington, DC * Sen. Jake Garn, Salt Lake City, UT * Harry Gatos, Cambridge, MA * Robert Germany, Houston, TX * John Getter, Houston, TX * Martin Gibbins, Seattle, WA * Kalaui Gilding, Honolulu, HI * Steve Gillett, Woodinville, WA * Ernest V. Gilmer, Jr., Huntsville, AL * Marion Givens, Los Angeles, CA * Peter Glaser, Cambridge, MA * Al Globus, Santa Cruz, CA * Lori Goetsch, Mt. Pleasant, IA * Nathan Goldman, Houston, TX * Donald Goldsmith, San Francisco, CA * Rigo Gonzalez, Denver, CO * Allan Goodman, Bethesda, MD * Don Gordon, San Francisco, CA * Sen. Slade Gorton, Olympia, WA * Dale Goudie, Seattle, WA * Chuck Gould, Downey, CA * Jonathan Gradie, Honolulu, HI * Gary Gray, Ann Arbor, MI * Richard Gross, Santa Clara, CA * Fred Haddock, Ann Arbor, MI * Thomas E. Hagglund, Denver, CO * Richard Haines, Los Altos, CA * William Hale, Washington, DC * Donald Hall, Honolulu, HI * George Hall, Alamagordo, NM * Tim Haller, Honolulu, HI * Betty Halliwell, Santa Monica, CA * Rolf Hamerquist, Seattle, WA * Karen Hamilton, Boulder, CO * Thomas A. Hanson, Cleveland, OH * Helen Hart, Boulder, CO * Charles Haskett, Houston, TX * Steve Hathaway, Mt. Vernon, IA * Philip Hattis, Needham, MA * B. Ray Hawke, Honolulu, HI * Kenneth H. Hayashida, Seal Beach, CA * Robert Haymes, Houston, TX * Daniel Hays, Huntsville, AL * Paul Hays, Ann Arbor, MI * Donald Hearth, Boulder, CO * Charles Helsley, Honolulu, HI * Gerard Hendey, Denver, CO * William Henley, Lakewood, OH * J. Patrick Henry, Honolulu, HI * Keith Henson, Redwood City, CA * Patricia Herringer, Boulder, CO * Jim Hess, Iowa City, IA * Albert Hibbs, Pasadena, CA * Grant Hicks, Walthan, MA * William Higgins, West Chicago, IL * John Hobson, Jr., Denver, CO * Pam Hoffman, Cleveland, OH * Joe Hopkins, Renton, WA * Kristen Hotaling, Denver, CO * Karen Howard, Athens, OH * Peter B. Humphrey, Honolulu, HI * Claudia Jabo, Cleveland, OH (on behalf of Rep. Mary Rose Oakar) * Lee Jackson, Houston, TX * George James, Falls Church, VA * Seth Jarvis, Salt Lake City, UT * Dawn Jenkins, Lakewood, OH * Kandah Jeyapalan, Ames, IA * Bryce Johnson, Rockford, IL * Richard Johnson, Los Altos, CA * Nicholas Johnson, Colorado Springs, CO * Christopher Jones, Honolulu, HI * Douglas Jones, Boulder, CO * Helen Kabat, Cleveland, OH * Frank Karash, Powell, OH * Larry Keating, Denver, CO * Paul Keaton, Los Alamos, NM * Tom Keaveny, Boulder, CO * Dan Keena, Tallahassee, FL * Jim Keene, San Francisco, CA * Alan Keister, Los Angeles, CA * Albert Kelley, Cambridge, MA * Hugh Kelso, Redmond, WA * Mike Kennedy, Boulder, CO * John Kierein, Boulder, CO * Curt Kinghorn, Salt Lake City, UT * Lou Kirch, Cleveland, OH * Jack Kirwin, Tucson, AZ * Mark Kliss, Boulder, CO * Kristoffer Knapp, Denver, CO * William C. Knuth, Anaheim, CA * Jeff Kooistre, Grand Rapids, MI * Clayton Koppes, Oberlin, OH * Robert Kowaliw, Brighton, UT * Ramesh Krishnayer, Boca Raton, FL * John Krug, Santa Cruz, CA * William, Kurth, Iowa City, IA * Tim Kyger, San Francisco, CA * Will Kyselka, Honolulu, HI * Louis L'Amour, Los Angeles, CA * William Lane, Newtonville, MA * W.E. Langlois, San Jose, CA * Joe Lannutti, Tallahassee, FL * Ken Largman, San Francisco, CA * Jeffrey Larson, Webster, TX * Dean LaRue, Seattle, WA * Peggy Lathlean, Friendswood, TX * Robert LeCoco, Billingham WA * Richard Lee, College Station, TX * Richard Lewis, Melbourne, FL * Stacy Lieder, Houston, TX * Jeffrey Linsky, Denver, CO * T.D. Lin, Skokie, IL * Michael Lipschutz, West Lafayette, IN * Robert Livingston, Tallahassee, FL * John Llewellyn, Houston, TX * John Locastro, Tallahassee, FL * John Logsdon, Washington, DC * Gloria Ann Lopez, Roswell, NM * Jack Lousma, Ann Arbor, MI * Vincent Lowe, Bellevue, WA * Carol Luckhardt, Ann Arbor, MI * Glynn Lunney, Seal Beach, CA * Mark Luther, Tallahassee, FL * Anne Lutz, Houston, TX * Mike Lyons, Cleveland, OH * Alan Mabe, Tallahassee, FL * Robert Macon, Houston, TX * Marthona Madsen, Holladay, UT * Mariana Madwell, Honolulu, HI * Lorenz Magaard, Honolulu, HI * Eugene Mallove, Washington, DC * Kerry Malpass, Boulder, CO * Chris Mandra, Waltham, MA * Gregg Mann, Colorado Springs, CO * Scott F. March, Oakland, CA * Amy Marsh, San Francisco, CA * Irl Marshall, Littleton, CO * Edward Marwick, Skokie, IL * Sen. Spark Matsunaga, Honolulu, HI * Richard Matsuura, Hilo, HI * Michael Matthews, Houston, TX * John Mauer, Houston, TX * Paul M. Maughan, Washington, DC * Randy Mynard, Los Alamos, NM * Mark McCann, College Station, TX * Thomas McCord, Honolulu, HI * Joe McDaniel, Tallahassee, FL * Craig McDonald, Houston, TX * Robert McFarland, Boulder, CO * Steven McGrath, Mountain View, CA * Stephen D. McIver, Seattle, WA * Rex Megill, Logan, UT * Michael Mendillo, Boston, MA * Michael Meyer, Tallahassee, FL * Thomas Meyer, Boulder, CO * MariAnne Milkman, Iowa City, IA * Roger Milkman, Iowa City, IA * Jeff Miller, Seattle WA * Michael Miller, Marion, IA * Robin Miller, Peoria, IL * Stan Miller, Cleveland, OH * Steven Miller, West Newbury, MA * Knox Millsaps, Gainesville, FL * Peter Molton, Richland, WA * Don Moody, East Wenatchee, WA * Randy Moon, Salt Lake City, UT * Gilbert Moore, Bingham, UT * David Moore, Houston, TX * Martin Moore-Ede, Boston, MA * Stanley Morain, Albuquerque, NM * David Morrison, Honolulu, HI * Art Morrissey, Englewood, CO * Cheri Morrow, Denver, CO * Douglas Morrow, Broomfield, CO * Frank Moss, Salt Lake City, UT * Bennet Mullen, Nacogdoches, TX * Richard Munoz, San Francisco, CA * William Nahumck, Painesville, OH * Kevin Nelson, Cambridge, MA * Marilyn Newton, Iowa City, IA * James P. Nibblett, Seattle, WA * Oran Nicks, College Station, TX * Steve Nixon, Houston, TX * David Norton, College Station, TX * Gordon Oakley, Huntsville, AL * Alcestis Oberg, Dickinson, TX * James Oberg, Dickinson, TX * Hermann Oberth, Feucht, Germany * Gary Oleson, Alexandria, VA * Eric Olson, Marynard, MA * Gayle Ormiston, Colorado Springs, CO * Warren Overton, Birmingham, AL * Mark O'Brian, Ann Arbor, MI * James O'Brien, Tallahassee, FL * George O'Neel, Grass Valley, CA * Robert Pace, Jr., Huntsville, AL * Scott Pace, Santa Monica, CA * Michael Papagiannis, Boston, MA * Allen Parker, Auburn, WA * Claire Parkinson, Greenbelt, MD * George Parks, Seattle, WA * Perry Pascarella, Cleveland, OH * Dorothy Paul, Iowa City, IA * Eddie Pearson, Dayton, OH * Jerome Pearson, Dayton, OH * Georgianna Pena-Kues, Albuquerque, NM * David Peters, Salt Lake City, UT * Randy Phelps, Cleveland, OH * Robert Pickar, Schenectedy, NY * G. Stephen Pittman, Fremont CA * William Plato, Cleveland, OH * William Pollard, Ann Arbor, MI * Yolanda Porter, Denver, CO * Mark E. Prado, Arlington, VA * Roger Pressentin, Seattle, WA * Linda Preston, Park City, UT * Jim Pridgeon, Seattle, WA * Greg Privette, Denver, CO * Brian Proea, Houston, TX * Charles Provost, Altanta, GA * Ray Puccetti, Cleveland, OH * Louis Quay, Washington, DC. * Don Quinn, Houston, TX * Marsha Rainey, Denver, CO * John Raitt, Logan, UT * Ken Randle, Salt Lake City, UT * William Ranken, Los Alamos, NM * Joe Redfield, Chicago, IL * Eberhard Rees, Huntsville, Alabama * Laura Reeves, Albuquerque, NM * John Reid, East Bay, CA * Victor Reis, McLean, VA * Eugene Rennekamp, Cedar Rapids, IA * Phillip Rennert, Fairfax, VA * Richard de Revere, Tallahassee, FL * Jim Rice, Huntsville, AL * William Richardson, Koloa, HI * Mark Ridderhoff, Clearfield, UT * John Robinson, Washington, DC * Buck Rogers, Ann Arbor. MI * Thomas Rogers, McLean, VA * Susan Rose, Boulder, CO * Carol Rosin, Washington, DC * Muriel Ross, Ann Arbor, MI * Russel Rucky, Cleveland, OH * Andrew Rudnick, Houston, TX * William Rudow, Boston, MA * John Rummel, Moffett Field, CA * Bennett Ruttledge, Washington, DC * Eric Sableman, Palo Alto, CA * Hrishikesh Saha, Huntsville, AL * Phillip Salin, Redwood City, CA * Horst Salzwedel, Palo Alto, CA * Leo Sandon, Tallahassee, FL * Stephen Sandstedt, Houston, TX * Albert Schaffer, College Station, TX * Richard Scheck, Beverly Hills, CA * Victor Schmidt, Washington, DC * Charles Schmitt, Washington, DC * Ed Schmitz, Los Altos, CA * Angus Schmoe, Issaquah, WA * Steven Schneider, Boulder, CO * Niels Schonbeck, Denver, CO * Dan Schultze, Iowa City, IA * Kenneth Schulze, Rocky River, OH * Steven H. Schwartzkopf, Moffett Field, CA * Donald Scott, Daly

City, CA * Robert Seamans, Cambridge, MA * J.J. Self, Santa Cruz, CA * Carolyn Sesplankis, Cleveland, OH * David Sheff, Iowa City, IA * George Shepherd, University Park, CO * Rolin Sidwell, Washington, DC * Teresa Siegwarth, Cleveland, OH * Gary Silver, Beachwood, OH * Rand Simberg, El Segundo, CA * Brent Simon, Cleveland, OH * Al Simonc, Honolulu, HI * William Sinton, Honolulu, HI * David Smernoff, Moffett Field, CA * Bill Smith, Huntsville, AL * Gordon Smith, Seattle, WA * Greg Smith, Honolulu, HI * Curtis Snow, Seattle, WA * Marcellus Snow, Honolulu, HI * William Sommers, Huntsville, AL * Norman Sperling, East Bay, CA * Robert Stahele, South Pasadena, CA * Michael Stamm, Redmond, WA * Malcolm Stamper, Seattle, WA * Thomas Stauffer, Houston, TX * Jill Steele, Denver, CO * Kurt Stehling, Chevy Chase, MD * Richard Stiennon, Southfield, MI * Carol Stoker, Boulder, CO * Dennis Stone, Houston, TX * Marie Stone, Renton, WA * Chuck Stovitz, Beverly Hills, CA * Ernst Stuhlinger, Huntsville, AL * Willem Stuiver, Honolulu, HI * Mark Sullivan, Boston, MA * R. Ivan Sumner, Monticello, FL * George Sutherland, Cleveland, OH * T.C. Swartz, Seattle, WA * Richard Sweetsir, Jacksonville, FL * David Swift, Honolulu, HI * Andre Sylvester, Houston, TX * Nicholas J. Szabo, Seattle, WA * Steven Tait, Cedar Rapids, IA * Harvey Tananbaum, Cambridge, MA * David Tarnas, Seattle, WA * Donald Tarter, Huntsville, AL * Jeffrey Taylor, Albuquerque, NM * Thomas C. Taylor, Wrightwood, CA * Rob Teames, Brighton, UT * Scott Thomas, Logan, UT * Brian Tillotson, Seattle, WA * Baldwin Tom, Houston, TX * Tilhamer Toth-Fejel, San Jose, CA * Julia Tracy, Seattle, WA * Nico S. Triantatilloo, Seattle, WA * Robert Truax, Saratoga, CA * Rick Norman Tumlinson, Washington, DC * Wanetta Tuttle, Albuquerque, NM * Chester Twarog, Ft. Devens, MA * Robert Twiggs, Ogden, UT * William Urban, Houston, TX * James Van Allen, Iowa City, IA * James Van Alstine, Huntsville, AL * Vernon Van Dyke, Iowa City, IA * Bill Vardamon, Huntsville, AL * Ray Viator, Houston, TX * John Wagner, Midvale, UT * Arthur Walker, Jr., Stanford, CA * Constance Walker, Denver, CO * David Wallace, Ann Arbor, MI * George Wallerstein, Seattle, WA * Betty Walton, San Francisco, CA * Bob Wardell, East Bay, CA * Gerald Ward, Newton MA * C. Flint Webb, Beverly, MA * Bernard Weddleton, West Newbury, MA * Harry Weisberger, Phoenix, AZ * Len Weiss, Silver Spring, MD (on behalf of Sen. John Glenn) * Roger Weiss, Ann Arbor, MI * Michael Werner, Moffett Field, CA * Hanns J. Wetzstein, Natick, MA * Harold M. White Jr., Chapel Hill, NC * Frank White, Newton, MA * Mark Whittington, Houston, TX * John Wildenthal, Houston, TX * Gary Williams, Logan, UT * John Williams, Huntsville, AL * David Williamson, Washington, DC * Brittain Wilson, Ann Arbor, MI * Charles Wilson, Sevens Hills, OH * Glen Wilson, Washington, DC * Laurie S. Wilson, Gamber, MD * Linda Wilson, Ann Arbor, MI * M.D. Wilson, Galesburg, IL * Roger Wilson, Boulder, CO * Rep. Timothy E. Wirth, Boulder, CO * Neil Wolff, Ann Arbor, MI * James Wood, Katy, TX * Nancy Wood, Houston, TX * Gordon Woodcock, Huntsville, AL * Philip Woodruff, Napa, CA * Lori Woodward, Fort Collins, CO * Jay D. Woosley, Seattle, WA * Elisa Wynn, Buffalo, NY * Howard Young, Detroit, MI * Marilyn Yvon, Livonia, MI

LETTERS AND COMPUTER RESPONSES: Nikki Aardema, Naperville, IL * Dennis Abad, Aurora, IL * Steve Abrams, Lexington, KY * Ali AbuTaha, Reston, VA * Anthony Adams, Richmond, VA * Catherine Allbaugh, San Bruno, CA * Judy Anderson, Palo Alto, CA * Melissa Andrew, Naperville, IL * Daniel Appleman, San Jose, CA * Albert Arking, Greenbelt, MD * John Bagby, Jr., Jefferson City, MO * Garland Bauch, Houston, TX * C.M. Bawol, Alamogordo, NM * Matthew Belmonte, Alexandria, VA * Greg Bennett, League City, TX * Bob O. Benn, Washington, DC * Linda Benson, Seattle, WA * Robert Bickford, Fremont, CA * George Blakeslee, Weston, MA * Becky Blitz, Naperville, IL * Fran Bloomer, King of Prussia, PA * Frank Borman, Miami, FL * Lewis Branscomb, Armonk, NY * Mark Brender, Washington, DC * Mark E. Brender, Washington, DC * George Brickner, Chicago, IL * Robert T. Brigantic, San Antonio, TX * William Brown, Weston, MA * William C. Brown, Weston, MA * Robert Brungs, St. Louis, MO * Leslie Bruns, Naperville, IL * Rep. Sala Burton, San Francisco, CA * Stephen Cain, Brooklyn, NY * Sharon Campbell, Seattle, WA * Mark Castleman, Normal, IL * Granville Cate, Baltimore, MD * Michelle Chang, Naperville, IL * Blaine Clemmens, Naperville, IL * Aaron Cohen, Houston, TX * Steven Cohen, Redondo Beach, CA * Steven M. Cohn, Redondo Beach, CA * April Cole, Aurora, IL * Michael Comberiate, Greenbelt, MD * Gordon Cooper, Beverly Hills, CA * Don Crossman, Hartford, CT * Malcolm Currie, El Segundo, CA * Andrew Cutler, La Jolla, CA * George Dalton, Boston, MA * Jamie Darby, Naperville, IL * Nivedeta Das, Naperville, IL * G.K. Dawson, Portola Valley, CA * Doug DeVries, Cupertino, CA * Sen. Christopher Dodd, Willamantic, CT * M. Dorfman, San Jose, CA * Charles M. Duke, Jr., New Braunfels, TX * Jason Dunn, Aurora, IL * Mike Duvos, Seattle, WA * Harry Eckert, Cherry Valley, IL * Daryl Edwards, North Olmsted, OH * Thomas Elifrit, Windsor, WI * Jerry Emanuelson, Colorado Springs, CO * Robert Eramia, Seattle, WA * Raymond Erikson, Palm Bay, FL * William J.D. Escher, Madison, WI * Jennifer Estrup, Naperville, IL * Kent Fairfield, Gaston, OR * Pat Fallon, Belmar, NJ * Dominick Felicio, Naperville, IL * Charles C. Filley, Houston, TX * Steven Flajser, Washington, DC * Leo Foley, Washington, DC * Gulliver Foyle, Lafayette, CA * Kristy Fracasso, Naperville, IL * Marsha Freeman, Leesburg, VA * Louis Friedman, Pasadena, CA * Stanley Friedman, New York, NY * Derrick Fries, Birmingham, MI * Mike Fulda, Fairmont, WV * Joanne Gabrynowicz, New York, NY * Timothy Gaffney, Miamisburg, OH * John Galt, San Francisco, CA * William Ganoe, Tucson, AZ * Giorgio Gaviraghi, New York, NY * Edward Gibson, Redondo Beach, CA * Jennifer Gilman, Naperville, IL * T. Keith Glennan, Reston, VA * Al Goldwater, Santa Cruz, CA * William Good, New York, NY * David Graham, Washington, DC * Gary Gray, Chicago, IL * Georgia Griffith, Lancaster, OH * Jim Grubs, New York, NY * Kathy Gullu, Naperville, IL * Greg Hallock, Naperville, IL * Walter Hammond, Huntsville, AL * J.J. Hanak, Troy, MI * Kim Hanratty, Naperville, IL * T. J. Hart, Whippany, NJ * Sen. Orrin Hatch, Salt Lake City, UT * S. Hatfill, Mattoon, IL * Jodi Heath, Naperville, IL * Gregory Helfrich, Bellevue, WA * Jim Heller, Naperville, IL * Frederick B. Henderson III, San Francisco, CA * Melanie Henderson, Naperville, IL * T.A. Heppenheimer, Palos Verdes Peninsula, CA * A. Hertzberg, Seattle, WA * R. W. Hesselbacher, Philadelphia, PA * Arthur Hoag, Flagstaff, AZ * Harold C. Hollenbeck, Englewood Cliffs, NJ * Brandi Horne, Naperville, IL * Brian Horwath, Naperville, IL * Donald Hubbard, Chevy Chase, MD * Peter B. Humphrey, Honolulu, HI * David Huntsman, League City, TX * Devrie S. Intriligator, Santa Monica, CA * James B. Irwin, Colorado Springs, CO * Robin Jackson, Washington, DC * Philip Jacobs, Norfolk, VA * Francis S. Johnson, Richardson, TX * Jenny Johnson, Naperville, IL * Sheldon Jolson, Forest Hills, NY * R.M. Jones, Rockford, IL * Ken Jopp, Saint Paul, MN * Mary Kay Keller, Naperville, IL * John Kennedy, Cincinnati, OH * Sen. John Kerry, Boston, MA * Joe Kestel, Naperville, IL * James Killman, Sherman, TX * Adrian King, Stanford, CA * Elbert King, Houston, TX * Christopher C. Kraft, Jr., Houston, TX * Saunders Kramer, Gaithersburg, MD * Robert Kretsinger, Charlottesville, VA * Billy LaBonte, Naperville, IL * Beth LaGrant, Naperville, IL * Edward Lantz, Gaithersburg, MD * Melissa Larsen, Naperville, IL * L.W. Lehr, St. Paul, MN * William B. Lenoir, Arlington, VA * Karyn Lentz, Aurora, IL * Patricia Leveille, Bend, OR * Brian Levenson, Naperville, IL * David Lloyd, San Francisco, CA * James A. Lovell, Chicago, IL * Michael Lyon, Parma, OH * Thomas F. Malone, West Hartford, CT * William Mankin, Atlanta, GA * Carrie Marcinkevicius, Naperville, IL * Yovette Markey, Washington, DC * Hans Mark, Austin, TX * Norah Martinez-Tower, San Mateo, CA * Luretta Martin, Tucson, AZ * Ralph E. Matkin, Murphysboro, IL * Joseph Mattaino, Jr., Alexandria, VA * Frank B. McDonald, Washington, DC * J. William McDonald, Louisville, KY * Walter A. McDougall, Berkeley, CA * Michael McGann, Baton Rouge, LA * William McLaughlin, Wilmington, DE * Rich Menella, Naperville, IL * Marvin Menter, Washington, DC * Wayne Metsker, Seattle, WA * Sen. Howard Metzenbaum, Shaker Heights, OH * Christina Meyers, Naperville, IL * Elizabeth Miller, La Jolla, CA * Jay Miller, San Francisco, CA * Lori Molter, Naperville, IL * Thomas H. Moorer, Washington, DC * Tricia Mueller, Naperville, IL * Dale Myers, Leucadia, CA * Rick Needham, Mercersberg, PA * Rep. Bill Nelson, Melbourne, FL * D. Ellis Neunherz, Granville, OH * Martin Nix, Seattle, WA * Richard D. Norton, Philadelphia, PA * Marie Oleson, Truckee, CA * Rep. Leon E. Panetta, Monterey, CA * Jon Pankow, Naperville, IL * Donald Parker, Houston, TX * Jenny Patzmann, Naperville, IL * Joseph N. Pelton, Washington, DC * Charles Pillard, Washington, DC * F.E. Potts, Tuscon, AZ * Frank Press, Washington, DC * Dale Raines, Lakewood, CO * Eberhardt Rechtin, Los Angeles, CA * Timothy F. Regan, Dallas, TX * Rande Repke, Naperville, IL * Roger Revelle, New York, NY * William Richardson, Kola, HI * Cortland Richmond, North Andover, MA * William Robbins, Sykesville, MD * Michael Robinson, Largo, FL * George S. Robinson, Washington, DC * Milton W. Rosen, Bethesda, MD * Stanley Rosen, Colorado Springs, CO * John Ruley, Dayton, OH * Cathy Runge, Plainfield, IL * Bennett Rutledge, Arlington, VA * Gilbert D. Rye, Washington, DC * Stephan R. Schmitt, Horsham, PA * Jeremy Schmutz, Naperville, IL * Cindy Schommer, Aurora, IL * David Schreiber, San Jose, CA * Milton Schultz, Williston, ND * Jesse Scinto, Ft. Collins, CO * David R. Scott, Lancaster, CA * Richard Seebass, Boulder, CO * Jennifer Seffernick, Naperville, IL * John Seghers, San Mateo, CA * James C. Selman, Sausalito, CA * Cornelius Seon, Brooklyn, NY * Erin Sheehan, Aurora, IL * Jon Shemitz, Ben Lomond, CA * Lee Shurie, North Hollywood, CA * Mark Silverstein, Laurel, MD * Gary Silver, Beachwood, OH * Donald K. Slayton, Houston, TX * George Slusher, Annapolis, MD * Harlan J. Smith, Austin, TX * Jerra Smith, Naperville, IL * Richard J. Smith, Washington, DC * James M. Snead, Beavercreek, OH * John N. Snell, Baltimore, MD * Mitch Snyder, Washington, DC * Jim Southwick, Naperville, IL * Gretchen Stanek, Naperville, IL * Lisa Stanek, Naperville, IL * Frank A. Stanton, Milton, MA * Matt Starbuck, Naperville, IL * Don Stitt, Pittsburgh, PA * H. Gordon Straw, II, San Jose, CA * Greg Sutherland, Santa Cruz, CA * Gregory S. Swann, New York, NY * Derron Swan, Naperville, IL * Kari Tangemann, Naperville, IL * Brad Taylor, Aurora, IL * Larry Taylor, Whittier, CA * Kirby Timmons, Los Angeles, CA * Jessica Tobin, Naperville, IL * Rep. Robert G. Torricelli, Hackensack, NJ * Rockwell Townsend, San Francisco, CA * Suzanne Traub, Cambridge, MA * Nick Turner, Boulder Creek, CA * James Turney, Richmond, VA * Brian Tvedt, Santa Clara, CA * Mona Tycz, Greenbelt, MD * Scott Ucker, San Carlos, CA * Mike Van Pelt, San Jose, CA * Johnny Van Styn, Cincinnati, OH * Ryan Vander Zanden, Naperville, IL * Rep. Harold L. Volkmer, Hannibal, MO * Rep. Robert S. Walker, Lancaster, PA * Rep. Vin Weber, Slayton, MN * Margot Walhke, Naperville, IL * Ryan Watson, Naperville, IL * Jennifer Weaver, Naperville, IL * Frederick West, Washington, DC * Frank White, Newton, MA * Jennifer Whitehead, Naperville, IL * Robert Wilk, Naperville, IL * Jeanne Wojtasiak, Naperville, IL * Thomas Wolfe, New York, NY * Gordon Wolman, Baltimore, MD * Rep. Ed Zschau, Los Altos, CA

"DEPARTMENT P" LETTERS: *In February 1986, a popular Sunday supplement published an article which ended with a suggestion that interested individuals write to us, among others, to express their opinion on whether or not the United States and the Soviet Union should jointly embark on a program to send people to Mars. The letters were addressed to "Department P" at the Commission which enabled us to keep track of those letters which were directly in response to the article. By February 28, when our report was completed, we had received hundreds of letters.* Sasha Akery, Homerville, GA * Francis Allbritton, Chehalis, WA * Richard Allen, Montgomery, AL * Joan Ammon, Pittsburgh, PA * Brandon Amo, Canton, NY * Christine Anderson, Springfield, MA * Robert Annear, Jr., Greenfield, MA * Tim Arnold, Chattanooga, TN * Joseph Audi, North Canton, OH * F. W. Auerbach, Long Beach, CA * Pat Ault-Duell, Goodland, KS * Stephen Babiak, Washington, DC * K. Donald Baer, Charleston, SC * Cheryl Ballou, Corona, CA * Suzanne Baltes, Graham, NC * Mike Baker, Las Vegas, NV * Dennis Banta, Anderson, IN * George Barany, Syracuse, NY * Linda Barclay, Grapevine, TX * Patrick Barker, Pratt, KS * John Bardsley, Huntington, NY * Geoffrey Barron, Pomona, NY * Chris Bartleson, Lehigh Valley, PA * Darrell Bartlett, Chico, CA * Etta Barton, College Park, GA * A.T.A. Base, Weslaco, TX * S. Bass, St. Louis, MO * Raymond Bates, Tampa, FL * Edward Bearsley, Eugene, OR * Glen Beatty, Little Rock, AR * Dianne Beeaff, Tucson, AZ * David Beedle, Hellertown, PA * John Beers, West Haven, CT * Gary Beizzalini, Oak Park, MO * Jim Berger, Winchester, MA * Chris Berkey, Lower Burrell, PA * Mr. & Mrs. Berlin, Odessa, TX * Bonnie Berman, Bowling Green, KY * Claudia Betro, Canton, OH * Milt Bevis, Quincy, FL * Olivia Bibb, Charleston, WV * R. Bickel, Kaneohe, HI * Marianne Bickett, Tempe, AZ * Regina BinChik, New Paltz, NY * Gloria Black, Rossville, GA * Henry Blankfort, Los Angeles, CA * Gary Boedefeld, Saint Louis, MO * Bill Boenigter, Casper, WY * Nancy Bogue, Madison, WI * Chuck Bokoskie, Safford, AZ * Harold Bolharner, St. Louis, MO * David Bowen, Kingsport, TN * Lena Bowen, St. Petersburg, FL * Karen Bowland-Hicks, N. Hollywood, CA * Lynn Bowman, Monte Sereno, CA * Holle Boykin, Quincy, FL * Karl Brandt, Upper Marlboro, MD * Martin Breeden, St. Louis, MO * Max Breinfalk, Fort Wayne, IN * Steve Brewster, North Las Vegas, NV * Stephanie Bridges, Phoenix, AZ * Mark Briggs, Manlius, NY * James Brill, Martinsburg, WV * Kenneth Britt, Easthampton, MA * Elizabeth Brown, Kensington, CA * James Brown, West Jordon, UT * Ginny Bruno, Albuquerque, NM * Phyllis Bryant, Auburn, NY * Robert Bryant, Chico, CA * Mike Buell, Portland, OR * Vito Buccina, Syracuse, NY * Elizabeth Buck, Evansville, IN * Michael Buckbee, Wadsworth, OH * Jean Burns, Long Beach, CA * Cyndi Bushluna, Denver, CO * Kathryn Butcher, Ann Arbor, MI * John Byers, Alexandria, VA * Vicki Callio, Camp Hill, PA * Celeste Calongne, Thorton, CO * Justin Camp, South Hadley, MA * Jay Campbell, Bronx, NY * David Cannard, Portland, OR * Carol Carlile, Cliffside Park, NJ * Bill Carlson, Appleton, WI * Lynn Carlson, Appleton, WI * John Carpenter, Athens, GA * George Carr, St. Petersburg, FL * Roderick Carr, Seattle, WA * Nick Carson, Youngstown, OH * Susan Case, Alexandria, VA * Sis. Marge Cashman, St. Paul, MN * Laura Casto, Arlington, TX * Daniel Castro, San Diego, CA * James Cecil, Martinsville, VA * Rob Chambers, Lake Helen, FL * Brian Chappell, Welch, WV * Sally Chappell, Bridgton, ME * Roy Chesseri, Belleville, NJ * A. W. Chistensen, Florissant, MO * Elisabeth Christ, Coppersburg, PA * Jack Christilaw, Livonia, MI * William Chumley, Parker, CO * Larry Clark, St. Joseph, MO * Ted Clark, Edinburg, TX * J. E. D. Cline, Woodland Hills, CA * Tom Cohen, Woodinville, WA * Kenneth Colby, Arlington, VA * Paul Cole, Ontario, CA * J. H. Coleman, Oklahoma City, OK * James Collett, Sunnyvale, CA * Nancy Collett, Sunnyvale, CA * G. W. Collier, West End, NC * Frank Collins, Port Rechey, FL * Moseley Collins, Okeechobee, FL * Terry Colvin, Sierra Vista, AZ * Dennis Concoby, Las Vegas, NV * Florence Conner, Tucson, AZ * William Copper, White Oak, PA * Jim Cordray, Champaign, IL * Christine Cortese, Kihie, Maui, HI * J. R. Costerison, Muncie, IN * Bernard Cote, Erie, PA * Todd Cottle, Austin, TX * Patricia Coulson, Knoxville, TN * Dan Craig, Nampa, IN * Peaches Cray, North Las Vegas, NV * John Creed,

Lincoln, CA * James Crim, Muncie, IN * Robert Crimmins, Vallejo, CA * C. Carter Croft, Tampa, FL * Kenneth Crowe, Birmingham, AL * Walter Crumpler, Victorville, CA * Gottfried Csala, Wilkes-Barre, PA * Gayle Cue, Billings, MT * Raymond Curiale, Long Island, NY * Ken Curtin, Laguna Hills, CA * Rick Czach, Tampa, FL * Jacqueline D'Agostino, Charleston, SC * Patrica Dana, Beaverton, OR * William Dana, Beaverton, OR * Howard Dashke, Caseyville, IL * Shirley Davis, Champaign, IL * Terre Davis, Auburn, CA * Charles Davisson, Charleston, WV * Wade Dazey, Santa Barbara, CA * Esmond Dean, Staten Island, NY * Edgar Decker, Prescott, AZ * Jennifer Dell, Las Vegas, NV * Norman DellaColetta, Scio, OH * John de Maagd, Santa Barbara, CA * David DeMarzo, Pittsburgh, PA * James Denney, Youngstown, OH * Mark Denro, Lexington, KY * Sally Denro, Lexington, KY * Charles Densmore, Gainesville, FL * Larry Deran, Fremont, CA * Michael DeRobio, Wexford, PA * James DeRyan, Spokane, WA * Darlyne Dewellyn, Athens, GA * Jacqueline Diamond, Santa Barbara, CA * Steven Dodge, Honolulu, HI * James Doherfty, Loveland, CO * Todd Donovan, Spring Glen, PA * Michael Doughton, Sacramento, CA * Bruce Dorsch, S. Lake Tahoe, CA * John Dprzibila, Herndon, VA * Jenny Drake, San Pedio, CA * Karl Draney, San Diego, CA * John Draper, Bakersfield, CA * Virgil Dube, Jacksonville, FL * James Duncan, Fairfield, TX * Dorothy Duquet, Yarmouth Port, MA * Agusta Durden, Havana, FL * Alice Dyal, Mt. Pleasant, FL * Kit Dyke, Maui, HI * Roy Eckman, Las Vegas, NV * Agnes Egan, Denver, CO * Patrick Elder, Olela City, OK * Thomas Elifritz, Windsor, WI * David Elkin, Albany, IN * Mrs. O. O. Elliott, Grandview, TX * Roberta Elliott, Del Mar, CA * Gary Ellis, Falmouthport, MA * Latia Ely, Las Vegas, NV * Richard Emanuel, Anchorage, AR * Ernest Emerick, Pocatello, ID * Lille Emery, Troy, MO * Thomas Emmel, Gainesville, FL * Celeste Engel, Victor, MT * William English, Burkeville, VA * Carol Eno, Mattydale, NY * Michael Erickson, Oshkosh, WI * Anthony Esler, Williamsburg, VA * Suzanne Ethridge, Norman, OK * Mary Fan, Chattahoochee, FL * Brian Fellingham, El Reno, OK * Audrey Fenner, Webster Groves, MO * Bruce Fergusson, Seattle, WA * Jill Ferguson, Junction City, KS * Thomas Filkins, Manassas, VA * Debora Finn, St. Petersburg, FL * Frank Fiondella, North Haven, CT * Paul Fisher, Lima, OH * Emerson Flannery, Eugene, OR * George Fleming, College Park, MD * Donald Flick, Brownsburg, IN * Carol Follett, Los Gatos, CA * Mr. & Mrs. Foreman, Oakland, CA * Joe Foran, Mesa, AZ * Donald Foreman, Fort Wayne, IN * Edward Forster, Santa Barbara, CA * Mr. & Mrs. Foster, Eugene, OR * Susan Foster, Portland, OR * Wendy Foster, Portland, OR * David Fox, Brookeville, MD* Norman Frank, Richland, WA * H. B. Franklin, Montclair, NJ * Alec Fraser, Heathsville, VA * Robert Frederking, Pittsburgh, PA * J. William Frey, Willow Street, PA * Joan Frey, Billings, MT * Karl Frey, Billings, MT * Fred Freyer, St. Simons Island, GA * Richard Frickmann, Goleta, CA * Dale Friend, Tampa, FL * Jean Friske, Peoria, IL * William Friske, Peoria, IL * William Fuchs, Centreville, VA * Amy Fuller, Lancaster, PA * Steven Fuller, Yoncalla, OR * Thomas Futtner, Alexandria, VA * Catalino Galvez, Oakland, CA * Robert Galyen, Arvada, CO * Trudy Gamble, Lubbock, TX * Jenny Garden, Skokie, IL * Roger Gardner, Clarksville, TN * Canid Gartner, Ukiah, CA * Scott Garver, Fort Wayne, IN * Ralph Garvis, Placerville, CA * Agnes Geelan, Fargo, ND * Betty George, Orlando, FL * Gregory Gibb, Eureka, CA * Scott Gibbson, Hickory, NC * Thomas Gibbson, Seattle, WA * G. Ernst Giesecke, Springfield, IL * David Gillespie, Louisville, TN * Gary Gimbel, Seguin, TX * Nina Gimond, Rockville, MD * Carol Glasser, Seattle, WA * David Gleason, Sulphur, LA * Kathryn Golding, Orange, CA * I. Goldman, New York, NY * Elizabeth Goodwin, Kankakee, IL * Emily Goodwin, Kankakee, IL * Jack Goodwin, Kankakee, IL * Paula Goodwin, Kankakee, IL * Charles Gossard, Phoenix, AZ * Neil Gowen, Loveland, CO * Mr. & Mrs. Graham, Macon, GA * Jeffrey Gramlich, Columbia, MO * Kathleen Grauer, San Diego, CA * John Graves, London, Kentucky * B.C. Gray, Huntington Beach, CA * H.L. Gray, Huntington Beach, CA * Randy Green, San Diego, CA * Peggy Gregory, Atlanta, GA * Scott Gregory, Quincy, FL * Kenneth Grimes, Hamden, CT * Lucy Grimm, Brockton, MA * William Grimm, Madison, WI * Michael Grogg, Roanoke, IL * Chester Grusinski, Mt. Clemens, MI * Catherine Guinn, Pfafftown, NC * Tom Hahn, Welch, WV * Philip Hall, Jr., Maplewood, NJ * Ronald Hall, Lowell, MA * Thomas Halloway, Evansville, IN * R. F. Halusan, Belleville, IL * Edna Hambey, Gadsden, AL * Patricia Hamilton, Tucson, AZ * Paula Harney, Granger, IN * Jean Harrington, Detroit, MI * Kristi Hart, Fort Wayne, IN * Linda Harter, Wallace, ID * Emily Hartzell, Cheraw, SC * Mr. & Mrs. Harwood, Hendersonville, NC * Mrs. Roland Hassbaum, St. Charles, MO * Crystal Hastings, North Las Vegas, NV * Philip Hawkins, Ashville, NC * Philip Hawn, Santee, CA * Stephen Hayman, Lafayette, LA * George Hazelton, Murfreesboro, NC * Carmella Heidrick, Clyde, KS * Art Heinrick, Lompoc, CA * Joan Heinrick, Lompoc, CA * Mrs. A. G. Heinsohn, Knoxville, TN * James Henderson, San Diego, CA * Christine Henning, Tempe, AZ * Rhoda Herman, Bethesda, MD * Doug Hermaner, Quincy, FL * Laurel Hepner, Billings, MT * Albert Hiener, Orinda, CA * Doris Hervey, Palenville, NY * Sonia Higbee, Salt Lake City, UT * Phil Higby, Youngstown, OH * Helene Hill, Grand Rapids, MI * Wayne Hill, Dallas, TX * Wesley Hiller, Santa Roas, CA * Emma Himeno, Honolulu, HI * Luther Hintz, San Jose, CA * Graham Hodges, Liverpool, NY * Peter Hoey, Flushing, NY * Ed Hoff, Sebastopol, CA * Grandma Hoff, Millersville, PA * Kenneth Hogan, Orland Park, IL * C. William Holmes, Salt Lake City, UT * Jennifer Hohol, Centerville, PA * D. A. Holliday, Addison, IL * Cecelia Honey, Tampa, FL * Wells Hoover, Takoma Park, MD * Virginia Hoppe, Canastota, NY * Steve Horowitz, Van Nuys, CA * John Houk, Purcellville, VA * Doug Hoveland, New Richmond, WI * Benjamin Hubbard, Brea, CA * Liza Hull, Garden Grove, CA * Lynn Hull, Garden Grove, CA * Jody Humble, Greensboro, NC * Carol Hummel, Maryville, TN * John Hunsinger, Jr., Decatur, GA * Denise Hutchinson, Dupont, GA * J. A. Huycke, Atlanta, GA * Randy Ingersoll, Yellowstone Park, WY * April Ingram, Dupont, GA * Franklin Ingram, Santa Barbara, CA * Robert Inskeep, Huntington Woods, MI * Kenneth Isbell, Allentown, PA * John Iverson, Salt Lake City, UT * Raegene Iverson, Salt Lake City, UT * Paul Jackson, Pico Rivera, CA * Tanya Jackson, St. Louis, MO * Elizabeth Jacobs, Yonkers, NY * Paul Janse, Pomona, CA * Chris Jasiewicz, Huntington Beach, CA * Mike Jasiewicz, Huntington Beach, CA * Ruth Jette, Stamford, CT * Carlton Johnson, Lock Haven, PA * Karen Johnston, Bloomington, IN * Gordon Jones, Los Angeles, CA * Margret Jones, St. Louis, MO * William Jones, Crawfordsville, IN * Merry Jorgensen, Redondo Beach, CA * Peter Kachur, Uniontown, PA * Gustave Kaitz, Monticello, NY * Caroline Kallas, Maywood, IL * Beth Kargel, Quincy, FL * Bill Kargel, Quincy, FL * George Kauffman, Fresno, CA * John Kauffman, Phoenix, AZ * Glenn Keaneny, Hershey, PA * Sarah Kenley, Noblesville, IN * Carol Kersten, St. Louis, MO * T. O. Killgrove, Frazier Park, CA * Julie Kimmel, Havana, FL * Joan King, Sautee, GA * Steven King, Fresno, CA * Thomas King, Silver Springs, MD * Irene Kirby, Seattle, WA * Clarence Kirkbide, Cumberland, OH * Erin Klinger, Muncy, PA * Dennis Klitzke, Lyndon Station, WI * Lari Knedel, Auburn, CA * Randy Knee, York, PA * Jim Knutson, La Crosse, WI * Almira Kopp, Casco, ME * Otto Kral, Hudson, WI * Mrs. A. J. Krechel, Hemet, CA * Harry Kramer III, Pittsburgh, PA * Richard Krieg, Ridgefield, CT * Ann Kriss, Austin, TX * Judy Kropp, Oakdale, CA * James Krupp, Wallinford, CT * Michael Kwasniewski, Brookfield, IL * T. Kwiecinolir, Seattle, WA * Steven Lampman, Liverpool, NY * Gabriel, Langdon, Bloomington, IN * Mr. & Mrs. Lango, Verona, NJ * Ron LaPierre, Sutton, MA * Lily Laser, Whippany, NJ * Sharon Lasseter, Quincy, FL * A. Lava, Anaheim, CA * Margot Lavoie, Liverpool, NY * Catherine Lawrie, Tijeras, NM * Randy Lawson, Mooresburg, TN * Steve Leach, Lancaster, PA * Arthur Leak, Colby, KS * Peter Leitner, Tampa, FL * Andre Lelievre, N. Weymouth, MA * Tom Lentz, Hammond, IN * Ace Leonard, Englewood, CO * Carol Leonhardt, Quincy, CA * Dana Lewis, Las Vegas, NV * Thomas Lewis, Canton, OH * Todd Lewis, Middletown, NY * Joseph Lichfield, St. Johns, AZ * Robert Licorish, Oakdale, CA * Richard Liebert, Whitestone, NY * Thomas Litchard, Clemmons, NC * Karl Lohr, Groton, CT * Wayne Longbein, Boerne, TX * M. Jean Lowe, San Jose, CA * James Lowe, Mountain Home, AZ * Sharon Lugn, Seymor, CT * Todd Lugn, Seymor, CT * Jack Lundy, Huntsville, AL * David Luthringshausen, Metaire, LA * William MacFarlane, North Conway, NH * Fran Madole, Prescott, AZ * T. Russell Mager, Tacoma, WA * Mr. & Mrs. Malis, Merrillville, IN * Geoffrey Mandel, Cambridge, MA * Lois Mandelberg, Arlington, VA * Christopher Martin, Houston, TX * J. Martin, Long Beach, CA * Joseph Martinez, McAllen, TX * Cindy Masek, Lincoln, NE * Michael Mash, Walled Lake, MI * Ross Mathis, Coupeville, WA * Walter Matthews, South Bend, IN * David Maxwell, Lynnfield, MA * Scott May, Northville, MI * James McCarty, Asheville, NC * Bobby McCaskill, Coats, NC * Mary McCombie, Sunnyvale, CA * Mary Lou McCord, Menasha, WI * J. David McCrabb, Stow, MA * Michael McCullough, Santa Clara, CA * Dennis McCurry, Clawson, MO * William McDonald, Albany, NY * Timothy McGauley, Grand Junction, CO * Ronald McGuckin, Croydon, PA * Mary McLane, North East, PA * Marilyn McLaughlin, West Fork, AR * Corby Mcneely, W. Palm Beach, FL * R. Jerrold Melville, Syracuse, NY * Jay & Linda Melvin, Woodside, CA * Mr. & Mrs. Melvin, Woodside, CA * John Milletics, Potterville, MO * Barry Miller, Dallas, TX * Eric Miller, York, PA * K. L. Milner, Las Cruces, NM * Craig Milsten, York, PA * Paul Minnich, Lancaster, PA * Adele Mirshak, Bath, PA * Warren Mirshak, Bath, PA * Ben Missler, Tualatin, OR * David Moe, Citrus Heights, CA * Fred Molz, Auburn, AL * Alicia Monroe, Quincy, FL * Claudia Montague, Havana, FL * L. R. Montesini, Victoria, Australia * Victor Monti, Yuba City, CA * Jane Monucure, Burlington, NC * Bill Moore, Oklahoma City, OK * Johnny Moore, Jr., Huntsville, TX * Patti Moore, York, PA * S. R. Moore, St. Joe, MO * Alan Mootry, Spokane, WA * Daniel Moran, South Plainfield, NJ * Robert Morewell, Wyoming, IL * Carole Morgan, Quincy, FL * Jimmy Morgan, Magnolia, MS * Mrs. Morin, South Hadley, MA * 1st Lt. Morit, Bismark, ND * William Mosher, Port Huron, MI * David Mullin, Washington, DC * Maryellen Mungovan, Syracuse, NY * Rosalinda Munoz, Cambridge, MA * Betty Murphy, Pittsburgh, PA * Dennis Murphy, Oregon, WI * Jonathn Murphy, Exland, WI * Darren Nance, San Diego, CA * Ann Nangle, Newburyport, MA * Ruth Nankivil, Santa Rosa, CA * Mr. & Mrs. Naughton, Madison, WI * Illana Naylor, Manassas, VA * Dean Nazario, Pompton Lakes, NJ * Roger Nelson, Los Lunas, NM * Debbie Nevitt, Santa Barbara, CA * Dwight New, Indianapolis, IN * Pamela Newby, Virginia Beach, VA * David Newsome, Oklahoma City, OK * Norman Nicol, Santa Rosa, CA * Lester Nichole, Tampa, FL * Matthew Niehaus, Raymond, IL * Julius Nitus, Orange, CA * Tom Nolan, Jr., Mobile, AL * Mim Noordam, Emmaus, PA * Michael Noto, York, SC * J. Ward O'Brien, Woodburn, OR * M. E. O'Brownee, Honolulu, HI * Sarah O'Hara, Tyler, TX * Diana O'Keefe, Oshkosh, WI * Janet O'Neil, Bellevue, WA * Jeffrey Offenhuane, Lexington, KY * Rick Oestrike, Robbinsville, NJ * Charles Oldham, Fayetteville, NC * Susan Olivarez, McAllen, TX * Nicole Otis, Bronx, NY * Bill Owens, Rocklin, CA * Jim Owens, Pontiac, MO * Amy Palm, West Salem, WI * Frank Palomares, North Las Vegas, NV * N. Palmeni, Queens, NY * Mary Pardee, Silver Spring, MD * Raymond Paris, Jr., New Salem, PA * Donald Parriott, Monroe, NY * Earnest Parker, Seattle, WA * Julie Parmenter, Southbridge, MA * Barry Parson, Daytona Beach, FL * Gordon Paul, San Jose, CA * Wayne Pavinich, Rustburg, VA * Wilbur Pearson, Jr., West Jordan, UT * James Pentz, San Diego, CA * William Perk, Carbondale, IL * Deborah Perkins, Quincy, FL * Thomas Perrin, Portland, OR * Elmo Peterson, Chicago, IL * Patty Peterson, Chamblee, GA * Richard Peterson, Goldsboro, NC * Wayne Peterson, Genesee, ID * William Peterson, White Bear Lake, MN * Jack Petree, Roanoke, VA * David Pevyhouse, Reedley, CA * S. Piro, Midwest City, OK * Myfanwy Plank, Santa Rosa, CA * Mary Pollom, South Bend, IN * Eugene Post, Daytona Beach, FL * Melissa Posten, Deptford, NJ * Linda Potter, Aurora, CO * Jan Pregel, Carbondale, IL * Carlton Puertas, College Point, NY * Steve Quai, Spokane, WA * John Quinlan, Jr., Mount Vernon, NH * George Rae, Hagerstown, MD * Laura Ranelli, Oradell, NJ * Tom Rasmussen, Chatsworth, CA * W. E. Rasmussen, Saint Paul, MN * Kenneth Rau, Woburn, MA * Vincent Rawlings, State Farm, VA * Richard Reichard, Johnstown, PA * James Renehan, Nashua, NH * Brenda Repper, Syracuse, NY * Ralph Ressler, Auburn, AL * Charles Revill, Grand Forks, B. C. * Curtis Reynolds, Las Vegas, NV * Tom Reynolds, Glassport, PA * Mr. & Mrs. Ribner, Newport News, VA * William Richards, Fort Wayne, IN * J. Richert, Etna, PA * Christine Rife, Harrisburg, PA * William Ringenberg, New Milford, CT * Sara Rittenhouse, Emmaus, PA * Steven Rivas, Owosso, MI * Robert Roane, Jacksonville, FL * Eileen Roberts, Las Cruces, NM * C. Brian Robbins, Alexandria, VA * Eleanora Robbins, Alexandria, VA * Mark Robbins, Salem, OR * Michael Robinson, Adelanto, CA * David Robison, Erie, PA * B. Roche, Mobile, AL * Kent Rodenbeck, Fort Wayne, IN * Julio Rodriguez, Temple Terrace, FL * Stephen Rogouski, Roselle, NJ * David Rollins, Arlington, VA * Beatrice Roper, Scranton, PA * Marilyn Roper, Bangor, ME * Greg Rose, Santa Rosa, CA * Kathryn Rose, St. Maries, ID * T. Rose, Springville, CA * Sanford Rosenthal, Charlotte, NC * Janet Ross, Kansas, WI * Paul Rowe, Barrackville, WV * Islene Runningdeer, New Ipswich, NH * Beth Rush, North Las Vegas, NV * Charles Russell, Onley, VA * Robert Ruthowoki, Clark, NJ * Chris Ryan, North Las Vegas, NV * George Ryan, Plattsburgh, NY * Susan Ryba, Santa Paula, CA * Tom Saffell, Banesville, OH * Danny Salamone, Elizabeth, NJ * Vera Salamone, Las Vegas, NV * Gary Sanchez, Albuquerque, NM * Carmine Sammarco, Melrose Park, IL * Carlton Schilcher, S. Londonderry, VT * Marjorie Schilcher, S. Londonderry, VT * Herbert Schlegel, NewBuryport, MA * Rudolph Schmeichel, Dallas, TX * K. T. Schmidt, Williamsburg, VA * W. Schmidt, Washington, D.C. * David Schnable, Speedway, IN * Freida Schnable, Speedway, IN * Kelly Schober, Chatsworth, CA * John Schoen, Hayward, CA * Herwig Schutzler, Lancaster, PA * Captain Schwedler, Stroudsborg, PA * Mary Sealfon, Middletown, NY * Ruth Seagren, Sun City, AZ * David Sekulsky, Wheeling, WV * Patricia Sessink, Franklin, MI * Danny Sessums, Zachary, LA * Steven Sharek, New Bedford, MA * Steven Sharer, Tyrone, PA * Marlene Shelby, Detroit, MI * Landis Shepherd, Ocala, FL * Mary Shepherd, Ocala, FL * Alan Shulman, Goffstown, NH * Frank Simons, Forth Worth, TX * Alfred Singer, Ruxton, MD * William Sizensky, Grafton, NH * Nancy Skillen, Lyons, IL * Nicholas Skinner, Provincetown, MA * Wilbur Sloat, Santa Rosa, CA * Harold Small, Boston, MA * Barbara Smith, Fort Worth, TX * Betty Smith, Santa Rosa, CA * Cory Smith, Bellevue, WA * Crawford Smith, York, PA * Ms. E. A. Smith, Virginia Beach, VA * Earl Smith, Santa Rosa, CA * Lawrence Smith, Holland, MI * Paul Smith, Columbia, TN * Roy W. Smith, Charleston, SC * Marcus Snyder, Jr., San Antonio, TX * David Sotka, Fort Wayne, IN * John Spafford, Westhope, ND * Carole Spencer, Redlands, CA * Kelly Spradlin, Utica, MI * Beverly Springer, Emmaus, PA * L. E. Stahl, Evansville, IN * K. L. Stanford, Norman, OK * Steven Stanley, Portland, OR * Sharon Steenbergen, Houston, TX * Robert Steinert, Bakersfield, CA * Brenda Sterman, Tucson, AZ * Carolynne Stevens, Richmond, VA * Michael Stevenson, Santa Barbara, CA * Frank Stoffers, Newark, DE * Bernard Story, Bethlehem, PA * Maxwell Stout, Austin, TX * Robert Stout, Royal Oak, MI * Royle Strom, Apache Junction, AZ * Fred Strong, North Hollywood, CA * E. Strothers, New Orleans, LA * Christopher Stubbs, Bakersfield, CA * Will Suber, Quincy, FL * W. Howard Sullivan, Norwich, NY * Jean Switzer, Chattanooga, TN * Louis Szabo, Landing, NJ * Michelle Szathmary, Cucamonga, CA * Marc Takacs, Huntington Beach, CA * Lillian Talbot, Sarasota, FL * C. B. Talley, Silver Spring, MD * T. D. Talley, Duncanville, TX * Susan Tamarkin, York, PA * Bonnie Taylor, Akron, OH * David Teel, Nogales, AZ * Carol Templin, Ritzville, WA * Anne Tenbensel, Santa Rosa, CA * Mr. & Mrs. Tennent, Washington, VA * Julia Ternak, Mulberry, FL * Ruby Thomas, Salt Lake City, UT * Joan Thompson, Beulad, CO * Joan Tifland, Silver Spring, MD * Ken Toll, Irvine, CA * Gregg Tolliver, Garden

Grove, CA * Joyce Tolliver, Garden Grove, CA * Maurice Toms, Hendersonville, NC * Roberta Tozier, San Diego, CA * C. H. Tracy, Ashland, OR * Katharine Tremaine, Santa Barbara, CA * John Tucci, St. Louis, MO * Charlotte Turk, Schiller Park, IL * John Tuttle, Seattle, WA * Ann Tyler, Tucson, AZ * Sam Tyner, North Las Vegas, NV * Terry Tyson, Redlands, CA * Ray Upchurch, Duncanville, TX * Cathy Urquhart, Londonberry, NH * Mike Valentino, Fontana, CA * John Vance, Ridgewood, NJ * Pamela Van Veen, Rowland, CA * Mr. & Mrs. Van Zandt, Bisbee, AZ * Louis Varricchio, Allentown, PA * Matthew Veazey, Abbeville, LA * Emiliano Vega, Sacramento, CA * Eric Vega, Sacramento, CA * Florence Verginio, Baldwinsville, NY * Greg Verginio, Baldwinsville, NY * Mr. & Mrs. Vetlesen, Sewickley, PA * Randolph Vikan, Seattle, WA * Eric Vogelvang, Orange, CA * Ron Volkman, Evansville, IN * B. Walker, Seattle, WA * Charles Walker, Falls Church, VA * Mary Walliser, Santa Paula, CA * Peter Watson, Greensboro, VT * Chester Ward, Jr., Owensboro, KY * Mr. & Mrs. Ward, Abington, MA * Mrs. Louie Ware, Staunton, VA * Robert Warren, South Bend, IN * Carrie Watt, York, PA * Ineke Way, South Bend, IN * Joel Weberman, Oak Park, MI * John Webster, Fair Oaks, CA * Virginia Weed, Anchorage, AK * Jonas Weil, St. Louis, MO * Anne Weinstein, East Middletown, VT * Bruce Wellard, Inkom, ID * Sue Welles, College Park, GA * Jim Werseles, Fayetteville, AR * Dr. & Mrs. Weston, Jr., Los Gatos, CA * Robert Westwater, Somerville, MA * Ben White, Houston, TX * Doug White, Lockport, NY * Elizabeth Whittington, Poland, OH * Fran Wienberg, Teaneck, NJ * David Wier, Mililani, HI * Linda Wilcox, Columbus, GA * Dennis Wilcutt, Glasgow, KY * George Wilkerson, Austin, TX * Mary Williams, Rocky Mount, NC * John Williamson, Scottsdale, AZ * K. Williford, Hampton Roads, VA * Nancy Wilson, Blackriver, NY * Orestes Wilson, Reading, PA * Warren Wilson, Primghar, IN * John Windhorn, Florence, SC * Laurence Winn, Phoenix, AZ * M. Wishard, Spokane, WA * Susan Wittke, Fort Wayne, IN * Andrew Wood, San Antonio, TX * Nancy Word, Cleveland, TN * Jerry Worley, Ashland, KY * Edward Worth, Port St. Lucie, FL * Marilyn Worth, Port St. Lucie, FL * Melisa Wright, Petroleum, WV * Guy Yates, Honolulu, HI * Roy Yates, Freeport, TX * Glee Yoder, Wichita, KS * David Yodhes, Allen Park, MO * T. James Zanotti, Novi, MO * Ron Zbiegien, Phoenix, AZ * Virginia Zinno, Middletown, NJ * Richard Zittel, Pueblo, CO * Jim Zuber, Canoga Park, CA * *All Saints Episcopal Church School, Florence, South Carolina* (John Burns, Susan Dudley, Daniel Jackson, Emily King, Austin Kirkland, Jordan Lauter, Dan Meier, Cassie Pairley, Katie Parry, Chad Stephens, Jane Ublett, Wanda, John Windhorn) *Castle View School, Riverside, California* (Megan Brown, Krista Carlos, David Derksen, April Harris, Kathy Nelson, Kristen Powers, Jason Riley, Justin Robey, Ryan Silvers, Gina Williams) *Clinch Middle School, Homerville, Georgia* (Sasha Akery, Torris Andrews, Antravious, Richard Arnold, Angie Ballwey, Jamie Bass, Mandy Bateson, James Bennett, Lewis Bennett, William Beverley, Glory Brand, Allonda Byant, Patty Campbell, April Davis, Shiela Darby, Brad Douglas, Kevin Edmond, Danny Franklin, Tobius Franklin, Denise Griffis, Pam Griffis, June Harris, Heath, Bill Hendricks, Melissa Hendrix, Tony Herrin, Kapiths Hodges, Denise Hutchinson, April Ingram, Jerome Jenkins, Jesse, Jason Kilcullen, Krystal, Brian Lee, Masheba, Michael, Kersha Mobley, Julie Musgrove, Nicole, Margo Paige, Tremayne Porter, Donald Raymond, Denise Reagan, Keuese Richardson, Stephanie Rivers, Heavenly Scott, Jeffery Stalvey, Michael Strickland, Jaylen Thomas, Keshia Lashonda Thomas, Mark Thomas, Tamica Thomas, Sebrina Williams) *Le Pera Elementary School, Parker, Arizona* (Arnold Arvizer, Javier Chaviea, Ronnie Clouse, Raut Forres, Naomi Leivas, Marisela Reyes, Maria Rubio) *Lynch Elementary School, Winchester, Massachusetts* (Sixth Grade Class) *Osterville Bay Elementary School, Osterville, Massachusetts* (Juinie Anderson, Denis Brandoo, Melissa Cotter, Tom Greer, Rebecca Gregoire, Jack, Rosemarie Lohee, Joey Machado, Jessica Mahannah, Danny McLaughlin, Dawn Pearson, Danielle Perchard, Hazel Richmond, Kenny Silva, Alexis Smith, Aaron Welles, Alan White, Jr.) *St. Pius School, Southgate, Michigan* (Diane Bastien, Mark Bomia, Leah Buono, Lori Dereniewski, Dan Digue, Elaine Edwards, Elias, Sara Feudner, Jennifer Fitzpatrick, Heather Forth, Kenneth Forth, Rosolino Gaglio, Derrick Gazie, Amber Grogg, Heather, Chris Hoffman, Matt Hoffman, Rebecca Killikeuc, Francis King, Shelly Kovacs, Joe Labadie, Thomas LaCombe, Michael, Allison, Miruzzi, Jennifer Mitroka, Marilyn Niebel, Teri O'Brien, Steven Parker, Mark Phillips, Paul Primeau, Brian Robert, Rose Sclafani, Amy Seneski, Mathew Skilliter, Jennifer Trent, William Urbanck, Kellylynn Walkneyer, Jeff Wallace, Melissa Wolfe, Beth Wozny, Brian Zimmerman) *Terry Elementary School, Selma, California* (Roleena Anderson, Gloria Campos, Vangie Cortis, Justin Davir, Dina, Maria Espinoza, Jatinder Gill, Jonathan Gomes, Jesse, Joe, Mike Keiser, Patti, Irma Perez, Layla Poe, Balvinder Purewal, Sundeep Purewal, Sunny Rai, Michelle Ramsey, Israel Rivers, Francisco Rodriguez, Laura Rizo, Ramandeep Sihotg) *Waverly Hall Elementary School, Waverly Hall, Georgia* (Shannon Brown, Telithia Brown, Jesse Capeheart, Chris Carter, Gina Cook, Michael Crooke, Michad Culpepper, Jay Doddins, Patrick Douglas, Belinda Faulkner, Thomas Galkatin, Kevin Ginn, Andreas Harvey, Kristi Hershman, Jocelyn Kelley, Melissa Luttrell, Tyreicus Marshall, Felcia Money, Wally Montgomery, Derek Neal, Natalie Powell, Michael Quinn, Wednesdi Selters, Chris Thomas, Rikki Trimm, William Turner, Lacoya Weaver, Lori Weaver, Michael Webb, Adam Williams, Tiawianne Williams, Lashay Willis, Shanecia West, Adam Wright, Victor Yearewood)

WITNESSES AND WORKSHOP PARTICIPANTS: COMMISSION MEETINGS—*May 15–17, 1985:* James A. Abrahamson, Strategic Defense Initiative Organization * Robert O. Aller, National Aeronautics and Space Administration (NASA) * James M. Beggs, NASA * Walter Boyne, National Air & Space Museum * Raymond S. Colladay, NASA * Charles W. Cook, U.S. Air Force * Philip E. Culbertson, NASA * Jennifer L. Dorn, Department of Transportation * Burton I. Edelson, NASA * Isaac T. Gillam, IV, NASA * John H. McElroy, National Oceanic and Atmospheric Administration * Jesse W. Moore, NASA * Kenneth S. Pedersen, NASA * *June 27–28, 1985:* Ivan Bekey, NASA * Joseph V. Charyk, COMSAT * Otho E. Eskin, Department of State * Dennis J. Granato, Department of Defense * Arthur F. Manfredi, Jr., Central Intelligence Agency * Ian W. Pryke, European Space Agency * Marcia S. Smith, Congressional Research Service * David W. Thompson, Orbital Sciences Corporation * *July 25–26, 1985:* Robert H. Brown, NASA Johnson Space Center (JSC) * Mark Cintala, NASA-JSC * Aaron Cohen, NASA-JSC * Mark K. Craig, NASA-JSC * Michael B. Duke, NASA-JSC* Owen K. Garriott, NASA-JSC * Gerald D. Griffin, NASA-JSC * Larry Haskin, Washington University * Carolyn Huntoon, NASA-JSC * Joseph P. Kerwin, NASA-JSC * Eugene F. Kranz, NASA-JSC * Joe Loftus, NASA-JSC * Ron Maynard, NASA-JSC * Brian Pacheco, NASA-JSC * Frank H. Samonski, NASA-JSC * Ernest E. Smith, Jr., NASA-JSC * Robert C. Ried, NASA-JSC * Carl B. Shelley, NASA-JSC * George R. Wittinghill, NASA-JSC * *August 21–22, 1985:* Arden L. Albee, NASA Jet Propulsion Laboratory (JPL), * Lew Allen, NASA-JPL * Graeme Aston, NASA-JPL * Dave Atkinson, NASA-JPL * Brian Beckman, NASA-JPL * Charles Beichman, NASA-JPL * Francis Bretherton, National Center for Atmospheric Research * Jo Bea Cimino, NASA-JPL * Duane F. Dipprey, NASA-JPL * Thomas M. Donahue, University of Michigan, * Robert E. Freeland, NASA-JPL * Margaret Frerking, NASA-JPL * C. R. Gates, NASA-JPL * Torrence V. Johnson, NASA-JPL * Carl A. Kukkonen, NASA-JPL * Dan McCleese, NASA-JPL * Dave Linick, NASA-JPL * Arden Meinel, NASA-JPL * David Morrison, University of Hawaii, Honolulu * Gregory A. Nelson, NASA-JPL * Kerry Nock, NASA-JPL * Edward C. Posner, NASA-JPL * Robert D. Rasmussen, NASA-JPL * V. Soumi, University of Wisconsin * Richard J. Terrile, NASA-JPL * Paul Weissman, NASA-JPL * Richard W. Zurek, NASA-JPL * *September 17–19, 1985:* Sam Baum, Department of Commerce, Bureau of the Census * Paul Bohannan, University of Southern California (Lunar Settlement Working Group) * Robert Brownlee, astronomer (Lunar Settlement Working Group) * Maxime A. Faget, Space Industries Inc. * Sydney Falk, Bickerstaff, Heath & Smiley (Lunar Settlement Working Group) * Ben Finney, University of Hawaii (Lunar Settlement Working Group) * Gareth Flora, Martin-Marietta Corporation * Joanne Irene Gabrynowicz, Helfenstein & Matza (Lunar Settlement Working Group) * Joseph Gavin, Grumman Corporation * Robert Goss, Astrotech International Corporation * David Grimes, Transpace Carriers, Inc. * Robert Hager, Boeing Aerospace Company * David Hannah, Space Services, Inc. * Eric Hanushek, Congressional Budget Office * William Hartmann, Planetary Science Institute (Lunar Settlement Working Group) * Stephen Haycox, University of Alaska—Anchorage (Lunar Settlement Working Group) * George Jeffs, Rockwell International Corporation * Eric Jones, Los Alamos National Laboratory (Lunar Settlement Working Group) * Christopher Joyner, George Washington University (Lunar Settlement Working Group) * Ronald Kutscher, Department of Labor, Bureau of Labor Statistics * John Long, Department of Commerce, Bureau of the Census * Alan Lovelace, General Dynamics Corporation * Brian O'Leary, Science Applications International Corporation (SAIC) * Wendell Mendell, NASA-JSC (Lunar Settlement Working Group) * Philip Quigg, foreign affairs specialist (Lunar Settlement Working Group) * Fred Singer, George Mason University * Stanley I. Weiss, Lockheed Missiles and Space Company, Inc. * *October 22–23, 1985:* Jay Boudreau, Los Alamos National Laboratory * Bernard Burke, Massachusetts Institute of Technology (MIT) * Martin Harwit, Cornell University * Stamatios Krimigis, Johns Hopkins Applied Physics Laboratory * Joseph Shea, Raytheon * Scott Swisher, Michigan State University * Rainer Weiss, MIT * Laurence Young, MIT * *November 19–20, 1985:* Margaret Augustine, Space Biosphere Ventures * John Billingham, NASA Ames Research Center (ARC) * Penelope Boston, National Center for Atmospheric Research * Ronald Bracewell, Stanford University * Robert Davis, American Institute of Aeronautics and Astronautics (AIAA) * William DeCampli, Stanford Medical Center * Von Eshleman, Stanford University * James French, NASA-JPL * Phil Hawes, Space Biosphere Ventures * Carl Hodges, University of Arizona * Joseph Kenner, New York University * Robert MacElroy, NASA-ARC * Chris McKay, NASA-ARC * Jon Miller, Northern Illinois University * Barney Oliver, NASA-ARC * Carl Sagan, Planetary Society * Gordon Smith, AIAA * Carol Stoker, NASA-ARC * James Tillman, University of Washington * Peter Wilkniss, National Science Foundation (NSF) * Michael Wiskershen, Stanford University * Rene Zentner, University of Houston * *December 16, 1985:* Clarence Brown, Department of Commerce * Kenneth W. Ciriacks, Geosat Committee * Richard Colino, INTELSAT * Robert Frosch, General Motors * John C. Fuechsel, National Ocean Industries Association * Frederick Henderson, Geosat Committee * Gregg Maryniak, Space Studies Institute * Samuel McCandless, National Ocean Industries Association * Ichtiaque Rasool, University of Paris * G. Wesley Rice, Geosat Committee * Vincent Salomonson, NASA Goddard Space Flight Center * John F. Yardley, McDonnell Douglas Astronautics Company * *Workshop on the National Academy of Sciences Space Science Board's Major Directions Study, August 2, 1985:* Don Anderson, California Institute of Technology * James Baker, Joint Oceanographic Institution * Bernard Burke, Massachusetts Institute of Technology * Thomas M. Donahue, University of Michigan * Larry W. Esposito, University of Colorado * Riccardo Giacconi, Space Telescope Science Institute * Donald Hunten, University of Arizona * Stamatios M. Krimigis, Johns Hopkins Applied Physics Laboratory * Joseph M. Reynolds, Louisiana State University * Frederick Scarf, TRW Systems * Scott Swisher, Michigan State University * David Usher, Cornell University * Rainer Weiss, Massachusetts Institute of Technology * *Life in the 21st Century Workshop, October 18, 1985:* Doug Bauer, Edison Electric Institute * Orville Bentley, Department of Agriculture * Alex Christakis, George Mason University * R. Morton Darrow, Darrow Associates, Inc. * Joe Duncan, Dunn & Bradstreet * Linda Forbes, United Way of America * Herbert Gerjouy, Program Strategies, Inc. * Walter Hahn, George Washington University * George Hazelrigg, National Science Foundation (NSF) * Madeline Hymowitz, NSF * Joe Kenner, New York University * Magda McHale, State University of New York * Michael Michaelis, World Future Society * Leik Myrabo, Rensselaer Polytechnic Institute * William Renfro, Policy Analysis Company, Inc. * Ralph Sanders, Industrial College of the Armed Forces * Dave Snyder, Consulting Futurist * Don Trilling, Department of Transportation * Rene Zentner, University of Houston * *Workshop on the Commercialization of Space (sponsored by AIAA), October 31, 1985:* Peter C. Badali, Honeywell, Inc. * Mireille Gerard, AIAA * James J. Harford, AIAA * Richard Hora, General Dynamics Corporation * Richard L. Kline, Grumman Corporation * Lester C. Krogh, Minnesota Mining & Manufacturing, Inc. * R. M. Mentzer, Ford Aerospace & Communications Corporation * Miles Mutnick, COMSAT * George D. Ojalehto, Science Applications International Corporation * James T. Rose, McDonnell Douglas Astronautics Company * Allan J. Rosenberg, General Electric Company * Daniel A. Ruskin, Lockheed Missiles and Space Co., Inc. * Jerome Simonoff, Citicorp Industrial Credit, Inc. * Arthur L. Slotkin, SDC Services Group * David W. Thompson, Orbital Services Corporation * Martin N. Titland, Fairchild Space Company * Stanley I. Weiss, Lockheed Missiles and Space Company, Co., Inc. * Albert Wheelon, Hughes Aircraft Company * Peter W. Wood, Booz Allen & Hamiliton Inc.

SPECIAL THANKS *Very special thanks are due to a number of people who provided us with untiring help throughout our deliberations or reviewed our draft report. Their knowledge, perspective, and vision have contributed greatly to our undertaking:* Joseph Allen, Houston, TX * Ivan Bekey, Washington, D.C. * Herbert Block, Bethesda, MD * Jack Butler, Huntsville AL * Charles Cook, McLean, VA * Kelly Cyr, Houston, TX * Daniel Fink, Potomac, MD * Eilene Galloway, Washington, D.C. * William Hartmann, Tucson, AZ * Diana Hoyt, Silver Spring, MD * Richard G. Johnson, Los Altos, CA * Brion Jones, Columbus, OH * Alan Landgraf, Columbus, OH * Reimar Luest, Paris, France * Gerald May, Washington, DC * Robert McCall, Phoenix, AZ * John McLucas, Alexandria, VA * Michael Michaud, Newport Beach, CA * Ron Miller, Fredericksburg, VA * Mary Morgan, Columbus, OH * George Mueller, Santa Barbara, CA * James A.M. Muncy, Arlington, VA * Kerry Nock, Pasadena, CA * Fred Paroutaud, LA, CA * Cynthia Penson, Columbus, OH * Thomas Pepper, New York, NY * Peter Perkins, Arlington, VA * Barney Roberts, Houston, TX * Thomas Rogers, McLean, VA * James Rulfs, Columbus, OH * Rebecca Rumbo, LA, CA * Gilbert P. Rye, Annandale, VA * Harrison H. Schmitt, Albuquerque, NM * Courtney Stadd, Chevy Chase, MD * H. Guyford Stever, Washington, DC * Richard Tresch-Fienberg, Cambridge, MA * Don Trilling, Alexandria, VA * Lillian Trippett, Washington, DC * Craig Voorhees, Bethesda, MD * Leonard Weiss, Silver Spring, MD * Frank White, Boston, MA.

BIBLIOGRAPHY

Adelman, Morris A., et al. *No Time to Confuse.* San Francisco: Institute for Contemporary Studies, 1975.

Akins, Faren, Mary Conners, and Albert Harrison. *Living Aloft: Human Requirements for Extended Spaceflight.* NASA SP-483. Washington, D.C.: NASA, 1985.

Allen, Francis R., et al. *Technology and Social Change.* New York: Appleton-Century Crofts, Inc., 1957.

Allen, Joseph. *Entering Space: An Astronaut's Odyssey.* New York: Stewart, Tabori & Chang, 1984.

Asimov, Isaac. *Change! Seventy-one Glimpses of the Future.* New York: Houghton Mifflin Company, 1981.

Barney, Gerald O. *The Global 2000 Report to the President: Entering the 21st Century.* Vols. 1 and 2. Washington: Council on Environmental Quality and U.S. State Department, 1977.

Beatty, J. Kelly, Andrew Chaikin, and Brian O'Leary, eds. *The New Solar System.* Cambridge: Sky Publishing, 1981.

Bekey, Ivan. "Tethers Open New Space Options." *Aeronautics and Astronautics,* Vol. 21, April 1983, pp. 22–40.

———. "Applications of Space Tethers." New York: American Institute of Astronautics, 1984. IAF-84-436.

———. "Space Station Operations Enhancement." New York: American Institute of Astronautics, 1984. IAF-84-43.

Bekey, Ivan, and Daniel Herman, eds. *Space Stations and Space Platforms—Concepts, Design, Infrastructure, and Uses.* New York: American Institute of Aeronautics and Astronautics, 1985.

Bernal, John. *The World, the Flesh and the Devil; an Enquiry into the Future of the Three Enemies of the Rational Soul.* London: K. Paul, Trench, Trubner and Co., Ltd., 1929.

Boston, Penelope, ed. *The Case for Mars.* San Diego: American Astronautical Society, 1984.

Botkin, James, et al. *Global Stakes—The Future of High Technology America.* New York: Penguin Books, 1984.

Brown, Harrison, James Bonner, and John Weir. *The Next Hundred Years.* New York: Viking Press, 1957.

Burke, James D., and April S. Whitt, eds. *Space Manufacturing 1983.* Advances in the Astronautical Sciences, Vol. 53. Proceedings of the Sixth Princeton/SSI Conference, May 9–12, 1983. San Diego: American Astronautical Society, 1983.

Calder, Kent E., and Roy Hofheinz, Jr. *The East Asia Edge.* New York: Basic Books, Inc., 1982.

Cetron, Marvin, and Thomas O'Toole. *Encounters with the Future: A Forecast of Life into the 21st Century.* New York: McGraw-Hill Book Company, 1982.

Chaisson, Eric, and George Field. *The Invisible Universe: Probing the Frontiers of Astrophysics.* Boston: Birkhauser, 1985.

Clarke, Arthur. *2001: A Space Odyssey.* New York: New American Library, 1968.

Cooper, Henry S.F. Jr. *A House in Space.* New York: Holt Rinehart and Winston, 1976.

Cortright, Edgar, ed. *Apollo Expeditions to the Moon.* NASA SP-350. Washington, D.C.: NASA, 1975.

Drucker, Peter, F. *America's Next Twenty Years.* New York: Harper Brothers, 1955.

Ezell, Edward Clinton, and Linda Neuman Ezell. *The Partnership: A History of the Apollo-Soyuz Test Project.* Washington, D.C.: National Aeronautics and Space Administration, 1978.

Faughnnan, Barbara, and Gregg Maryniak, eds. *Space Manufacturing 5: Engineering with Lunar and Asteroidal Materials.* Proceedings of the Seventh Princeton/AIAA/SSI Conference, May 8–11, 1985. New York: American Institute of Aeronautics and Astronautics, 1985.

Fisher, John C. *Energy Crises in Perspective.* New York: John Wiley & Sons, 1974.

Froehlich, Walter. *Space Station: The Next Logical Step.* NASA EP-213. Washington, D.C.: NASA, 1985.

Furnas, C.C. *The Next Hundred Years: The Unfinished Business of Science.* New York: Reynal & Hitchcock, 1936.

Gale, William, ed. *Life in the Universe: The Ultimate Limits to Growth.* Boulder: Westview Press, Inc., 1979.

Goldsmith, Donald, ed. *The Quest for Extraterrestrial Life—A Book of Readings.* Mill Valley: University Science Books, 1980.

Grey, Jerry, ed. *Space Manufacturing Facilities (Space Colonies).* Proceedings of the Princeton/AIAA/ NASA Conference, May 7–9, 1975, and includes Proceedings of the Princeton Conference on Space Colonization. New York: American Institute of Aeronautics and Astronautics, 1977.

———. *Space Manufacturing Facilities II.* Proceedings of the Third Princeton/AIAA Conference, May 9–11, 1977. New York: American Institute of Aeronautics and Astronautics, 1977.

Grey, Jerry, and Lawrence A. Hamdan, eds. *Space Manufacturing IV.* Proceedings of the Fifth Princeton/AIAA Conference, May 18–21, 1981. New York: American Institute of Aeronautics and Astronautics, 1981.

Grey, Jerry, and Christine Krop, eds. *Space Manufacturing III:* Proceedings of the Fourth Princeton/ AIAA Conference, May 14–17, 1979. New York: American Institute of Aeronautics and Astronautics, 1979.

Hartmann, William, Ron Miller, and Pamela Lee. *Out of the Cradle.* New York: Workman Publishing, 1984.

Hartmann, William K. *Moons and Planets.* Belmont, Calif.: Wadsworth Publishing Company, 1983.

Kahn, Herman, William Brown, and Leon Martel. *The Next 200 Years: A Scenario for America and the World.* New York: Morrow, 1976.

Kahn, Herman. *World Economic Development 1979 and Beyond.* Boulder: Westview Press, 1979.

Lee, Hahn Been. *Future, Innovation and Development.* Seoul: Panmun Book Company Ltd., 1982.

Lewinsohn, Richard. *Science, Prophecy and Prediction: Man's Efforts to Foretell the Future—From Babylon to Wall Street.* New York: Bell Publishing Company, Inc., 1961.

Logsdon, John, M. *The Decision to Go to the Moon: Project Apollo and the National Interest.* Cambridge: Massachusetts Institute of Technology, 1970.

McDougall, Walter. A. *The Heavens and the Earth: The Political History of the Space Age.* New York: Basic Books, Inc., 1985.

Mckay, Christopher, ed. *Case for Mars II.* Proceedings of the Second Case for Mars Conference, July 10–14, 1984. San Diego: Univelt Inc., 1985.

Miller, Ron and William K. Hartmann. *The Grand Tour: A Traveler's Guide to the Solar System.* New York: Workman Publishing, 1981.

Minsky, Marvin, ed. *Robotics.* Garden City: Omni Press, 1985.

Morrison, Philip, ed. *The Search for Extraterrestrial Intelligence.* NASA SP-419. Washington, D.C.: U.S. Government Printing Office, 1973.

Napolitano, Luigi, G. ed. *SPACE 2000.* Selection of Papers Presented at the 33rd Congress of the International Astronautical Federation. New York: American Institute of Aeronautics and Astronautics, 1983.

Nisbet, Robert. *History of the Idea of Progress.* New York: Basic Books, 1980.

O'Neill, Gerard K. *The High Frontier: Human Colonies in Space.* New York: Morrow, 1976.

————. *2081: A Hopeful View of the Future.* New York: Simon and Schuster, 1981.

O'Neill, Gerard K., and Brian O'Leary, eds. *Space-Based Manufacturing from Nonterrestrial Materials.* Technical Papers from the 1976 Summer Study at NASA/Ames Research Center. New York: American Institute of Aeronautics and Astronautics, 1977.

Orwell, George. *1984.* New York: Harcourt Brace Jovanovich, 1949.

Preiss, Byron, ed. *The Planets.* New York: Bantam Books, 1985.

Ramo, Simon. *What's Wrong with Our Technological Society and How to Fix It.* New York: McGraw-Hill Inc., 1983.

Sagan, Carl. *Cosmos.* New York: Random House, 1980.

Schwartz, Michiel, and Paul Stares, eds. *The Exploitation of Space.* London: Butterworth & Co., 1985.

Shelton, William. *Soviet Space Exploration: The First Decade.* New York: Washington Square Press, 1968.

Shklovskii, I.S., and Carl Sagan. *Intelligent Life in the Universe.* New York: Dell Publishing Co., 1966.

Simpson, Theodore, ed. *The Space Station: An Idea Whose Time Has Come.* New York: IEEE Press, 1985.

Smith, Marcia. *Mars: The Next Destination for Manned Space Flight?* U.S. Library of Congress. Congressional Research Service. CRS Report 84-20. Washington, D.C.: U.S. Library of Congress, 1984.

Smith, Marcia, Jane Gravelle and David Whiteman. *Insurance and the Commercialization of Space.* U.S. Congress. Senate. Committee on Commerce, Science, and Transportation. Washington, D.C.: U.S. Government Printing Office, 1985.

Smith, Marcia, et al. *Soviet Space Programs 1976–1980* (with supplementary data through 1983). 3 Volumes. U.S. Congress. Senate. Committee on Commerce, Science, and Transportation. Washington, D.C.: U.S. Government Printing Office, Vol. 1—1982; Vol. 2—1984; Vol. 3—1985.

Smith, Marcia, and Daniel Zafren. *Policy and Legal Issues Involved in the Commercialization of Space.* U.S. Congress. Senate. Committee on Commerce, Science, and Transportation. Washington, D.C.: U.S. Government Printing Office, 1983.

Solberg, Carl. *Conquest of the Skies: A History of Commercial Aviation in America.* Boston: Little, Brown and Company, 1979.

Trefil, James. *Space Time Infinity.* Washington, D.C.: Smithsonian Books, 1985.

U.S. Congress. House. Committee on Science and Technology. *Assess Potential Gains and Drawbacks of Civilian Space Cooperation with the Soviets.* Washington, D.C.: U.S. Government Printing Office, 1985.

U.S. Congress. House. Committee on Science and Technology. *Authorizing Appropriations for Landsat Commercialization (Report to accompany H.R. 2800)*. Washington, D.C.: U.S. Government Printing Office, 1985.

U.S. Congress. House. Committee on Science and Technology. *Background Materials on US-USSR Cooperative Agreements in Science and Technology*. Washington, D.C.: U.S. Government Printing Office, 1975.

U.S. Congress. House. Committee on Science and Technology. *Briefing on Mars Exploration*. Washington, D.C.: U.S. Government Printing Office, 1976.

U.S. Congress. House. Committee on Science and Technology. *Civil Land Remote Sensing Systems*. Washington, D.C.: U.S. Government Printing Office, 1981.

U.S. Congress. House. Committee on Science and Technology. *Commemoration of the International Geophysical Year (Report to accompany H. Res. 514)*. Washington, D.C.: U.S. Government Printing Office, 1982.

U.S. Congress. House. Committee on Science and Technology. *Commercialization of Land and Weather Satellites*. Washington, D.C.: U.S. Government Printing Office, 1983.

U.S. Congress. House. Committee on Science and Technology. *Commercial Space Launch Act (Report to accompany H.R. 3942)*. Washington, D.C.: U.S. Government Printing Office, 1984.

U.S. Congress. House. Committee on Science and Technology. *Establishing a Solar Power Satellite Research, Development, and Evaluation Program (Report to accompany H.R. 2335)*. Washington, D.C.: U.S. Government Printing Office, 1979.

U.S. Congress. House. Committee on Science and Technology. *Establishment of a Solar Power Satellite Research, Development, and Demonstration Program (Report to accompany H.R. 12505)*. Washington, D.C.: U.S. Government Printing Office, 1978.

U.S. Congress. House. Committee on Science and Technology. *The Expendable Launch Vehicle Commercialization Act*. Washington, D.C.: U.S. Government Printing Office, 1984.

U.S. Congress. House. Committee on Science and Technology. *Extraterrestrial Intelligence Research*. Washington, D.C.: U.S. Government Printing Office, 1978.

U.S. Congress. House. Committee on Science and Technology. *Future Space Programs*. Washington, D.C.: U.S. Government Printing Office, 1978.

U.S. Congress. House. Committee on Science and Technology. *Future Space Programs: 1981*. Washington, D.C.: U.S. Government Printing Office, 1981.

U.S. Congress. House. Committee on Science and Technology. *Future Space Programs: 1975*. Washington, D.C.: U.S. Government Printing Office, 1975.

U.S. Congress. House. Committee on Science and Technology. *H.R. 7412—The Space Industrialization Act of 1980*. Washington, D.C.: U.S. Government Printing Office, 1980.

U.S. Congress. House. Committee on Science and Technology. *Initiatives to Promote Space Commercialization*. Washington, D.C.: U.S. Government Printing Office, 1984.

U.S. Congress. House. Committee on Science and Technology. *International Cooperation and Competition in Space*. Washington, D.C.: U.S. Government Printing Office, 1984.

U.S. Congress. House. Committee on Science and Technology. *International Space Activities, 1979*. Washington, D.C.: U.S. Government Printing Office, 1979.

U.S. Congress. House. Committee on Science and Technology. *The International Geosphere/Biosphere Program, 1984*. Washington, D.C.: U.S. Government Printing Office, 1985.

U.S. Congress. House. Committee on Science and Technology. *The Land Remote-Sensing Commercialization Act of 1984—H.R. 4836 and H.R. 5155*. Washington D.C.: U.S. Government Printing Office, 1984.

U.S. Congress. House. Committee on Science and Technology. *The Land Remote-Sensing Commercialization Act of 1984 (Report to accompany H.R. 5155)*. Washington D.C.: U.S. Government Printing Office, 1984.

U.S. Congress. House. Committee on Science and Technology. *Landsat Commercialization*. Washington, D.C.: U.S. Government Printing Office, 1985.

U.S. Congress. House. Committee on Science and Technology. *NASA's Five Year Plan*. Washington, D.C.: U.S. Government Printing Office, 1983.

U.S. Congress. House. Committee on Science and Technology. *NASA's Space Station Activities*. Washington, D.C.: U.S. Government Printing Office, 1983.

U.S. Congress. House. Committee on Science and Technology. *National Space Policy*. Washington, D.C.: U.S. Government Printing Office, 1982.

U.S. Congress. House. Committee on Science and Technology. *The Need for a Fifth Space Shuttle Orbiter*. Washington, D.C.: U.S. Government Printing Office, 1982.

U.S. Congress. House. Committee on Science and Technology. *The Need for Increased Space Shuttle Orbiter Fleet*. Washington, D.C.: U.S. Government Printing Office, 1982.

U.S. Congress. House. Committee on Science and Technology. *Review of Materials Processing in Space*. Washington, D.C.: U.S. Government Printing Office, 1983.

U.S. Congress. House. Committee on Science and Technology. *Review of the National Aeronautics and Space Act of 1958*. Washington, D.C.: U.S. Government Printing Office, 1983.

U.S. Congress. House. Committee on Science and Technology. *Review of the National Aeronautics and Space Act of 1958, as Amended*. Washington, D.C.: U.S. Government Printing Office, 1984.

U.S. Congress. House. Committee on Science and Technology. *Review of Space Shuttle Requirements, Operations, and Future Plans*. Washington, D.C.: U.S. Government Printing Office, 1984.

U.S. Congress. House. Committee on Science and Technology. *Satellite-Directed Navigational Guidance for Aircraft (Report to accompany H. Con. Res. 190)*. Washington, D.C.: U.S. Government Printing Office, 1983.

U.S. Congress. House. Committee on Science and Technology. *Solar Power Satellite.* Washington, D.C.: U.S. Government Printing Office, 1978.

U.S. Congress. House. Committee on Science and Technology. *Solar Power Satellite.* Washington, D.C.: U.S. Government Printing Office, 1979.

U.S. Congress. House. Committee on Science and Technology. *Space Commercialization.* Washington, D.C.: U.S. Government Printing Office, 1983.

U.S. Congress. House. Committee on Science and Technology. *The Space Industrialization Act of 1979.* Washington, D.C.: U.S. Government Printing Office, 1979.

U.S. Congress. House. Committee on Science and Technology. *The Space Nuclear Reactor Program.* Washington, D.C.: U.S. Government Printing Office, 1983.

U.S. Congress. House. Committee on Science and Technology. *Space Industrialization.* Washington, D.C.: U.S. Government Printing Office, 1977.

U.S. Congress. House. Committee on Science and Technology. *Space Shuttle Requirements, Operations and Future Plans.* Washington, D.C.: U.S. Government Printing Office, 1984.

U.S. Congress. House. Committee on Science and Technology. *Transfer of Civil Meteorological Satellites (Report to accompany H. Con Res. 168).* Washington, D.C.: U.S. Government Printing Office, 1983.

U.S. Congress. House. Committee on Science and Technology. *United States Civilian Space Policy.* Washington, D.C.: U.S. Government Printing Office, 1980.

U.S. Congress. House. Committee on Science and Technology. *United States Civilian Space Policy.* Washington, D.C.: U.S. Government Printing Office, 1981.

U.S. Congress. House. Committee on Science and Technology. *U.S. Science and Technology Under Budget Stress.* Washington, D.C.: U.S. Government Printing Office, 1982.

U.S. Congress. House. Committee on Science and Technology. *U.S.-Soviet Satellite Accord: SARSAT/ COSPAS Search-and-Rescue Program.* Washington, D.C.: U.S. Government Printing Office, 1984.

U.S. Congress. House. Committee on Science and Technology. *US-USSR: Key Issues in Scientific Exchanges and Technology Transfer.* Washington, D.C.: U.S. Government Printing Office, 1978.

U.S. Congress. Senate. Committee on Commerce, Science, and Transportation. *Agreement Governing the Activities of States on the Moon and Other Celestial Bodies.* Washington, D.C.: U.S. Government Printing Office, 1980.

U.S. Congress. Senate. Committee on Commerce, Science, and Transportation. *Civil Remote Sensing Satellite System.* Washington, D.C.: U.S. Government Printing Office, 1980.

U.S. Congress. Senate. Committee on Commerce, Science, and Transportation. *Commercial Space Launch Act.* Washington, D.C.: U.S. Government Printing Office, 1984.

U.S. Congress. Senate. Committee on Commerce, Science, and Transportation. *Hearings on the Future of Space Science and Space Applications.* Washington, D.C.: U.S. Government Printing Office, 1978.

U.S. Congress. Senate. Committee on Commerce, Science, and Transportation. *The Moon Treaty.* Washington, D.C.: U.S. Government Printing Office, 1980.

U.S. Congress. Senate. Committee on Commerce, Science, and Transportation. *Operational Remote Sensing Legislation.* Washington, D.C.: U.S. Government Printing Office, 1979.

U.S. Congress. Senate. Committee on Commerce, Science, and Transportation. *Space Law: Selected Basic Documents.* 2nd edition. Washington, D.C.: U.S. Government Printing Office, 1978.

U.S. Congress. Senate. Committee on Commerce, Science, and Transportation. *A Symposium on the Future of Space Science and Applications.* Washington, D.C.: U.S. Government Printing Office, 1978.

U.S. Congress. Senate. Committee on Commerce, Science, and Transportation. *U.S. Civilian Space Policy.* Washington, D.C.: U.S. Government Printing Office, 1979.

U.S. Department of Commerce. Bureau of the Census. *Historical Statistics of the United States.* Washington, D.C.: U.S. Government Printing Office.

U.S. National Academy of Sciences. National Research Council. Assembly of Mathematical and Physical Sciences. Astronomy Survey Committee. *Astronomy and Astrophysics for the 1980's.* Washington, D.C.: National Academy Press, 1982.

U.S. National Academy of Sciences. National Research Council. Space Science Board. *Report on Space Science 1975.* Washington, D.C.: National Academy Press, 1976.

U.S. National Academy of Sciences. National Research Council. Space Science Board. Committee on Solar and Space Physics. *An Implementation Plan for Priorities in Solar-System Space Physics.* Washington, D.C.: National Academy Press, in press.

U.S. National Academy of Sciences. National Research Council. Space Science Board. Committee on Space Biology and Medicine. *Life Beyond the Earth's Environment—The Biology of Living Organisms in Space.* Washington, D.C.: National Academy Press, 1979.

U.S. National Academy of Sciences. National Research Council. Space Science Board. Committee on Solar and Space Physics. *Solar System Space Physics in the 1980's: A Research Strategy.* Washington, D.C.: National Academy Press, 1980.

U.S. National Academy of Sciences. National Research Council. Space Science Board. Committee on Earth Sciences. *A Strategy for Earth Science from Space in the 1980's. Part I: Solid Earth and Oceans.* Washington, D.C.: National Academy Press, 1982.

U.S. National Academy of Sciences. National Research Council. Space Science Board. Committee on Earth Sciences. *A Strategy for Earth Science from Space in the 1980's and 1990's. Part II: Atmosphere and Interactions with the Solid Earth, Oceans, and Biota.* Washington, D.C.: National Academy Press, 1985.

U.S. National Academy of Sciences. National Research Council. Space Science Board. Committee on Planetary and Lunar Exploration. *Strategy for Exploration of the Inner Planets: 1977–1987.* Washington, D.C.: National Academy Press, 1978.

U.S. National Academy of Sciences. National Research Council. Space Science Board. Committee on Planetary and Lunar Exploration. *Strategy for the Exploration of the Primitive Solar-System Bodies— Asteroids, Comets and Meteoroids: 1980–1990.* Washington, D.C.: National Academy Press, 1980.

U.S. National Academy of Sciences. National Research Council. Space Science Board. Committee on Gravitational Physics. *Strategy for Space Research in Gravitational Physics in the 1980's.* Washington, D.C.: National Academy Press, 1981.

U.S. National Aeronautics and Space Administration. *America's Next Decades in Space: A Report for the Space Task Group.* 0-365-738. Washington, D.C.: U.S. Government Printing Office, 1969.

U.S. National Aeronautics and Space Administration. *A Forecast of Space Technology 1980–2000, NASA SP-387.* Washington, D.C.: NASA, January, 1976.

U.S. National Aeronautics and Space Administration. *NASA 1986 Long-Range Program Plan.* Washington, D.C.: NASA, August, 1985.

U.S. National Aeronautics and Space Administration. NASA Advisory Council. *Planetary Exploration Through the Year 2000: A Core Program.* Washington, D.C.: NASA, 1983.

U.S. Office of Science and Technology. President's Science Advisory Committee. Space, Science, and Technology Panel Report. *The Next Decade in Space.* 0-378-385. Washington, D.C.: U.S. Government Printing Office, March, 1970.

U.S. Office of Technology Assessment. *International Cooperation and Competition in Civilian Space Activities.* Washington, D.C.: Office of Technology Assessment, 1985.

U.S. Office of Technology Assessment. *Civilian Space Stations and the U.S. Future in Space.* Washington, D.C.: Office of Technology Assessment, November, 1984.

U.S. Office of Technology Assessment. *U.S./Soviet Cooperation in Space: A Technical Memorandum.* Washington, D.C.: Office of Technology Assessment, July, 1985.

U.S. Space Task Group. *Report to the President: The Post-Apollo Space Program: Directions for the Future.* Washington, D.C., U.S. Government Printing Office, September, 1969.

Von Braun, Wernher. *Space Frontier.* New York: Holt Rinehart and Winston, 1963.

Von Braun, Wernher, Frederick Ordway, and Dave Dooling. *Space Travel: A History—An Update of the History of Rocketry and Space Travel.* New York: Harper & Row, 1985.

Webb, David C. *Trends in the Commercialization of Space.* Washington, D.C.: Aerospace Industries Association, 1985.

World Bank. *World Development Report, 1983.* Washington, D.C.: Oxford University Press, 1983.